MW00930582

Praise for The Fifth Way

"Reading *The Fifth Way* is like spending time with the author, Dave Brisbin, who has a gift of making simple the complicated religious mess we have collectively made of Christianity. He is a voice in the wilderness and a breath of fresh air. If you consider yourself a follower of Jesus, then *The Fifth Way* may help you discover the path your heart has long been seeking."

Chris Falson
Singer/Songwriter/Composer, Author: Planted by the Water—The Making of a Worship Leader

"We have arrived at a fascinating moment in history. At the same time religious institutions have developed a science of spiritual growth, Christians are discovering that is not what they want. Rather than be herded from one stage to another, believers are asking whether there is another way to walk with God that depends more on Spirit than structure and in practice is more organic than programmatic. Dave Brisbin's answer is 'Yes! There is *The Fifth Way*.' Of all the books in the Christian marketplace today why should you read this one? To renew your mind, refresh your heart, and restore your soul."

Chuck Smith, Jr.
Author and Spiritual Director for Reflexion—A Spiritual Community

"Dave and I met briefly at year twenty in my Christian journey and now here we are again at year forty. Our lives have merged again at an important crossroads, not just for ourselves but for the entire global community. It is time to enquire after the 'road that leads to good' and, as a result, to find 'soulrest' that will provide us with the energy of Jesus Christ to finish our passage upstream against increasingly stress-filled times. Dave proposes a *Fifth Way*; for what it's worth, I think he's right."

Graham Kerr
Former media person (Galloping Gourmet), Author: 'Flash of Silver, the leap that changed my world'

"Dave Brisbin's 'The Fifth Way' is intelligently poetic and masterfully crafted to shed light on a blue print for living *now* in alignment with original biblical intent. It supported me to deepen my personal relationship with Christ and reaffirm that my spiritual purpose is to be the love that *I am* in each moment of this day."

Richard Gibbs
Former NBA Basketball Player, Addiction Specialist

"By all reasonable accounts the Christian church is in decline right now. Consequently, I am grateful that David Brisbin is championing a fresh take on the Aramaic Jesus, an approach which may turn things around for Christianity and provide the wholesome insight of Christ to a new generation of believers. As such, I see Brisbin's book as an extremely important contribution in a world where it seems as if pastors themselves are perhaps too squeamish about the messy details of Bible scholarship. In contrast, *The Fifth Way* courageously applies the latest in Bible scholarship to trace out, in a very personal manner, the implications of living a Christian life that reflects the unquestionable Jewishness of the Aramaic Jesus."

John C. Drew, Ph.D.,
Author/Blogger: American Thinker, Breitbart.com, PJMedia, FrontPage Magazine.

"I hate to admit that I am not what you would call an avid reader. But when I met Dave Brisbin and our conversation came around to his book, just the way he talked about it made me want to get my hands on it. When I did, I didn't delay in reading the first chapter. I was hooked. But I didn't read it fast. It's not that type of book. I savored each chapter, set it down and let it sink in. I was anxious to read on to the next but I felt that what I was reading demanded time to think about it, maybe even to read it again before going on. Dave writes beautifully but more than that, he thinks beautifully. He draws the reader to take a journey with him to investigate how we have tried to know God, solve life's difficulties, and see if there is another way. And there is. I am so anxious to share this book with all of my friends and family."

Lindy Boone Michaelis
Singer, Daughter of Pat Boone, Author: Heaven Hears

"I'm just 30 pages into *The Fifth Way*, and I'm disappointed...I was looking for an editing job, for a profitable project. Instead, what I've found is some of the best writing I've *ever* read. I can't imagine giving any advice. I will continue to read because your intellect, perception, observations, and writing skills compel me to do so, but I can't imagine charging you for my time. I should pay you for allowing me to read this inspired manuscript."

Jerry Granckow
Book Editor, Author: In Search of the Silver Lining

"A few months ago I was introduced to your ministry though a friend who loaned me *The Fifth Way*. I am on page 300 and have advised her that the book is now on *permanent loan to me*. I understand she resupplied on her visit last week. Many of us sense this authentic Jesus and loving God but *The Fifth Way* brings into focus and expresses concepts and principles in a way that is extraordinarily insightful. Thank you for this book and for your ministry."

Allen Smith
Director, World of God Ministries, Inc.

"It's not often that one can say 'This book changed my life.' But this book changed my life. Where others either consciously or sub-consciously promote division in the name of God, Dave teaches unity and the importance of connection with God and *all* people, regardless of one's chosen faith. Unlearning suspect teachings of the past while coming to a deeper understanding about the true meaning of love, the importance of not judging those around us, and the value of being present in each moment has been a blessing that is hard to put into words. Because of Dave's book, I have a better understanding of who Jesus *really* was and what he was trying to teach us. I enthusiastically encourage you to begin your journey along *The Fifth Way*."

Doug Corbin
President, Paragon Charitable Services Group, Inc.

"Dave Brisbin's writing continues to create a powerful bridge between historical Christianity and the challenge of faith in modern life. His judicious research makes for a rich feast of background facts, and his use of personal anecdotal accounts makes factual research material relevant in a way only a spiritual writer could possibly do. *The Fifth Way* is a must-read for Christians and skeptics alike. Anyone who has ever wanted to know more about the centering value of Christian experience will benefit from Brisbin's determination to paint a picture of Christ that only a true scholar-artist could create."

Michael Hoffman, M.A., Dr.AD
Addiction Specialist, Author: The Thirsty Addict Papers—Spiritual Psychology for Counselors

"*The Fifth Way* gives us a closer look at the Semitic mind of Jesus Christ through careful research and understanding of Palestinian Aramaic, the everyday language of Jesus Christ. Dave Brisbin gives us the four basic philosophies that dominated the lives and thought of everyone in first century Israel. He gives us an understanding of the Greek mind that shapes the Western world today, leaving the gap between Semitic and Western languages, Eastern and Western thinking. Dave shows us a new way, the way of Yeshua Ha Mashiach, Jesus the Messiah, a 'Fifth Way,' one of living out faith, connection with God, and the Kingdom of God. *The Fifth Way* will give you a fresh understanding and depth of relationship with the heartbeat and thinking of Yeshua Ha Mashiach. Reading this book will expand your experience with Yeshua, our Jesus, and lead you to thinking differently, in a 'Fifth Way.'"

Dr. Michael Erickson
Sr. Pastor, Big Bear Four Square Church

"*The Fifth Way* is a 'must read' for anyone seeking to learn more about the life and teaching of Jesus Christ. It is invaluable as a reference and a 'must have' for anyone in full-time ministry. The stories are engaging and relevant. The teaching is objective and well supported by references. I highly recommend this book and am looking forward to reading it again. Great job, Pastor Dave!"

Dr. Ken Pierce
Physician, Missionary, Worship Leader, Author: Wise@Heart

THE
FIFTH
WAY

A Western Journey to the
Hebrew Heart of Jesus

DAVID BRISBIN

The Fifth Way
A Western Journey to the Hebrew Heart of Jesus

Published in the United States of America
theeffect
27122A Paseo Espada, Suite 924
San Juan Capistrano, CA 92675
www.theeffect.org

13-digit ISBN: 978-1-4993-4166-9
10-digit ISBN: 1-4993-4166-0

Cover photography © 2010 by Peter Zelei

Printed in the United States of America

For Marian, Caitlyn, Megan, Sean, and Brennan...
those who know me best and love me anyway.

Contents

THE TRUTH
THE TERMS OF THE WAY

THE LIFE
ON THE WAY

Acknowledgments

THE WRITING OF THIS BOOK HAS BEEN A JOURNEY IN ITSELF, AND NO journey occurs without traveling companions and those we meet along the way. I want to thank all those around me who encouraged me to write including so many at theeffect faith community who have cheerled through the process and David Stacy and Frank Billman for their help and support in preparing this current edition. I also want to thank Jeff Larson, my friend who faithfully read along with the initial writing of the manuscript, editing and discussing at every stage. Jeff didn't live long enough to see the project through with me, but his enthusiasm and description of the journey he engaged, of the journey we engaged together with these words as excuse, have been enough.

And of course, I want to deeply thank my wife, Marian, who wrote on a sticky note the call for me to write the book I'd been talking about for years before that. I'm looking at that note right now—her constant reminder—and though she has called herself an author's widow over the years, she has never failed to support and encourage and love me through it all.

I've casually read so many authors express these same sentiments of gratitude and indebtedness for the support of husbands, wives, editors and friends in the writing of countless books...

Now I understand.

Author's Note

IF THE ANCIENT HEBREWS ARE RIGHT, IF WE HUMANS LIVE OUR LIVES between heaven and earth—between the poles of unity and individual form, connection and apparent separation—then as we work to bring heaven to earth and earth to heaven, our lives will necessarily oscillate between the two. And if *that* is true, then the success of our lives can be measured simply by our ability to love the oscillation. Never either-or, always both-and...a learning to love rain *and* shine; day and night; the theology, doctrine, ritual, and ethics of religion *and* the wordless, contemplative unknowing of present spirituality. Never full resolution, always an embrace of seeming opposites—a looking at life through our own eyes, then infinite eyes, and back again.

This book will attempt to model that oscillation as it alternates chapter by chapter between the objective and subjective, logical and emotional, conceptual material and personal experience expressed in biographical snapshots and a string of journal entries dated from 1990 to 1994. Though two decades apart, the conceptual material carries a line of thought gleaned from the experience and disturbance reflected in those entries, and neither would exist without the other.

Because Jesus was addressing the herenow of his Kingdom and rarely anywhen or where else, our spiritual journeys along his Way always play out against the backdrop of each moment of our daily lives. And so, the strategies we need to live on earth must operate side by side with the one we need to experience heaven here on earth...

..they must oscillate as well.

Just as there are four cardinal directions in which we can move across the earth, there are also Four Ways in which we move our earthly agendas: *yield, manipulate, exit, and destroy*. From nations and armies to churches and husbands and wives, when faced with stubborn objects standing between us and our heart's desire, we can yield to the power in our path, manipulate or influence it, flee it, or tear it down.

Since the beginning of time, these four have been the only tools available and the only ones needed. There are certainly combinations in between, just as there is northwest and southeast, but the four remain—and in each of us one predominates. The Four Ways work well and are essential to meeting the needs of physical survival, but we are not just physical creatures. Jesus is showing us, through life and message, the futility of trying to live spiritually abundant lives through physical means motivated only by need. The tragedy of Western history is that the church lost that message early on, using these Four Ways institutionally as tools for obtaining things Jesus lived and died insisting we already possessed.

If we listen with Hebrew ears, we can hear Jesus begging us to engage a completely different way...a Fifth Way.

Instead of the Four Ways moving about the plane of the earth's compass, the Fifth Way of Jesus travels at another angle, a non-earthly angle, because rather than driven by need, it begins at the awareness of abundance. It takes the Four Ways and turns them inside out, downside up, and backside front. Where the Four Ways seek relevance, power, and attention to achieve their ends, the Fifth Way freely gives those desires away to make them real qualities in the lives of others—because we'll never know whether something is really ours to possess until we can freely give it away—because objects of our deepest desire can only and ever be *received*...never taken.

This Fifth Way, this Way of Jesus is the only way to the Father, to the unity and contentment of God's love, because only by beginning to match the quality of that love, will we ever know it really exists, that we are beloved.

And until we know we are beloved, we will always live in fear.

The Gospel According to Lou

There are moments when life makes sense.

BIG MOMENTS. DEFINING MOMENTS. MOMENTS THAT SEEM TO clarify, even justify other moments of your life. Sometimes you sense you're in a big moment. Try to take note, mark it. But I think most times you don't. Or can't.

I had a moment like that a few years ago. And I didn't realize how big it was holding my wife's hand in the hospital room visiting Lou. I couldn't know at the time for sure, but certainly was aware of the possibility that it would be the last moment I would spend with Lou.

Lou was old, and he was sick. He was tired of the dialysis and had finally said no more. Big dark patches of blood lay just under his skin and covered much of his arms and the parts of his legs exposed by gown and sheet. I was shaken by his appearance, but Lou seemed unaware and undeterred. He smiled his trademark smile, the one that seemed to split his face into two halves and said you were the only person in the world at that moment...the one with the gap between the front teeth that I'd seen so many times as he'd greet me in the aisles on a Sunday morning.

I loved Lou. I loved him, and I loved the idea of him. As he had gotten sicker, I'd taken to visiting him in the convalescent home, and we'd had time to talk in ways that Sunday mornings couldn't hold. I'd gotten to know more than just the smile, but had learned that the smile went all the way to the bone with Lou.

1

In the moment my wife and I were with him, we talked about many things; most were inconsequential though, because the big thing was hard to put into words. And when it was obvious he was tired and needed to sleep, we got up to go, and he took a hand from each of us and squeezed and looked at us with a squeeze too, with the intensity of something he really wanted to convey.

With the smile spreading across his face again he said,

"Love each other. Just...love each other."

He paused for a beat, then added,

"And kid around a little."

We smiled and hugged and left and three days later he was dead.

Lou died exactly two weeks before my ordination as a pastor. Thoughts and time had been filled with preparation for the event and especially for the message I was to give, and by the time we had stepped around the curtains of Lou's bed, I had an outline in mind and thought I knew what I wanted to say that Sunday. But in the days that followed our visit and his death, the bigness of that moment with Lou became clearer and clearer until I realized that Lou had already said it all—everything I was trying to say—in just twelve words. It was a gospel according to Lou. Complete, intact, beautiful in its brevity. I couldn't say it any better, and any more said would only be commentary. Twelve words.

Chapter one, verse one: Love each other, just love each other.

Chapter one, verse two: And kid around a little.

That moment with Lou helped make sense of many other moments—to begin to understand something I'd been suspecting for some time through the years of study and preparation, but hadn't quite been able to formulate mentally or verbally and certainly not in twelve words.

Lou was the same person living or dying: all his parts, physical, emotional, spiritual, worked seamlessly together to produce that smile. I don't know how long it took him to get to the smilepoint; I didn't know him as a young man or even a middle-aged man, but for as long as I knew him, he made a complete statement with his life. I'm not saying that Lou never had a bad moment, a black day or a brown day...of course he did. But he had gotten to a point in his life where at any given moment he could provide whatever was most needed by any person in his path. In a body ravaged by diabetes and managed with dialysis, Lou had become content. More often than not.

Lou loved us and loved to kid around with us. His love was the way he had decided to live his life, but his kidding around was the way we knew we were loved. His playfulness made his love real, not the love itself, because love is never transferred directly—the effect love has on our choices is all that can ever be felt by another. We often say that love is a decision, and so it is, in part. Love may have been Lou's decision, but his kidding around was the proof that he actually liked the decision he made...that his decision had transformed him from someone who practiced love to someone who had fallen deeply *in* love.

Lou was transformed. And that made all the difference.

The writings we hold sacred in Judeo-Christian Scripture give us image after image of the centrality of transformation—from being born again to drinking living water to becoming like little children. They all point in the same direction: radical change. All we may do in the name of God, however well meaning, is meaningless without true transformation that changes us from the inside out and makes the experience of our lives radically different. Without transformation, love remains a decision and lots of hard work. *Be ye transformed*, and love becomes play.

Thoreau wrote that most men lead lives of quiet desperation and go to the grave with the song still in them. What is it about the Gospel, the Good News, that isn't good enough anymore to actually transform our lives from being characterized by fear to being characterized by contentment...and from there, to being able to play at love? What did Lou know that we don't? Was there some wonderful joke God told him that kept him smiling and laughing every time he recalled the punch line?

I think so. I think God kept Lou laughing because Lou had finally seen God as God is. Lou couldn't tell us the joke, you had to be there, but we could see it written on his face and in his life. And in his gospel. But is Lou's gospel consistent with the other four?

☉ ☽ ♁ ♁ ♁

The Gospels tell us that *Yeshua*—the Hebrew name of Jesus—wept. They never mention that he smiled or laughed, but does that mean he never did? One characteristic of Scripture is that if a thing was commonly known by the people, it was not explicitly stated; it was already understood. If you live in a desert, a sunny day is nothing of note—but a rainy day makes all the headlines. Yeshua is said to have wept twice, big news because as Lou helped teach me, the rest of the time he was smiling and laughing. Everyone knew that about him, it didn't have to be written down.

When Yeshua says we must be like little children to enter the Kingdom of Heaven, what do we think that means? Look at children playing in a schoolyard and look at yourself at work. Is there a difference? If Yeshua came to give us entrance to Kingdom, could he give us anything he didn't already possess himself?

We need to read between the lines here.

We need to see that Yeshua was always the first guy in the pool, running ahead of his friends, urging them on from over his shoulder, and showing them with his life what it meant to live in the richness of Kingdom. He drew crowds with the sound of his laughter and the brilliance of his smile long before the force of his words. In fact, his words had force *because* of the sound of his laughter and the brilliance of his smile.

Instead of the somber and stoic Jesus typically portrayed in our paintings and films, the one standing ram-rod straight, arms outstretched and eyes lifted heavenward, speaking King James English, we need to see a laughing, smiling Yeshua with an arm draped about the shoulders of anyone close. When we read about Yeshua reprimanding his friends for keeping the children away from him, we need to resist the typical image of him perching one child on his knee and patting her on the head while the others quietly circle up and watch. Yeshua would have been rolling on the ground with all of them at once, kicking up dust, tickling and wrestling and giving horseback rides. Undignified? You bet. We could all do with a little less dignity and a lot more fun.

We are so busy seeing Yeshua as God, that we miss seeing him as a man: a man in love with life—completely integrated and fearless. Yeshua had his black days and brown days too, but he was characterized by contentment...because he knew his Father, and the news was good.

I am not now where Lou was when he died. But I do have the desire to get there. A burning desire that has taken me a good distance along the Way to the smilepoint. And on my black days and brown days, when I seem to be losing my Way, I cling to my desire like a piece of wood on open water, and I pray as Thomas Merton once did:

> My Lord God, I have no idea where I am going. I do not see the road ahead of me. I cannot know for certain where it will end. Nor do I really know myself, and the fact that I think that I am following your will does not mean that I am actually doing so.
>
> But I believe that the desire to please you does in fact please you. And I hope I have that desire in all that I am doing. I hope that I will never do anything apart from that desire. And I know that if I do this you will lead me by the right road though I may know nothing about it. Therefore will I trust you always though I may seem to be lost and in the shadow of death. I will not fear, for you are ever with me, and you will never leave me to face my perils alone.

Desire is the critical first piece, the engine that drives us toward something we realize is yet unrealized. Without it, nothing further takes place. Desire is pleasing to God in and of itself, but desire is only the first step to being characterized by contentment. Our desire, no matter how fervent and passionate, can be shunted off in unprofitable directions by our mistaken notions of the Way. God continues loving us and being pleased by us and our desire, but our lives will not reflect that love in contentment and playfulness until we start to know who God really is and what that means to our moments.

And so we come to the part about counting the cost, picking up our crosses, being crucified with Christ...and images predictably form in our minds of toil and sweat, blood and death. We ask each other if we would be willing to die for Christ as he died for us. But the real question being asked is not whether we'd be willing to die for Christ, but whether we are willing to *live* as he did—focused on life and celebration. Are we willing to live abundantly by being willing to let die everything in us that would keep us from entering transformed lives characterized by contentment?

The Good News is only as good as we actually believe it is, and we'll only know whether we really believe the news is good when we become characterized by contentment ourselves. When we have really fallen in love with each other and God, our lives will bear the marks of the death of our desperation, and we really will be like people raised from the grave of our fears.

Lou understood this. Maybe not technically or theologically, but deeply and personally and in a way he could articulate so beautifully.

Love each other...just love each other.

But trying our best to love each other remains all work and no play for too many of us.

And kid around a little.

Without the kidding around, without the sense of fun and play and celebration, how is it that we're really in love? The two are inseparable—each one defining and proving the existence of the other. If we're really in love, then we're also at play. And if we're really at play, in that moment, we're also in love.

Lou knew this too, and in that moment we had with him, that big moment, he tried to squeeze into our hands and eyes and ears what took him a lifetime to comprehend.

There's only so much anyone can really tell you, but I can tell you that in that big moment, my life made sense. And in the moments that have followed, I have found more and more truth in Lou's gospel.

I can't do any better than Lou did; I'm not going to try. But what does it take to get to the point in life where you can state the Gospel with authority, straight from your heart in only twelve words?

This book is about the journey to that moment.

THE GATE

THE WAY TO THE WAY

It's fascinating the things we remember.

>Even more fascinating, the power of the things we don't. And all our things, remembered or not, remain deep in our bones, affecting us in ways large and small, intended or not, helpful or not.

>Growing up in a church setting, it's easy to miss the point that religion and spirituality are two very different things. They occur together from time to time, but the strength of their relationship rests entirely on the person doing the occurring— and as children, we're mostly just doing what we're told.

>The Catholicism of my youth was a patchwork of dormant memories and unremembered attitudes by the time my first marriage ended twentysome years ago...

>Hadn't been to Mass since the day before I left the monastery I had entered out of high school—nearly fifteen years. *Bless me father for I have sinned...* I can still feel the sway of cassock and surplice hanging from my shoulders, close my eyes and look down into a brass chalice—watch the ripple of altar lights through heavy, sweet wine. I don't remember learning a thing about marriage and divorce and remarriage through twelve years of Catholic education: of catechism and altar boyism, high school Latin and theology...even less from the Order's house of formation on the edge of those endless cornfields southwest of Chicago. But half a life of steeping in a culture and a faith actually alters the DNA, and just the slightest nudge stands us back up against our ancestral selves.

>A divorce is more than slight. Breaks all the rules set deepest down. I don't know if it's worse to divorce or be divorced upon. Perpetrator or victim. I've had my heart broken before

and since, and though broken may hurt harder, I think breakers hurt longer. At least Catholic ones.

>I remember hearing somewhere that people should mate for life...like pigeons or Catholics. I'd forgotten I was still Catholic, but my *soul* remembered and punished me...for being divorced, for forcing my three year old daughter into a purgatory between mom and dad, collecting the million hurts she'd spend her youth and perhaps middle age trying to outrun. Catholics don't divorce; annul, but not divorce.

>For fifteen years I hadn't done any of the things Catholics do, and now that I was doing things Catholics didn't, whatever faith my DNA remembered had no power to heal or comfort.

It could only punish.

Warriors and Gardeners

The quality of the means we use
must match the quality of the ends we seek.

OR BETTER, THE QUALITY OF THE MEANS WE USE *ALWAYS* MATCHES the quality of the ends we *produce*. Like breeds like; we reap what we sow, get out what we put in. We won't get olives from fig trees, and if the ends we seek are the unity and contentment of true spiritual formation, we need to know that we can't work for unity and contentment without first acting unified and contented.

A young man tells me in low tones that he's praying that the Lord comes back soon: today would be fine with him. His finances are so upside down, he doesn't know how he's going to make it to next month. I can almost see his knuckles whiten as he grips the wheel and stares down the rest of his life like the barrel of a gun. A woman in her sixties confides that even after forty years of service in the church, she still wonders if she's really going to heaven.

Anxious people.

A student says he's been worried ever since attending a Pentecostal/charismatic service, which was so bizarre to him that he couldn't help ridiculing it afterwards. Did he blaspheme the Holy Spirit, commit the unforgivable sin, he wants to know? Another says he's afraid that in the end times he may take the mark of the beast by mistake and be damned forever. I tell them both that God's not like that, that they couldn't possibly commit an unforgivable sin without knowing exactly what they were doing, which is the only possible definition of unforgivable in the first place. I can see they remain unconvinced and uneasy.

Frightened people.

A pastor tells a study group that he holds his arms outstretched, palms up in times of praise and worship in order to show God that his hands are clean and acceptable—as a child would show his mother he washed his hands for dinner. But I'm thinking when my two-year-old son comes to me with arms outstretched and palms up, he just wants to be picked up and held.

Guilty people.

It's fascinating, the things we remember. Even more fascinating, the power of the things we don't. And the things our souls remember that our minds do not, tend to punish us. We are shaped much more by the pain and trauma we experience than the love and care. Pain creates unremembered attitudes toward others, situations, life itself that color our perception and form the basis for choices we don't plan or understand.

As if paraphrasing Thoreau, snapshots of contemporary life in our churches betray our desperation, quiet or unquiet, in nearly every frame. Whether anxious, frightened, or guilty, it all comes down to fear because all these emotions are the manifestations, the acting out of fear—fear of some sort of loss. We're afraid we're not going to get what we want or what we need, and at the deepest levels, we're afraid of simply not being acceptable to others or God. We lead fearful lives and wonder why we never arrive anywhere else, as if fear could ever breed anything that doesn't look like itself.

Yeshua has given us a blinding glimpse of what a life looks like when the news is really good and the realization dawns that we can approach each moment from an attitude of abundance rather than need, from the contentment of knowing we are already connected to everything that matters rather than the fear of always wanting. Until the quality of the means by which we live our lives begins to match the quality of the life Yeshua led, that Lou led beyond his smilepoint, we will never make the leap from fear to contentment to playful love.

Often within our churches, the problem compounds as beliefs and practice reinforce our fears and sense of unworthiness rather than the unconditional acceptance of the Good News. If there's to be any hope of changing unremembered attitudes, we must begin with conscious principles that are pointing in the right direction.

⊙ ⊙ ⊕ ⊕ ⊗

Is there a primary metaphor for our spiritual lives?

If so, then we seem to have collectively decided as a church that it's the image of the warrior that suits us best.

We speak of being soldiers for Christ, we put on the full armor of God as we prepare ourselves and our children to take and occupy the land—we even organize ourselves in paramilitary fashion. Our imagery is largely imperialistic in nature, an invasive, conquering mentality in which foreign lands and foreign hearts and minds must be bent to the will of God. We say we do this in love, for the eternal good of those in our path, but if they don't see it that way, we must fight until they do.

And in the fighting, we understand that we will be attacked by the enemy. In fact, we often say that one way of knowing that we're on the right track is to measure the amount of opposition we face as the enemy finally begins to take notice of our accomplishments on the field of battle.

This is the image and metaphor toward which we've gravitated, but it is certainly not the only one in Scripture. In fact, Yeshua never uses it. He seems to have preferred a very different image in his teachings—that of the gardener or farmer. Instead of fluttering banners, snorting horses, and deafening drums, there is the quietly bent back of the gardener breaking up the soil, preparing the ground for seed, squinting into sun and wind for hints of coming weather. Yeshua's stories and images speak of a flowing in concert with tides and wind rather than a strident opposition, a watching of the succession of seasons with feet and hands deeply embedded in dark earth, feeling it turning underneath bringing sun and rain and all the essentials of life. Instead of a sudden, violent bending into submission, there is a slow and steady, infinitely patient tending and nurturing into fullness.

So are we warriors or gardeners?

Of necessity, we are at times one or the other or both. But as we follow the life of Yeshua through the Gospels, we see much more gardener than warrior. There is that patient tending and growing of relationships, a willingness to let everyone and everything take whatever time needed to come to fruition. Yeshua is always present and vigilant, but never coercive: plants ripen in the due course of their season and no amount of force on the gardener's part can change that fact. The gardener's success is in intimately knowing the seasons and the times and the tending in order to be a part of that flow and to be standing in the right place at the right time when the heavy fruit falls.

What are the ends we ultimately seek?

To forever lead the anxious, frightened, guilty life of the warrior? To be constantly on guard for the enemy, always ready to strike or be stricken, living in the daily presence of death? Of course not, that was always only means to a different end...but the metaphor we choose shapes us, creates itself in our image.

The quality of the means we use must match quality of the ends we seek because at any moment in our lives, the quality of our means is all the experience there is. There are no ends. A task has means and ends, but not life. Life is not a task; it's a single, ongoing moment of lived experience that only and ever matches the quality of our means, our metaphor.

Maybe, then, we are reluctant warriors who fight when we must, but always with a wistful eye over our shoulders longing for the silent fields of home, for the moment we can literally beat our swords back into plowshares and take up the work we love.

This is just how it feels to begin walking the Fifth Way after walking the first Four Ways our entire lives. Like falling into the arms of a loved one after an exhausting and frightening ordeal, the Four Ways of striving against overwhelming power and insurmountable odds, fighting always uphill, upwind, and upstream with our ancient weapons—*to yield, manipulate, exit, and destroy*—are as much a joy and relief to leave behind as a battlefield littered with our dead. To stride out of the smoke, to feel the wind at our backs instead of our faces, to glide downhill and pick up speed, to be content to let the earth turn without pushing are all hallmarks of the Fifth Way as opposed to the first four, of the gardener as opposed to the warrior.

For many weary warriors out there, it's time to come home.

We progress at the pace of pain.

>If that's true, then the fifteen years between monastic order and marital divorce provided impetus that very nearly over-shot any landing. Paced by the pain of divorce, I entered a personal purgatory: atonement by misery for the next three years or so...isolating in a nearby town, going to work, coming directly home again to bare walls, unpacked boxes, lunchmeat dinners.

>My best friend was the bicycle I rode with a vengeance every day after work as if I could sweat out hurtful things before the sun went down. But as hard as I could ride or run, suicidal scenes played continuously across the back of my mind: how the slightest tug on the wheel could end all this, how if I did it just right the insurance company would still pay.

>I know it was only a divorce. Show of hands almost any-where and most will be in the air for at least one breakup somewhere, somewhen. People have gone through so much worse, have done so much worse. And as true as that is, in the painful moment, it's just as meaningless. Pain is like per-fume. Open the bottle anywhere and soon you smell it eve-rywhere. Without something to counter, our greatest pain, no matter how small, fills to overflowing. And of course, divorce and daughter weren't the sum of my pain, just the natural result of nearly twenty years of constant fear.

>Why? How to account for all this pain, all the fear? There should have been trauma, lots of trauma.

But I can't remember any.

Spiritual Common Sense

Faith isn't rational, but it isn't irrational either.

FAITH IS AN ASSUMPTION WE MAKE ABOUT TRUTH THAT ALLOWS US to go out and experience that truth. Call it extra-rational...common sense still applies.

Before it was beaten out of us by the creeds, doctrine, and dogma of the church, before it was leached out of us by the relativism, nihilism, and materialism of secular philosophy and humanism, there was a spiritual common sense that we were all born with, and which, if we squint and strain, can still be glimpsed flitting around the edges of our awareness. It's that part of us that asks all the "wrong" questions, the ones that "lack faith," the ones that make teachers squirm or angrily reprimand their students. But the questions persist, even if we stop asking them. They don't dissipate when there are no answers to be found. And if we've learned to be satisfied with a particular school of thought, a church, or a theology, there's still something underneath that remains unsettled, unsettling—which is exactly what makes the teacher defensive and angry at having the edges of the veneer pried up by impertinent but common-sensical students.

Passionate common sense is the check and the balance, the only foothold against a slide into superstition and spiritual irrelevance. It seems we need permission once again to legitimately use our common sense in the realm of the spiritual...then let's give it, because in terms of our faith, there are many common sense questions to ask. Like a child shaking off the question of how Santa could possibly descend every chimney during a single night in favor of the promise of Christmas morning, we shake off questions about God's nature and the presence of evil, about sin and judgment, salvation and damnation, scripture and science in favor of the promise of a secure faith. It's pure irony that in the name of faith we should stop asking such questions, when to stop asking is the first sign that we are no longer serious about our journey of faith, about following the Way of Yeshua.

Recently, a 17-year-old son challenges his father, wanting to know if what his father believes is actually true, or just what he believes.

What a question!

The perfect question. The central question. Are such questions only being asked by 17-year-olds...those of us too young, too naïve, too unschooled to have lost the spiritual common sense with which God birthed us—the very tool he gave us to bring us back to himself? We should all be asking the same question, not just of others, but of ourselves. Is what we believe really true, or just what we've decided to believe? What we've learned to accept? What we've let others decide for us?

Many of us have stopped asking common sense questions, or never began in the first place. We have simply accepted the received tenets of our faith on faith, so the task is left to our children, the 17-year-olds among us with the audacity to look behind the curtain. And they *are* looking and asking. Their whole generation, aided by a few of their elders, is looking and asking, and the rest of us are uncomfortable, perhaps defensive...and increasingly irrelevant to their search. Call it postmodern thought or emerging church or blatant heresy, we can try to resist, but it's all about the common sense God gave each of us inevitably reasserting itself after too much time away.

All new human ideas and questions begin as heresy, advance to orthodoxy, and end in superstition, to paraphrase Thomas Huxley. But because something is shunned as heresy doesn't mean it's also not *true*. And accepting something as orthodox doesn't *make* it true. And of course, by the time orthodoxy devolves to superstition, all common sense and critical thought is lost.

Prevailing opinion has nothing to do with truth. The two are as far apart as the east is from the west—intertwined only in the mind of the person who has lost touch with common sense.

☉ ⊙ ⊕ ⊕ ⊘

Some things in life are not transferable.

Each one of us is responsible for his or her own journey to truth. No one can take it for us, and no one can give us his or hers. The ruby slippers Dorothy wears can take her home at any moment, but no one can tell her how they work; she has to find out for herself.

We will be convinced of the truth of something only when we have gone out and *become* convinced, submitted it to rigorous testing in the laboratory of our lives. People were amazed at Yeshua's teaching because he taught with authority, not as the Pharisees and Scribes taught. That is, Yeshua was the same person living or dying...his truths were part of the reality of his life and not a classroom exercise.

Taste and see that the Lord is good, the Psalms tell us. Taste and see, not sit and think. For us, as much as for the ancients, we need to get out of our minds and classrooms and into the streets of our lives to find God playing among us.

If we're afraid of looking heretical in someone's eyes, we'll never ask the first question, postulate the first idea, or set out on our own journey to truth. Thank God Yeshua and his followers weren't afraid to be called heretics or drunkards or gluttons: or Francis of Assisi, Galileo, Martin Luther, or a 17-year-old boy challenging his father's beliefs. If we're afraid to ask the most basic, most common sense questions, we'll never be able to answer the most relevant question, "Who am I," which itself only has meaning as we come to know ultimate reality in the person of God. And without knowing who

God is, the true radical nature of love, we'll never "enter the Kingdom," live the transformed life toward which Yeshua is trying to guide us. We'll never understand how God and love, Kingdom and transformed life are really all the same thing. Find one; find them all.

When I was preparing to enter a seminary graduate school, several pastors I knew tried to talk me out of it, saying that modern seminaries are where people go to lose their faith rather than learn about it. But how valuable is a faith that is dependent on the maintenance of ignorance? Such a faith is indistinguishable from superstition. If our faith can only thrive in the absence of the knowledge of its origins, history, and competing theological concepts, then what is it we really have to hold on to?

And what are we afraid of?

Losing truth? Finding truth in the unfamiliar? Yeshua told us to ask, seek, and knock. Ask and it will be given, seek and you will find, knock and it will be opened. What are we afraid of? The search for what is really true is the search for ultimate reality. Reality as it really is. God as God really is. No matter where that Way takes us, it will be a good journey, because even if we find ourselves somewhere we never imagined, God precedes us. Or in the words of T.S. Eliot, "And the end of all our exploring will be to arrive where we started and know the place for the first time."

Just as home-again Dorothy realizes she never needs to leave her own backyard to find her heart's desire, once we've followed our own yellow Way awhile, we can say with Yeshua that the Kingdom is not out there somewhere to be found by observation and discovery, but is within us, among us, and in our midst—or in the rendering of his native Aramaic language, *legau men*, moving dynamically from inside to outside.

If our desire is the engine, then our common sense is the rudder.

Those of us who are most invested in any school of thought, who've spent the most time studying, training, practicing, are the ones most in need of asking that 17-year-old's question because our common sense may have the most layers of accumulated dust. We can use our common sense as a sort of divining rod—the forked branch fabled to vibrate in the presence of water—to guide us to the right questions that will lead us not necessarily to the right answers, but to the right *experiences* that will convince us of the truth. There really is no other way, which is what Yeshua meant when he said he was the Way, that no one comes to the Father but through him...through that Way of living life as he lived and experienced it.

From the lips of Shakespeare's Hamlet: *there are more things in heaven and earth than are dreamt of in your philosophy*...because the most important questions are not so easily asked. What do you ask when you don't know what you don't know? *Why* would you ask when what you do know seems to be all there is? But if we are simply willing to begin the journey, there will come the shattering moment we get the first glimpse of a little man behind a green curtain working the controls of a world we never knew existed.

No matter how fleeting the glimpse, it can't be unseen, and everything is forever changed.

I'm adopted.

>Was that trauma enough? The beginning of pain and fear? Did I remember my birth mother somehow? Did something happen before adoption and memory took hold, some mishandling or abandonment that survived just beyond periphery? My adoptive parents were good people, careful, caring, but cool to the touch, living always somewhere down the hall. I remember them fighting only twice; I wish they'd fought more so I could see—heated up, revealed things. Especially my father. Everything I know about him, I know from others or through the letters and news clippings that came in a box posted from Nebraska after his mother died. He was a boy scout; he won awards for model airplanes built from scratch with leather seats and working electrical lights. I read that part over and over. Where did they all go? Why didn't he build anymore? I was a cub scout, built models of cars, planes, and ships with plastic parts that came from toy stores, but he never sat with me or let on about a skill I couldn't imagine.

>Looking at pictures in the box with the news clippings— family and faces from another world—was I supposed to feel a connection? Would people of blood have felt it? I put the pictures back next to the clippings. Naturally introverted, awkward, bookish, invisible in elementary school, I came straight home every day to my encyclopedias and maps of the solar system. Was that alienation enough to blame?

>There was a period of bedtime molestation, but it was brief, and when I resisted loud and long enough, it went away— nothing like the horror stories you read about. But did it fundamentally alter my view of the adults in my life, my place with them? It didn't seem so at the time, and even now it

fights for validation in my mind like a half-remembered dream. But when I got to seventh grade and my first crush on a girl, I was so teased by mother and sister that I consciously decided it wasn't safe anymore—better not to let on, start living always down the hall. Was that the moment fear began, or just another moment on top of all the others? Maybe it doesn't matter how fast or how far, just how long.

Because pain is like perfume; eventually it fills you up.

The Process of Kingdom

This is not a book of answers.

In terms of life and meaning and spirituality, there is no such thing. The deepest questions in life are not so much answered as experienced. Not so much understood as undergone. The most profound truths are not offered directly and succinctly, but like a figure coming out of the mist, are slowly defined by a gradual grasping of an ability to ask more and more incisive *questions*—each new question leading to another and a step closer to the whole.

But this is not a book of questions either.

Neither questions nor answers, this is a book about the terms of the Way between the two—an attempt to understand *the process* by which we experience the truths of life and begin to see them more clearly. It's about Yeshua's Aramaic message, his teaching of the Way to truth and life, what he calls entering the Kingdom of Heaven.

Yeshua said the Gate that opens to the Way that leads to life is narrow. The Way is narrow too and before the narrow Way can be traveled, the narrow Gate must be negotiated first. That is, we must understand enough of the nature of the journey to even realize we're standing at the Gate, the unassuming trailhead that directs the first step. Yeshua said few go by this Gate and this Way, and this is true. Most of us are so consumed with finding answers to life's questions that we completely miss the Way that stretches between the two.

Then Yeshua says that *he* is the Way, the Truth, and the Life. Three single-syllable images that have fueled endless debate and theological exertion for two thousand years can still clear a room today, because apparently the Way of Truth and Life is a *person* and not a thing. If the Way is a person, we have to know the person before there's any hope of knowing the Way. Looking at Yeshua's teaching from a first century, Aramaic point of view—as if for the first time—will begin to bring the person out of the mist, tracing the unmistakable outlines of the shape of his Way back to Father, to Kingdom.

Whenever he was studying a block of marble, Michelangelo said he envisioned the finished sculpture, say a horse, standing inside the stone as if frozen in ice. He could walk around it and see it from every angle and in every detail until it was as real to him as the raw block. Then all that remained to do was to remove everything that was not the horse. The process was slow, but sure in the hands of the master sculptor. Stroke by stroke, chip by chip, the excess stone was removed to reveal what had always been there standing in the heart of the stone.

For us, trying to sculpt our lives into the Kingdom of Heaven, the process is similar. If we look at our lives as a raw block of stone, our Kingdom-self is already there, fully formed, standing within. We know where it is, because Yeshua told us where to look. All that remains is to remove everything that is not Kingdom in our lives.

But here's where analogy breaks down. It's not *we* who actively do the removing. Attempting to do so directly only focuses us on the negative space, the parts we don't want in our lives, locking us more firmly into non-Kingdom. It's a focus on the person/Way of Yeshua to the exclusion of everything else that chips away all that excess material. If we, like Michelangelo, focus on the positive space, on the finished product standing within, running our fingers over every curve and detail, living with its image intimately etched in our spirits day in and out, at some point we suddenly realize there is nothing else left in our lives. Our lives have *become* Kingdom—Kingdom, shaped and sculpted by the natural abrasion of our passage along the Way.

But also like Michelangelo, we must have a clear image of what that positive space really is. For Kingdom to be realized in our lives, we must know what it is and what it looks like to the last vein and muscle; we need to know its shape and the shape of the journey leading there.

"He who has ears, let him hear," was a favorite expression of Yeshua that speaks to this need for the willingness to radically shift our worldview. We need new ears to hear.

> Heaven is waiting for us,
> but we don't have to wait for heaven.

The Kingdom of Heaven is not heaven—not as we think of heaven—the heaven of afterlife. Yeshua's Kingdom is the quality of life being lived *herenow* by those who experience God's intimate presence in the moments of their lives. It's the life lived by those who have awakened from their dreams to find their reality infinitely more wonderful. The realization of that reality, knowing God that intimately *is* the transformation, the rebirth, the entry into Kingdom—the smilepoint between love as decision and love as play.

While we focus on the therethen of heaven, Yeshua is calling us to refocus on the herenow of Kingdom. The heaven of the next life is still there waiting for us, but we don't have to wait for death to experience moments of unity and timelessness right herenow in the relationships we grow in Kingdom. Yeshua told us all that the waiting was over way back in Mark 1:15—that Kingdom has already arrived. These herenow Kingdom moments are the very substance of heaven: the herenow *is* the therethen for which we long, and by Yeshua's definition, Kingdom is *always* herenow and can never be anywhen else.

If Yeshua is telling us that our spiritual life is not about the acquisition of heaven in the next life but something immediate and herenow that *extends* into the next life, that changes everything. Or nothing, if we don't follow his implications to their radical conclusions.

We need new ears to hear.

Yeshua said the Kingdom of Heaven is like a man who finds a treasure buried in a field, goes off joyfully, sells all he has, and buys that field. This captures it perfectly. Because the essential truth is this:

the man already knows where the treasure is buried before he ever sets off to claim it.

The first and most difficult obstacle to grasping the shape of our journey is becoming convinced that the location of the treasure is really no mystery at all. Yeshua has told us exactly where it is and then tells us over and over in image and story and parable how to claim it. This is our red X marking the spot. Our big clue. Like a decoder ring from a cereal box, Yeshua gives us this first piece, the meaning and location of Kingdom, through which we can decipher all the rest of the puzzling pieces we'll find along the Way.

But for our decoders to work, we need to understand what the first hearers of Yeshua's message would have understood, immersed in the language, culture, and society of their day. Stripped of all we imagine from a modern viewpoint thousands of miles and years away and restored to its original Hebrew/Aramaic roots, Yeshua's Way, the Fifth Way, emerges not as an answer to a question, but an experience of the presence of God in this present moment.

This Fifth Way is not a thought to be contemplated, but an action to be lived.

The Fifth Way is not a creed or a doctrine to believe, but a way and a quality of life to enjoy.

Yeshua takes all these concepts, bundles them up, and calls them the Kingdom of Heaven, the centerpiece and framework of all his teaching. The Way to the Kingdom can't be thought through, it can only be lived through, which means we can only find the Way once we're *on* the Way—in motion, breaking out with the deepest desire to claim Kingdom, as God also desires. And making our desire the same as God's desire is the very definition of answered prayer and the shape of the Way.

If all this sounds incomprehensible, that's a good start. Let the paradoxical, staggering sayings of Yeshua fall uncritically on your mind for a moment: the last shall be first and the first last, hate your father and mother, gouge out your eye, to name a few—and you get a glimpse of the bewilderment of many of his first followers, a bewilderment we still share, if we're honest. That's fine, as it should be. The worst place to start is the place from which you think you already have all the answers—for then, what incentive is there to break out into unfamiliar territory?

We won't be off searching for buried treasure. It's already found, safely tucked away and waiting for us, which is where the joy comes from. Now comes the painful process of chipping away, selling all we have that is not Kingdom: the dying to self, the emptying, the unlearning, which is the essence of the inside out, downside up, backside front process of the Fifth Way. The Way that will give us all the resources we need to buy that field.

Once the field is ours, the treasure is ours.

Once the treasure is ours,
questions and answers pale in comparison.

I divorced in fear because I married in fear.

>Every decision I made, I made in fear—to somehow lessen, protect, comfort. I didn't know I was afraid, didn't experience fear directly, but looking closely at memories as if at details in a faded snapshot, there is always evidence of discomfort and depression, forensic marks of an obsessive need for something *else*. There was always something else I was supposed to be doing, somewhere else I was supposed to be living, someone else I was supposed to *be*—that what and where and who I was, was just not good enough. There are probably a thousand reasons for every emotion, but ignorance of them is no excuse; the emotion persists. Looking back, a thousand cuts, large and small, bled a fear that was relentlessly driving me to be always other than whatever I was.

>I called it virtue, living by process of elimination—entering and quickly exiting every relationship, job, school, vocation at the first sign of imperfection... But it was just fear.

>Afraid in high school, I had no idea what to do as graduation approached, and entered the monastery to stay close to the monks who taught me and had given me a hand to hold in the dark. Fear is always motivating but never a purpose, and I can still hear the voice of my closest friend in the house of formation, the only one of us first year postulants who seemed appropriate there, asking one night long after lights out: *why are you even here?*

>With only fear as purpose, the question was a landmine in a living room—devastatingly unanswerable, a fuse burning down to the moment I left... The house. The cornfields. The Church. With only fear as purpose, the next fifteen years trying to carve out a career in music, writing, recording, earning a

degree, teaching middle school, climbing a corporate ladder, getting married, having a child led only to those bare walls and unpacked boxes...a silent bicycle standing guard.

>Fear motivates. So does pain. The pain of picking up and handing off my daughter once or twice a week was always present, but fear blinded me to the added injury of bringing her home to bare walls and unpacked boxes, of macaroni and cheese dinners heated in the only pot I owned. I didn't deserve a home...couldn't see past the guilt that kept me guilty of not building one for her.

>I remembered I'd started a journal in a yellowed, hard-bound notebook with an ancient Bell Labs logo on the cover. The first entry was dated when my daughter was only forty-one days old. I'd intended to write a life letter to her, but after a few ragged entries, the book remained mostly blank. Four years later, book in hand, it seemed important to continue—to explain what had happened, make verbal amends or at least a record that would wait quietly for a four year old to grow into its pages.

>With justification and penance initially filling my pen, I began to write again. But as entries piled up, something began to happen on those pages: pain pushing past fear into the first stirring of flat sails, first blips on a flat line screen.

The Wellfrog

You cannot speak of ocean to a wellfrog,
the creature of a narrower sphere.
You cannot speak of ice to a summer insect,
the creature of a season.

Chuang Tzu, 4th Century BCE

ARE YOU AWAKE? OR ARE YOU DREAMING? RIGHT NOW, AS YOU SIT
or lie there reading this page, are you really sitting or lying there
reading or just dreaming that you're sitting or lying there? Look
around you. Is what you see really "real" or just images projected
from within your own mind?

What seems so obvious at first blush is really not so and the question not as silly as it seems. None of us experiences the world
around us, reality, directly. We experience it through our senses—
senses that measure temperature, pressure, light, and chemical
substances and convert those measurements into electrical impulses
that travel to different parts of our brain. The brain then interprets
those signals as images, sounds, tastes, smells, and touch. It's like
watching a program on television; the television receives electrical
signals and converts them to project images that you see on the
screen. But as you watch, you really have no idea where the signals
originated—from across the globe or the next room. All you have is
what's on the screen.

We are separated from reality in the same way, moving through
the landscape of our world the way a video game player moves

through the software of his. Our brains have no way of knowing whether the signals they interpret as sight and sound, taste and smell and touch are coming from external sources through our senses or are originating in another part of the brain itself.

In dreamtime, stored information from our experiences—memories—are called up, pieced together, and played across the screens of our minds. To the dreamer, dreamscape is as real as landscape. But sometimes we awaken inside our dreams. And if we wake just enough to realize we're dreaming but not enough to end the dream, we can experience our dreamtime from a more fully conscious state. Such dreams, lucid dreams, are a rare look behind the curtain of our consciousness, and some people actually practice the skill of cultivating them. Lucid dreamers train themselves to constantly question their consciousness—beginning in the waking state and moving to the dream state—looking intently throughout every day's details to spot clues or cues: whether color and perspective and the laws of physics are in normal operation or if the impossible is playing out before their minds' eyes betraying the dream masquerading as reality.

It's all about a constant questioning—what is the state of the reality around me? What's going on in every detail? Am I really awake? If the waker doesn't learn to question while awake and able to make conscious choices, the dreamer won't be trained to question when sleeping, and discrepancies between landscape and dreamscape remain undetected.

Most of us are quite content to let dreams be dreams, and life can be lived quite fully while taking our state of consciousness at face value. But our senses are only the first of two filters that separate us from true reality. The senses convert external stimuli into electrical impulses and send them to the brain, but the brain has to interpret those impulses into meaningful bits of information. How does it do that? How does the brain know what red is or what wet means? How does the brain tell us we like the chemical composition of doughnuts and hate that of broccoli? How do we decide one face is beautiful and another is not? Or know in a glance that this person is angry and that one in love?

The brain's ability to interpret information can't be separated from our ability to think, and our ability to think can't be separated from the sum of our knowledge and experience. In other words, everything around us, everything we've ever seen, heard, learned, and lived through has shaped and is shaping the way we *interpret* everything around us—everything we see, hear, learn, and live through. It's a closed loop. Circular logic. Like using a word in its own definition. Our current understanding of life and reality is the second filter, the dictionary through which we understand life and reality as it plays out before us.

This is the well Chuang Tzu speaks of and, like it or not, we're all wellfrogs obliviously swimming and croaking within the confines of the view we hold of the world around us—our worldview. And since the worldview that each of us holds is the very definition of reality itself, we can't directly separate it from our interpretation of reality. We don't see it as a point of view; it's just the way things are. It's the very ground on which we walk, the air we breathe, and so it forms the perfect prison: a prison with invisible walls; a prison that gives the illusion of freedom; a prison from which no escape seems necessary.

> The hardest thing you'll ever do is change your worldview.
> Second hardest is realizing you have one.

You cannot speak of ocean to a wellfrog because the wellfrog has no concept of anything existing outside the cylindrical column of air it breathes, the bright circle of light that appears high overhead at regular intervals, the narrow pool of water it occupies. For the wellfrog, there is no other "there" out there. If the sum of all experience includes only the narrow cylinder of the well, how could the concept of the vast expanse of limitless ocean ever enter the frog's mind?

Our wells are shaped by both our personal and collective experiences. By the time we are seven years old or so, much of the well has already been built around us as we experience the parenting ability or lack of it from the adult figures in our lives. The hurts and traumas and joys and play; the love and acceptance or indifference and abuse; the education and travel or lack of wider experience all play their parts in determining how we view other people—their motives, their value, their skin color, their perceived threat or connection to us—and how we view the world...our place in it.

The choices we make as adults, for better or worse, are pre-conditioned by the strategies we learned as children to meet and survive the challenges and the people we faced early on. Is the world a friendly place? Can the people we encounter be embraced as basically having our best interests at heart, or are they predators to be feared and outmaneuvered? Is our fundamental place in life part of and contributing to the flow of humanity around us, or do we stand outside that flow, passed by, ignored, even extorted by it?

How is our early worldview affected by the ensuing experiences of our lives? Typically, it is reinforced, as our choices become self-fulfilling prophecies all made within a certain frame of reference that recreate and repeat themselves over and over with each new/old choice. The abused tend to abuse; children of divorce tend to divorce; children of alcoholics tend to drink or over-compensate and over-control their surroundings and others; daughters marry their fathers and sons marry their mothers in order to regain or gain for the first time what they had or needed as children. The sins of the fathers are passed on from generation to generation.

But as powerful as our personal experiences may be, they are still only a frame within a frame, couched within the larger collective experiences of the culture and society around us. And those collective experiences are in turn a frame within an even larger frame of the history and worldview of our civilization. Our culture and society, through media, music and arts, schools, churches, law, and government institutions instill and install in each of us the back-drop of values, ethics, mores, and rules of community against which our personal experiences have any relevance or meaning at all.

The larger history and worldview of our civilization itself gives voice to the very way we visualize the nature of our universe and our place in it, the way we think about thought and existence itself. "Cogito ergo sum: I think therefore I am," Descartes famously stated in answer to these most basic of questions.

And though we can trust the first filter of our senses to present us with a relatively accurate representation of physical reality, the second filter of our worldview must be continuously examined and questioned, like a lucid dreamer, if we ever hope to peer over the edge of our wells to the wider reality beyond.

>Almost Chicago. In flight from Boston. Should be arriving in about an hour or so. Boston is a wonderful city. At least in the fall. I've only seen it in the fall. Both times. It was cold, but not freezing. Men in suits and topcoats, women in suits and top-coats and gloves. Much more formal than California. East Coast, sophisticated, historical. Such a deep sense of history and identity—place. I felt a part of something definable. The architecture is beautiful; such a side-by-side mixture of old and gleaming new. Water all around, bridges, tunnels. Wonderful seafood. And people. With hard accents and different atti-tudes and ways. I loved it. I wish I could've stayed longer, soaked it in. At least I was very aware for as long as I was there—appreciated it.

>So if you haven't been yet, honey, go to Boston in the fall. See what you think. These are my impressions now from a past you can't even remember; who knows what you'll find. But whatever it is, be aware. I don't think I can tell you any-thing more important than to always be as aware as you can of the moment in which you're standing.

>Right now, as you're reading this, try to imagine a young, un-certain man who was your father, but doesn't exist anymore, in a plane somewhere over the blackness of Lake Michigan writing to his daughter not as she is asleep in her crib, but as she will be, the woman who doesn't exist yet—these two peo-ple, so far apart in time and space, growing together slowly until they meet in these pages.

>And these pages carrying you along, if I can be a faithful writer, in accelerated time until the pages catch up to you. The you now/then. The you sitting there, reading. Where? Your home, apartment, dorm room, barracks, space vehicle?

With whom close to you? Husband, lover, sisters, brothers, children.

To me the possibilities are endless. To you they are simply your life. Present, past, future all meeting together at one point. But not just this point, all points.

>I think all time is always with us. The past is the present is the future. It's all here. Many better minds than mine think, have thought, the same thing. But we can only experience it in this life one moment at a time—and that moment for us is always the present. But it is also always the meeting point of all time. Our time. God's time.

>Don't waste moments. Don't neglect them; take them for granted. I'm finally realizing how precious my moments are. They are like my children, proceeding from me for better or worse, with a stamp on them; a stamp I put on them through my participation in them.

>And I don't even think it matters so much what I or you or anyone does with their moments as long as we are aware of them. With wide open eyes, we recognize that a moment has passed and left an impression on us.

An impression we call a memory, but is really just an acknowledgment that we were alive.

Sunrise and Sunset

In the most general terms, there are two basic worldviews human-kind has produced. We call them Eastern and Western, oriental and occidental, and like sunrise and sunset there almost had to be just two, as they represent the two basic ways in which each of us as a person approaches life: intuitive-intellectual, feeling-thinking, right brain-left brain. And just as the sun rises first in the east and then sets in the west, we begin our lives as children in the east of our intuition and grow toward the west of our intellect—always remaining a mix of the two, though one predominates.

As it is with each of us as individuals, so it has been with the civilizations we have created. Our most ancient civilizations, those of China and India, Mesopotamia and Egypt rose with the sun in the near and far east, and with them rose the Eastern worldview, the older of the two, presiding over our infancy as a civilized race. And those most ancient civilizations, characterized by their worldviews, were not considered "Eastern" at the time; they were just all there was until there was something with which to contrast.

The ancient Greeks are credited with taking a decidedly westward turn in the first millennium BCE, and through the philosophy of Heraclitus, Socrates, Plato, Aristotle, and their attendant schools of thought, formed a very different way of looking at life, nature, religion, science, art, politics, language...it was a new theory of everything that contrasted sharply with Eastern thoughtforms.

Again generally, where the East saw the universe, God, and man as a unified whole, the West saw them as duality, distinct parts in opposition to each other: good and evil, body and spirit, light and dark. And so where the East saw nature as an organic body living and growing around us, the West saw it more as a machine, a mechanism that could be reduced to and understood as individual moving parts. Where the East saw the community, the group, as the basic unit of society and the individual as existing to serve the community, the West saw the individual as the basic unit with the community existing to serve and protect the "rights" of the individual. This Western focus on individualism extended into the afterlife where individuality was immortalized in contrast to Eastern thought which tends to see individuality dissolving as a drop returning to the sea of unity. The West tends to see time as a line segment with a beginning and end, while the East sees it as a circle, a snake eating its tail symbolizing the merging of beginning and end, the unity of all time.

These Western concepts of the basic nature of reality—duality, reductionism, individualism, linear time—all gave rise to a very different worldview, which gave rise to a very different culture containing very different religious, scientific, legal, and political systems. These systems all turned out to be very good at describing the mechanics of the physical universe, manipulating and harnessing the power of the physical world, and creating new technologies through applied sciences. The Greeks believed supremely in the superiority of their philosophy and culture, and with the conquests of Alexander the Great, exported that culture throughout the Eastern world. Then, influenced by the Greeks, the Romans took their joint cultures westward and gave birth to the Europe that conquered the Americas and most of the rest of the globe in the Colonial period, erasing aboriginal cultures and Westernizing everything in its path, just as the Greeks had done two millennia before.

But though the Western worldview tends to be very good at understanding and manipulating the physical world, it is not very good at understanding and following the world of spirit. Here, the Eastern worldview, with its emphasis on unity, community, and a cyclic concept of time is much better suited to bring us into heightened spiritual awareness, which is exactly why Yeshua told us we must become like children—recapture the worldview of our intuitive youth—if we want to enter Kingdom.

More important though, for our purposes, is the realization that the ancient Hebrews were an Eastern people, with an Eastern mindset and worldview. Their culture and religion and language were entirely Eastern in concept and can only be properly understood through that lens. So most important then, is to understand that

Yeshua, as a product of and teacher to his people, was an Eastern man himself.

We have so Westernized Yeshua (we call him Jesus, from the Greco-Roman version of his name) and his message (as translated from Eastern Hebrew/Aramaic into Western Greek and English) that even the thought of him as an Eastern man seems blasphemous. But the fact remains that Yeshua lived among and taught an Eastern people in an Eastern culture and mindset in a typically Eastern way. A way much better suited to the communication of spiritual principles than the way through which we now find ourselves trying to understand his ancient message.

At the bottom of our Western wells, we can't conceive of another there out there from which Yeshua speaks, a vast and limitless ocean of spiritual possibilities, so we interpret his message as best we can—understanding his words through the filter of our modern worldview and so changing the meaning of his most basic concepts into forms that would be unrecognizable to both Yeshua and his first hearers.

This is not an indictment or a criticism; it is simply a statement of our nature and the nature of reality. It's not that West is bad and East is good or vice versa; each worldview has its strengths and weaknesses, and as with each of us as individuals, a balance between the two would be ideal. The point is, we are all *captives* of our worldviews, whether Eastern or Western or anything in between, and to wish it were not so, would be to deny the reality of our lives.

As hard as changing a worldview may be, it's not impossible. But changing worldviews is really not the goal as much as embracing another at the same time—gaining dual citizenship. Like learning a second language, we need to also become fluent in Yeshua's childlike Way of viewing the unseen things of Spirit if we really want to follow. And as with language, there are no shortcuts. We either live the process of immersion until our very thoughts are transformed or we do not.

Some things in life are not transferable...at least not directly.

>I started saying bedtime prayers with you a few weeks ago. At first you wouldn't say anything—too shy. So I prayed your prayer for you, one line at a time and asked you to repeat after me. You did. After a few times, you wanted your turn, and of course I had to repeat after you. Only fair. Then I started praying for myself first and you for yourself after. And if I forgot about prayers, or you thought I was forgetting, I'd hear, Daddy, you forgot something... Then, Wednesday night—this is Friday—when you were praying you said, I really love you Jesus, because you're so nice. I like talking to you all the time and I like listening to you. This really struck me—you listening to Jesus. Most of us think prayer is just talking, and I find myself not taking enough time to listen myself. So after you were done—a very long prayer—I asked you how Jesus talked to you.

>You said that you know when he's talking to you, but you didn't hear him, or a voice. It was inside your head. And he would tell the right things to do and say. Sometimes you knew it was just you thinking of the right things, but sometimes it was him. And then you said sometimes you played games.

>Games? Yes, you two have a game you play. It's sort of like "duck-duck-goose" but just for two, and the duck-duck person doesn't chase but the other person does—or maybe the other way around. And sometimes people looked at you funny when you were playing. When do you play? At lunch and snack break at Kid's Korner.

>I can't tell you how much all this means to me. Jesus said, unless we become like little children, we will never enter the Kingdom. You are teaching me what this means. You have such faith. The faith of a child. The heart of a child.

The Fifth Way

You believe in God so completely that you play games with
him in the middle of the day in the school yard.

If I could have faith like that, I really could move mountains.

Between Heaven and Earth

> We are all connected; we are all alone.
> We are alone in our connectedness,
> in finding connection with each other.

In this life, we're never fully alone, and we're never fully connected either. We're never fully alone because there's a Spirit of Unity, *Alaha*, guiding us, and yet we're never fully connected as long as we're breathing inside these individual and material bodies that keep us firmly entrenched in space and time and at arm's length from one another. We're never fully alone because our humanness makes certain experiences common to everyone, but we're never fully connected because our perceptions create unique filters that color each of those experiences uniquely.

And the most important thing we can discover in our aloneness—the only thing worth having and the reason why we're here: connection, unity, oneness—cannot be transferred or transmitted to another. Frustrating, but so *necessary*. For only when the journey has been personally experienced, is it really ours to keep, as with everything we find along the Way. To be connected, to be in unity, means to have traveled alone to the doorstep of another—and know the place for the first time.

The ancient Hebrews called this fact of life heaven and earth, *shemaya* and *a'ra*. Today's quantum physics calls it wave and particle: heaven—the place of unity, of wave-like connection between everyone and everything, and earth—the place of particular individuality and form. Humans were understood to be occupying the space *between* heaven and earth, capable of both wave-like unity and particle-like form.

Our job as humans is to bring heaven to earth and earth to heaven, to merge the two without losing the essence of either. *Your Kingdom come, your will be done—on earth as it is in heaven* means that the purpose of our journey between heaven and earth is to find unity with each other despite the separateness of our individual forms and yet to maintain our sense of self within that unity. Human self-awareness may end our stay in Eden as we eat from the tree of the knowledge of good and evil, but self-awareness is the part of us created in God's image and powers our ability to choose between heaven and earth in the first place. Or more accurately, to continually oscillate between the two, between unity and separation, between *Alaha* and *hataha*, God and sin. *Alaha*, the Aramaic name of God, actually means unity, and *hataha*, Aramaic for sin, was understood as separation itself. The opposite of all God is.

But as the Gate and Way that lead to life are narrow, few people find the unity that is possible *herenow* in this life of form and individuality because few learn to see past themselves as particle (self, individuality, separateness) to the wave (other, connectedness, unity) lying beyond. Some never begin the journey at all, having become convinced there *is* no wave. Others who begin, never learn to see themselves as *part* of the wave...usually because they've been taught either explicitly or implicitly that the wave of unity awaits them in heaven, but is not possible here on earth—that earth is mere preparation for the unity to be experienced in the afterlife. Nothing could be further from the teaching of the ancient Jews or of Yeshua *as* an ancient Jew.

To bring heaven to earth—to bring unity and connectedness to individual form and matter, to merge the particles into the wave—is another way of looking at Yeshua's Way of "entering the Kingdom of Heaven."

This Way of Yeshua is all about unlearning and learning, and each is as important as the other. From whatever moment we embark, there is something to unlearn and something to learn—in that order, because no one comes to the table completely empty...and the worst place to start is the place from which we think we already have the answers. Yeshua's teachings can form the signposts and milestones of our journey, but they are only as good as our ability to let go of everything we think we know in favor of what really is. That's the unlearning, and some will have more to unlearn than others. To empty all that out and stand naked again in the Garden is a very good place to start. The only place really, for if we don't first become like those little children, we can't enter Kingdom at all.

○ ◐ ⊕ ⊕ ⊘

It's in this process of unlearning and learning that the differences between East and West become most stark. As the West tends to see the universe in straight lines, as discreet segments that can be pulled apart, rearranged, strung together as desired, we as Westerners tend to think in straight lines as well. We understand life in terms of cause and effect, logical conclusions proceeding from logical premises. At the bottom of our wells, we look for straight lines to be thrown down to us, segments of rope to grasp that will directly pull us out of the darkness and into the light. But what we're missing here is that while such direct methods work perfectly well in pulling physical bodies from physical wells, they have little traction with spiritual bodies and mental wells.

When the student is ready, the teacher appears.

If you analyze the teaching of Yeshua, you realize it's not straight at all, but curved. You see him not so much teaching as simply making students ready. Yeshua rarely, if ever, answers a direct question with a direct answer. When questioned, he typically answers with another question or a story or an image. "Who is my neighbor?" and Yeshua tells a story of man attacked by robbers and a Samaritan, of all people, who helped him. "Who is the greatest in the Kingdom of Heaven?" and Yeshua brings over a child and puts her on his knee. "Good teacher, what must I do to inherit eternal life?" and Yeshua wants to know why the questioner calls him good in the first place.

Yeshua knows that just by virtue of asking such questions, the student is not ready, is not looking in the right places for truth, and so sends him off in other mental directions. Like a Zen master, Yeshua answers questions with questions or complete non-sequiturs—non-linear responses designed to force straight-line thinking into curved paths. He knows it's not the answer that is important; it is the ability to begin a journey, to think in new and indirect ways that is key.

Stranded at the bottom of our wells, we ask for a line to be thrown down to us and what we get is a shovel full of dirt dumped on our heads. What an insult. We ask again; another shovelful. Why won't he answer? Another shovelful. But if we don't stop asking, if we're willing to keep shrugging off shovelful after shovelful, we eventually realize that the floor of the well is now several feet higher as the dirt piles up, and we begin to see the nature of things. It's not a direct reaching down that lifts us to a new vantage, but an indirect layering up. The experience of working through images and stories, parables and symbols, of watching spiritual principles being acted out in real life, living through joyful times and painful times speaks to our subconscious spirit in a way logic can never reach.

Spirit by its very definition and nature is *ruha*, Aramaic for wind, breath, and spirit—all at the same time. It is the wind that Yeshua said blows to and fro with no one knowing where it's going or where it originated—not reachable by logic or the language of logic. It must be snuck upon, outwitting the overpowering conscious mind by dropping another layer of dirt into our dark well. Call this process *endarkenment*: as Neil Douglas-Klotz explains, the Aramaic word for the light of creation, the light of Genesis 1 that makes sense of the darkness and chaos is *nuhra*, and the swirling, chaotic energies of the darkness are *heshuka*. But in Eastern, Hebrew thought, light and dark are not mutually exclusive opposites or dualities, surrogates for good and evil as in the West, but a continuum of complementary and necessary energies.

Nuhra is like the straight, bright rays of the sun, while *heshuka* is the swirling, unpredictable, powerful energy of wind and water. Or like *yauma*, day and *lailah*, night, light and dark alternate as times of action from event to event and times of repose for assimilation and retrospection. It's the difference between the waking and dream state, between the conscious and the subconscious: both are necessary, and it is through the meeting of light and dark, *nuhra* and *heshuka*, conscious mind and subconscious spirit, that true creation or re-creation, transformation, takes place. When what our spirit has "learned," day by day and layer by layer, finally breaks through into conscious thought, we really know that thing.

We want to seek transformation through enlightenment alone, bringing the straight rays of *nuhra* down to illuminate the darkness at the bottom of our wells. But the true course, the way of Yeshua's teaching, is to bring the darkness up into the light: endarkenment leading to enlightenment. It's the only way—the straight rays of *nuhra* won't penetrate the curved walls of our well, so we must rise up to meet them. It is a slow process, an indirect one. It doesn't even feel like a process at all, or like learning in any way we understand learning. It just feels like living. Living our daily lives between heaven and earth with all their mundane details...beginning to notice things that we didn't see before, relationships between dots that previously seemed unconnected.

Then one day, we react to a situation much differently than we ever have before. We make a choice that we've never made before and realize that the old programming has broken down, freeing us to go somewhere we've never been before. A ray of *nuhra* warms our faces as the teacher appears, and a glimpse of the vast ocean opens before us at the precise moment we hit the smilepoint.

Our lives *themselves* are the Way, the curved path of endarkenment that slowly fills our wells and lifts our vantage. There is no other teacher: the living of our lives and the process of enlightenment are not separate; they are one and the same. Seeing our lives with this purpose, matching our choices and strategies to this purpose will determine our ability to flow between heaven and earth, between the Four Ways and the Fifth.

As we live our lives with the engine of our desire in one hand and the rudder of our common sense in the other, the Way begins with a willingness to unlearn, a common sense questioning of what it is we believe about our reality and why we believe it—a testing and a prodding and a desire to break out into the next open space. And the next...

And since our worldview, our version of reality, was built with Western tools—logic and language—we're going to have to use the same tools to help pry open those airy spaces before we can ever attempt to see the ocean through Yeshua's eyes.

But the tools of logic can only take us so far and to be purposefully on our Way, we'll need to proceed as the Israelites did through the wilderness between heaven and earth...with alternating doses of light and dark, *nuhra* and *heshuka* , enlightenment and endarkenment, spirituality and physicality, thinking and feeling, a pillar of cloud by day and of fire by night—a journey with no physical dimension and no sense of passage, but a journey punctuated by exhilarating moments of darkness rising into light, bringing milestone and measure of our progress.

THE WAY

THE SHAPE OF THE JOURNEY

>Just got in from my run. Still dripping, very hard to hold the pen—for some reason my hand is unsteady. I did get up early today, but my run was not good from an exercise standpoint: walked a lot. Tired. Ran last night and my legs are still very flat. Wasn't too good from a communion standpoint either.

>That is, a few months ago I was feeling a real joy during my runs. Being part of the early morning. Being part of the dawn. Running through it, celebrating it with my legs. I would simply thank God for my legs. That they were strong enough to carry me. To allow me to move through his dawn. To see how much beauty still remains of his original dawn. To feel a tiny part of what it must have been like for the first man to walk with God fully in the cool of the day through the Garden in perfect fellowship.

>Outside the Garden, even at 5:30 AM there were still buses and stoplights and power lines blocking the orange clouds in the east. But light is beautiful in the horizontal way it cuts across the trees just after dawn, and in these last few months, I felt close enough and part enough to know that the Lord was running with me then. Not as strong as that time in Malibu at Serra—the night that I asked him to run with me and could almost hear his footsteps and was almost sure I would see his form in the moonlight if I turned and looked—but close enough for mid-town Huntington Beach.

>This morning I didn't feel that closeness at all. My mind was racing in a thousand places at once, irritated by the scrapings of the details and people of the last few weeks. And words came to my mind and stuck. *Tolerance.* I was thinking that was the key. *Patience.* So many of us trying to find our way in difficult situations. *Understanding.* Moving out to try to grasp what was being said, communicated. To see the value and

beauty in another person's thoughts and ideas and beliefs. *Love*. To reunite. To feel at one. To come back to that center place that is at once full extension and full equilibrium. All encompassing but very personal. Close.

>Tolerance. Patience. Understanding. Love. They were words that came unasked out of my thoughts. My words? My thoughts? And I said them over and over trying to dispel my irritation with a mantra of these words. Then it struck me that these words were also in the exact and proper order of ascendancy. That the only way we approach true love is by this path in this order. And that each step broke down walls and barriers in the heart that prepared for the next step. That tolerance and patience create the possibility of understanding. Not the understanding of complete knowing of the other, but a compassionate understanding of acceptance. From that flows love—complete identification.

>It was then I realized these weren't my thoughts or my words at all. I have to learn to trust the smallness and stillness of the Lord's voice within me. My faith is small, so his voice seems so also. I'm becoming convinced that as I learn to trust and believe, that I will be able to appreciate more and more of God's true proportions.

>As I turned the corner to head home, the eastern sky in front of me was becoming light—raked with scalloped clouds getting their first color. The Lord's prayer came to mind as a ragged line of crows cut across my vision. Silhouettes. But then I suppose crows are always silhouettes. I thought about how this light, this moment was just that, a moment. The earth incessantly turning, and this angle and shade of light already changing into another angle and shade.

>And I thought about you. Always changing, have changed every time I see you. Can't stop it. Freeze it. All such moments, life, are so ephemeral. These moments we treasure passing and becoming moments we do not. And then moments we do.

>And I thought about heaven. Maybe heaven is just a moment we treasure like any of these. But forever.

>I guess it was a pretty good run after all.

Beyond Theology

Everything has a name.

GOD GAVE ADAM THE AUTHORITY TO NAME ALL THE ANIMALS IN the Garden, and we've been naming everything since. And since in ancient Hebrew thinking, the authority to name something, like a child or an animal, was a symbol of the dominion held over that something, there's a psychological lesson here for us all. To this day, Jews won't speak the name of God as a sign of respect and to avoid showing any possible dominion over the Mighty One. But the rest of us continue to name everything in sight—especially in the area of theology:

There's Dispensationalism and Covenant Theology. There's Systematic Theology and Biblical Theology. There's Soteriology and Eschatology, Theism and Deism and even Finite Godism. Pantheism, Panentheism, Polytheism, Henotheism, Atheism, Gnosticism, and Agnosticism. How about Hermeneutics, Hypostatic Union, Arianism, Semi-Arianism, Modalism, Docetism, Nestorianism, and Pelagianism? You can be a Premillennialist, Postmillennialist, or Amillennialist. A Pre, Post or Mid-Tribulation Rapturist. A Futurist, Preterist, Historicist, or Idealist. You can practice Calvinism, Arminianism, Wesleyanism, Lutheranism, or Catholicism. You could be Eastern Orthodox, Evangelical, Pietist, Quaker, Shaker, LDS, JW, Four Square, Denominational, Non-Denominational, Congregational, or just plain Baptist. Or Anabaptist...

You could look all these up to see what they mean, but that's not really the point. We have spent so much time and energy trying to describe, categorize, subdivide, and explain every aspect of God and his nature—to exert control and dominion over God and our relationship with him, if only by simply attempting to comprehend him, that we don't even know what each other is talking about anymore—let alone actually agreeing on anything. And with all those theological terms flying, we have forgotten that while God gave us permission to name the animals of the Garden, he didn't give us permission to name *him*.

How could he? How could we?

God told Moses from the burning bush that his name was *hayah asher hayah* that is, "I am that I am." How can we really get any closer than that? How do we describe raw, ultimate existence—that which simply is—any more clearly? How do we, using finite tools such as language and the laws of physics describe what is by definition infinite? Our limited languages and concepts and equations melt all over the dashboard long before temperatures and velocities ever reach the neighborhood of infinity.

It's turtles all the way down...

One really ancient cosmological model tried to understand how the world worked by explaining that the earth was resting on the back of an enormous turtle. But when asked what the turtle is resting on, the basic answer was that it's "turtles all the way down." As you toy with the mental image of an infinite stack of turtles descending into blackness like two mirrors placed face-to-face, you immediately get the sense of the futility of logically trying to prove the unprovable. There always has to be one more turtle. But at the same time, there can't be of course, and so the tiny space between the end of our last turtle and the beginning of the abyss, is all the space God needs...to be God.

"Where were you when I laid the foundations of the earth? Declare, if you have understanding," the Lord challenges Job from the whirlwind. Some things are not meant to be proven, or as Paul Campos writes, "The argument between those who treat science as a religion and those who want to make religious belief amenable to the methods of science can produce no winner, or even a coherent disagreement."

Whenever we try to explain the infinite in finite terms, that is, try to "prove" spiritual principles or even the existence of spirituality or God by logical means, it's turtles all the way down. There's always a point where logic runs out, a line we can't cross, an abyss into which we finally must simply jump. The infinite is by definition, infinite, and so can't be defined in finite terms. The two are mutually exclusive. Logical principles can only describe logical processes, and infinite processes aren't logical—they're, well, infinite.

If the spiritual could be proven, what's the use of faith? Or ask it this way: why is faith so highly prized in Scripture? Because in this finite life of logic there is no other way to approach the infinite or God or our spiritual selves except by faith. We can move logically to within just a few nanoseconds of the moment of creation, but when temperatures and velocities approach infinity, we must take that leap.

It's interesting that those who claim atheism, those who say categorically that there is no God, are taking just as much a leap of faith as those of us who believe there *is* one. God's existence can't be either proven or disproven logically. The only logical response to God is agnosticism—the big shrug, the "I just don't know." So why spend so much time trying to "prove" the existence of God or Noah's ark or the ark of the covenant, the validity of creation science or end-times prophecies, or (fill in the blank here)? There seems to be a need in us to have a turtle to stand on, something solid under our faith. But if it's provable, it's not faith after all.

Let's be honest and stop all this.

We can prove God *to ourselves*, but not to anyone else. God lives in a place that is beyond theology, beyond anything that can be named. We can know that we know that we know through our direct experience and connection to our God, but we can't transfer that assurance to anyone else. That's their job, not ours. The best we can do is show them the *effect* of our assurance on the quality of our lives and let them interpret that as they will.

The whole concept and process of theology then is simply the creation of our best expression of the inexpressible, our attempt to make sense of things we just can't fully know herenow. Or better, it's a way of describing the action of God we experience directly in our lives. After the pure experience comes the need to express it to others in some way, but our theology is always only partially accurate at best, and complete nonsense probably more than we'd ever want to imagine. Yet we fight wars both large and small, kill, excommunicate, and generally hurt each other's feelings over the theoretical models of God we construct—not realizing or admitting that no one has it all right anyway. Do we really think that any one of us has it all right? That we really have God all figured out? As Thomas Aquinas said, "A comprehended God is no God at all." And from Brennan Manning, "I wouldn't want a God I could understand." If we could comprehend God, if we could fully understand who and what God is, he would then cease being God for us.

And yet we can't help trying. Something in us compulsively wants to know. Actually, that's a good thing, an essential thing; we're just going about it in the wrong way.

God seems to place a lot of stock in us knowing him. The book of Ezekiel uses the phrase "knowing God" over seventy times in various formulations. The key, of course, is knowing what it means to know God as Ezekiel did. We assume that it means to have a correct thought about God in our minds, to comprehend, to understand, to be able to describe.

But for Ezekiel and his fellow ancient Hebrews, this line of thinking ends at the last turtle. In fact, it's not the act of thinking at all that takes us any farther than that.

>When are you coming back for us Lord? Will it be as soon as so many people say? Will I live out my life? Will my daughter live out hers? I can't help asking even though you've told us that we can't know, shouldn't know. But you also said we'd know the seasons--and they seem to be upon us. I can't help asking--we all can't.

>I feel disappointed in myself today, this week. So weak, undisciplined, unfaithful. But most distressful--joyless much of the time. I should be filled with the joy of your company, Lord. With you in my life, there is nothing that can touch my soul with permanent harm. With you the world's pain pales in the white light of your love--becomes understandable, transcendable.

>I love you, Lord. But I don't show it. I love you, but I don't live it. I love you, but I don't give it back...except in small, widely-spaced moments.

>Draw those moments out for me, Lord. Add a few more day by day and draw those out for me too, until the spaces in between--the dry deserts in between--become the small, widely-spaced moments and then disappear altogether so that my life can be a continuous living prayer to you.

>Joy within pain.
Comfort within sorrow.
Hope within despair.
Until you come again.
Or until you take me home
to fold me in your arms.

Knowing God

To "know" in Hebrew is expressed by the word *yada*. In Aramaic, the same word is *yida*. Both words come from the same ancient root meaning "hand," and since Semitic words were formed out of the meaning of their roots, understanding root meanings provides the cultural context for the word. The idea here is that to know something is not to think it, but to handle it, to have such long-standing experience and familiarity that you can feel its shape in your hands.

The hammer and saw in the hands of the journeyman carpenter have worn calluses around their shapes through years of constant use. The carpenter can feel the weight of the tool in his hands even when they are empty...can feel the swing or stroke that addresses the wood just as the musician can feel the instrument, the strings or keys under her fingers. A lover can feel the face of his beloved, and his hands ache to hold her familiar form when she is not present.

Knowing God has nothing to do with mental concept and everything to do with constant use, with the easy familiarity of long relationship. Like the way well-worn jeans wrap around your hips or the way couples long married begin to look like each other and finish each other's sentences. It's about intimacy that can only be found through the experience of being intimate. And if that isn't enough to get the concept across, to "know" was also a Hebrew euphemism for sexual intercourse, for making love. When Adam knew Eve, when a husband took his wife into his tent and knew her, there was ultimate intimacy between them, ultimate knowing.

This is the kind of knowing Ezekiel is talking about. It's the kind of knowing Yeshua is talking about when he tells us there will be those who say "Lord, Lord," and expect to enter the Kingdom but will not, because they and God don't know each other. Not because their theology is wrong, but because they've never taken God into their tents and worn the shape of his form into the palms of their hands, never experienced the sensation of having their very muscles remember the feel of God in their embrace.

This kind of knowing has nothing to do with terms and concepts. It has nothing to do with theology at all. It is purely and simply intimate, ongoing relationship with God as reflected in our relationships with each other. The two are inseparably linked.

Knowing theology is not knowing God.

Living together, hanging our toothbrushes side by side; that's the kind of knowing Ezekiel would recognize.

>Down by the pool near the waterfall in semi-darkness listening to the water. Are you in the water, Lord? When the leaves move high overhead, are you in the trees? Where are you? Where do I go to listen? What do I listen for? How do I listen? Do I strain? Do I relax? Is it obvious? Subtle?

>Elijah in the cave hiding from Jezebel knew how to listen--what to listen for. Even in his despair and self-pity, his desire to die, to give up. He knew the sound of your voice. When the wind tore into the mountain, he knew you were not there. The earthquake, the fire--the same. But when the still voice, the whisper barely displaced the air at the back of his cave, he wrapped his mantle around his face and went out to meet you. I love that image. Silent compliance. Obedience. Submission.

>I look down and I see ants on the ground swarming over something. Carrying off pieces of it in the long snaking column back to their queen. Such great activity, effort. So completely silent. I look--no sound. Yet I imagine if I was suddenly ant-size, standing near, the sound would be of a fierce battle or frenzied construction site. Tearing, scraping, scuffling, buzzing. I'd put my hands over my ears and run.

>But hearing nothing, I sit and watch. Soundproof. My ears are too big for such things. The mass of my eardrums cannot be moved, vibrated by such small variations in air pressure. If I could somehow thin them out, refine them, a new world of sound would open up until I could hear the ants.

>I think that's where you are, Lord. Right in front of me like these ants. Shouting, talking, waving at me right before my face.

>But I hear only what I'm capable of hearing. See what I've learned to see. Relate as my spiritual, emotional maturity dic-

tates. I think your revelation is all around me and I walk right past–through—in despair because I can't find it.

>Does it frustrate you, Lord? That I am so deaf and blind? That my ears and spirit are too thick and heavy to be moved by your calls? Do you get tired of waving your arms and shouting from behind the glass I put up between us?

>Elijah knew how to listen. Yet still despaired. I can't hear, and despair too. Whose despair is blacker? The despair of knowledge or ignorance?

>Elijah came out of his cave at your call.

>I only pray that I hear when you call me out of mine.

Making it Personal

Theology may pale next to Hebrew knowing, but it is still essential when properly placed in life. A friend of mine wrote what he called a "personal theology" of God's ultimate plan and the reason we're here on this planet. His theology itself was to me of less importance than what it did for him in his life, allowing him to see the beauty and necessity of his circumstances, however difficult, in fulfilling what he saw as his purpose.

All theologies begin as personal theologies—attempts to express an inexpressible experience of the infinite in a finite life. And any theology only becomes useful once it has become personal.

Theology is not an end in itself. It's a process of training the mind to accept a certain concept about God, to mentally assent to that concept. It's a way of clearing a path to belief. But belief is not an end in itself either. In the New Testament, the Aramaic word for believe is *'ete'men*, and for faith, *haimanuta*. Both of these words contain all the meanings associated with our concepts of belief, faith, and trust—all present simultaneously in each Aramaic word. Whenever Yeshua speaks of believing or having faith, what he's really driving at is *trust*: confidence, firmness, integrity between thought and action, living and choosing as if something were already true. Try substituting "trust" for "faith" or "belief" wherever you find those words in the New Testament and see how it deepens the message. In fact, *'ete'men* is related by root to the Hebrew word *amen*, which is also an affirmation of confidence and trust.

Far from being an end in itself, belief is merely the first step in the journey to trust. Belief allows the mind to accept and assent. When belief deepens, the mind allows the body to take action consistent with the belief. Belief that has become action is called faith: "Faith without works is dead," as James wrote. And when faith deepens through repeated experiences of the trustworthiness of God, it becomes trust—the confidence that holds fast even when the circumstances of life seem to contradict the belief with which we started.

But hear this: we cannot will ourselves to trust.

We can't just scrunch up our faces, ball up our fists, and grunt out trust. No amount of mental effort will do. Trust is experiential. We must *repeatedly* experience the trustworthiness of anything in order for us to trust it, whether a person, a parachute, or a principle. That's why it takes so long to restore trust when it is broken in a relationship. The process of experiencing trustworthiness must be repeated, not at the point from which the relationship resumes, but even further back—now having to overcome the experience of the betrayal as well.

> Belief is idea.
> Faith is action.
> Trust is experience.

I believe that this parachute will brake my fall and save me from hitting the ground at 120 miles an hour. But I don't have faith in the parachute until I actually jump out of the plane at 12,500 feet. And I don't trust the parachute until I've personally experienced enough successful jumps that I actually start to enjoy the ride.

Belief deepening to faith is the only means by which we can experience trust. And trust is the only means by which we can transform our lives from a base of fear to a base of love, because only trust allows us to see beyond our circumstances and take the risk that our fear would normally abort. "Faith without works is dead" means that someone who is instinctively, reflexively caring for children and treating others with respect and love is someone who has made the full journey from belief to trust—someone I want to know, someone I'll stand shoulder to shoulder with anytime, anywhere. Francis of Assisi is credited with saying, "Preach the Gospel continuously. *Use words where necessary.*" Amen...'ete'men.

Once we arrive at trust, the mental stuff just doesn't matter anymore; it was all only vehicle after all. Our theological abilities don't matter to God's knowing us and accepting us, except as the means by which we get to the point that caring for children and showing respect and love for each other becomes vitally important. Getting to that point. *That* matters, because that is the essence of true relationship, of knowing each other and God.

How do we get there? How do we develop a personal theology?

A brown-robed Franciscan priest once told me exactly how when I was trying to argue a theological point with him years ago. Before I could even get all my wonderful words out, he held up his hand in the universal stop sign and said, "All I can tell you is what I've become convinced of. Go become convinced of what you're convinced of." I thought it was an evasion at the time. Now I know it's the only honest answer we can ever give and the only Way to live this life.

Our personal theology will come out of our personal experience of God, our trust. There is no other way to learn such a thing, because such a thing is not transferable between humans. We may find ourselves lined up with someone else's conceptions, but we all must arrive under our own steam.

Teaching theology really is a contradiction in terms, but at the same time, in order to help anyone get to the point that they are willing to let go of everything they think they know in order to become convinced of what God is really showing them, we need the classic tools of theology at least to deconstruct old forms if not to try to construct new ones...to take us down to ground zero, to the present moment where God really lives.

The Chinese philosopher Chuang Tzu said, "The purpose of a fish trap is to catch fish. Once the fish is caught, the trap is forgotten. The purpose of a rabbit snare is to catch a rabbit. Once the rabbit is caught, the snare is forgotten. The purpose of words is to convey ideas. Once the ideas are grasped, the words are forgotten. Where can I find a man who has forgotten words? He is the one I would like to talk to."

The purpose of theology is to catch God...to get us to the point of falling back into his embrace and experiencing who he really is and not who we might imagine him to be. And once God is caught, the theology can be forgotten. In this way, theology is properly formed and useful. If not, then not. Theology is not and never should have been a litmus test for our acceptability to God. Or to each other. That's abomination. We can properly use theology to build belief, and belief to promote faith, and faith to produce experience and trust in God. Then wrapped in his embrace, as Paul Harvey always said, we get the rest of the story.

Where can I find a person who has forgotten theology?

Alone again.

>Starting over, freshly motivated to pick up trail and scent at the edge of those cornfields right where I left them, I began searching for meaning in every direction except Christianity— Catholic or otherwise. Been there, done that. Eastern philoso- phy and religion, especially Taoism and Buddhism; metaphys- ical and occult thought and practice: ancient religions, pyramidology, astrology, channeling, remote viewing, clair- voyance, lucid dreaming, astral projection; meditation and brain biofeedback tools; Church of Religious Science; nearly a year in the Mormon church working through the steps of investigation all held successive sway as candidates for a truth that receded like a horizon. One by one they intrigued, engaged, and faded as I realized whatever truths I found were not the whole truth I needed.

>Then one of my employees invited me to her church. I accepted without much thought and found myself on a Sunday morning standing in a converted industrial warehouse with a couple hundred people, their arms raised and singing to a full band on a stage dominated by a grand piano and the big voice of the worship leader. When the whole group burst out simultaneously in tongues, I was transported back to the charismatic Catholic prayer meetings to which my mother dragged my high school self after she had been born again.

>It felt like coming home, but to a home in which I'd never actually lived. So radically different was the culture that I had no time to think about the faith at first. That came later. Jesus was recognizable here, something like the Catholic Jesus, but alien too. Unbloodied and down off the cross, he remained unseen on the edges of things, as if observing all that ware- house activity as I was.

77

>Here was everything I said I needed. And here was the Sunday the pastor asked everyone who wanted to give their hearts and lives to Jesus to raise their hands. I can still see the blurred image of my daughter looking up at me from my lap wearing the braids I'd braided and the short flowered dress with the white tights and shiny black shoes I struggled her into that morning...why are you crying, Daddy? I couldn't have answered even if I'd known, but my hand was in the air, and the pastor was half shouting in my ear past the music to see him after the service. And after, whisked into a side room to repeat a quick prayer of dedication—the sinner's prayer I later learned—the pastor clapped me on the back, stood to leave, and was halfway to the door before I stopped him asking what had just happened, why I didn't feel any different. He didn't actually check his watch, but dutifully walked back to sit beside me saying that fact was, I'd accepted Jesus into my heart. Feelings would come later... The door was slowly swinging closed.

>Whatever feelings he was expecting didn't come, even though concerned members prayed over me for Holy Spirit baptism, which I'd never heard of, didn't understand, and must have repulsed; they kept asking and praying. But I was making friends, and within a few months I was one of the musicians on the stage with the grand piano and the big voice, bringing recognition and acceptance from the group that elbowed past any non-feeling or non-spirit baptism. The pastor was everyone's papa and extended another hand to hold in the dark that I clung to as I began working a discipleship program and having first thoughts about becoming a pastor myself, about the symmetry of circling around from maybe monk to maybe pastor.

Expressing the Inexpressible

Catching God, knowing him, only occurs along the Fifth Way and is much less like a classroom lecture than a concert hall performance—much more poetry than prose. Until we've learned to move from warrior to gardener, to let go of the power and control we imagine, we'll try to catch God through the Four Ways with their concrete objectives and strategies. But the experience of God is not objective, linear, and cognitive, but subjective, allusive, immersive, and figurative. Image-based as opposed to word-based. Uncontrollable. Outrageous... It's not a straightforward proposition for heaven and earth to interface, and human language can never carry the full weight of the experience; it can only point toward it.

But to have such experience is also the need to share it, so how do we express the inexpressible and share our experience with each other along the Way? Ancient Easterners understood this dilemma and wrapped their message around God in ways we Westerners don't readily understand or accept today.

Trying to read Hebrew Scripture as if it were the front page of the New York Times, we look for truth about God in ways that were never encoded. Not realizing that much of the Bible is actually poetry—since Jewish poetry doesn't rhyme or follow set meter and is often translated into English as prose—we look for objective facts and figures where only metaphor, simile, and highly figurative allusions live. Then missing the point, we draw "factual" conclusions never intended from passages meant to be evocative and immersive, conveying truth like music, aimed more at subconscious spirit than conscious mind.

Ancient Jews employed what scholars call "block logic," which—as opposed to Greek logic that moves in straight lines from premise to conclusion with only one thing being true at a time—allows contradictory statements or concepts to lie side by side unresolved and unharmonized. We wonder at how God can harden Pharaoh's heart in one verse and Pharaoh hardens his own in the next or how God never leaves or forsakes us in one passage, and David and Yeshua wail, "my God, my God, why have you forsaken me" in others. We work hard to resolve such seeming contradictions or use them to discredit scripture itself without realizing that for the Jews, straight spiritual lines didn't exist: such paradoxes were part of the unresolved nature of life that looked one way from man's point of view and another from God's. It wasn't important or even possible to resolve everything when dealing with the infinite; it was only important to learn to live richly between heaven and earth—to thrive in the unknowing through trust.

Life doesn't resolve.

Any apparent resolution is only the momentary beginning of a next cycle, so any expression of life, if it's accurate, won't resolve either. If we're ever going to break the hold the Four Ways have on our minds and imagination and begin to walk the Fifth Way, we need to begin right here.

The way we look at Scripture is a reflection of the way we look at life. We have been dissecting life, taking it apart and trying to control the pieces for so long, that we truly believe the same process will yield the spiritual answers we seek. But the control we imagine over life is illusory, and the use of religion and Scripture to control the things of spirit even more so. Life and spirituality can't be controlled or objectively expressed—they can only be experienced. As they are. In their entirety. As soon as we break off pieces and imagine the pieces represent the whole, we deceive ourselves.

We look for intellectual accuracy to lead us to spiritual truth, but to the ancients, *everything* was spiritual; everything, all life and all events in life were infused and directed by God, and so the only way to begin to understand life and spirit was to be equally infused and directed. When we read the Scriptures today without an understanding of the most basic facts of ancient life, we miss the path to inexpressible experience, trying to understand God through the Four Ways instead of knowing him along the Fifth.

The Four Ways are physical and logical. They make perfect sense as both reaction to the difficult terrain of life and vehicle to navigate and travel. But they work in two dimensions: they propel us only across the surface of our physical world. When viewed from above, from a spiritual and symbolic point of view, there *had* to be a first four ways, just as certainly as there are four cardinal directions: north, south, east, and west.

The Four Ways are the ways of the earth, and point in every possible earthly direction; the Fifth Way, one more than four, is the Way of our initiation beyond the physical—the Way of the Kingdom, *malkutha*, of Heaven, *shemaya*—and points in an entirely different direction.

>*O God, who art the truth, make me one with Thee in everlasting love. It wearieth me oftentimes to read and listen to many things; in Thee is all that I wish for and desire. Let all the doctors hold their peace; let all creation keep silence before Thee: speak Thou alone to me.*

Thomas À Kempis

>I put this here because I can't do any better. And it so perfectly captures my state of mind. And I can't believe I just happened to read it today.

>True to my form, I am trying so hard to learn. I read the Scriptures; I talk to my pastors; I look for ways to go back to school for theological training; I go on retreats: I meet a priest who introduces me to a bookstore where I find Merton and Nouwen who lead me to Anthony and the Desert Fathers and Augustine and Aquinas and Camus and Dante and Maritain and Eckhart and John of the Cross and Hopkins and so many others I've never read who speak of Aristotle and Plato in the classical languages I can't read; and the preachers on the radio speak of Moody and Wesley and Calvin and Luther while I watch the fish and dove bumper stickers go by on the freeway with Jesus being sung to me a thousand different ways in songs that begin to all sound alike making background for talk shows that try to explain basic doctrine to confused callers debating fine points of theology and social values--pre-millennium, post-millennium, pre-trib rapture, pro-life/choice, gay rights, family values, moral decay, church and state, Catholic and Protestant, conservative and liberal, Mutt and Jeff...

>Turn it off. Shut it up. Snuff it out. Noise by any other name sounds the same.

83

>I stand in front of the congregation at church Sunday mornings, my microphone between us. We sing. We sing loud. We sing loud into amplifiers that make us louder--almost loud enough to be heard over the drums and piano and guitar. Well over the congregation who sings back at us.

>I sing the words of praise; think of the notes I must hit. I watch the people sing and sway and clap and sometimes dance and sometimes cry. And I wonder if anything is going on here. *What are we doing*, I asked you last Sunday in the midst of all that noise, in the midst of my noisy week, trying to think through my cluttered brain.

>Then down in front, kneeling at the steps, an elderly woman is transfixed in prayer. Eyes closed, mouth moving, hands upraised. What is she feeling? Is it real? Is it you, Lord? The pastor comes by and lays his hand on her shoulder for a moment before moving on. And the look on her face makes me smile and frees up a tear to be wiped away.

>And I know that you put that look on her face, and I thank you for allowing me to help by being part of her experience. I don't get a chance to ask her, but maybe she gets that same look on her knees by her bed with her hair in a net and only a round, wind-up clock clicking away as accompaniment. And maybe all this is just *unnecessary*.

>And it is. And I know it. But you use it anyway and give it the meaning it could never have on its own. But I realize more and more that I won't find you very often in the noise, Lord. And when I do, you won't speak to me as clearly or long-ly as you do on these silent pages. Not that you couldn't, but I can't hear as well, listen as well.

>I'm finding myself; who and how I am, through the measure of your presence in my life. Those activities, those modes and methods that bring me close to you are those that match the nature of my spirit--my silent spirit that doesn't speak, but knows when it's home, or at least getting close.

>So I will use the apparent magnitude of your presence as my sextant to guide myself through the maze of books and sermons and songs and T-shirts and Christian gift shops that I may stumble across on my way home to you.

The Four Ways

To yield, manipulate, exit, destroy...

SEEMS UNCANNY THAT WHENEVER I MENTION THE FIFTH WAY TO someone, the first question, even before asking for some sort of definition, is "What are the first four ways?" This is quite intuitive really, because in order to fully understand the Fifth Way, we need to understand the first four...first.

The answer is both historic and timeless. Stepping into the diverse Jewish world in which Yeshua lived and taught, it is impossible to avoid the "four philosophies" of Israel in the first century. Historically, any Jew of the day was in constant contact with these four philosophies and the four groups they represented, and Yeshua was in near constant confrontation as well. But even now, we are all in constant contact with these same four philosophies, and Yeshua's confrontations are exactly the same as those of anyone, anytime who decides to follow the Fifth Way.

By the dawn of the first century CE, Israel had experienced over five hundred years of near-continuous foreign domination—from the Assyrians and Babylonians to the Persians, Greeks, and Romans. Only for a short time beginning in the mid-second century BCE, did Israel regain a limited self-rule after the Maccabean Revolt wrested control of Judea away from the Greeks and established the Hasmonean dynasty. These Jewish kings ruled in the shadow of Greece and Rome for about a hundred uneasy years before the Romans took control shortly before the birth of Yeshua.

The national consciousness of the people of Israel was seared with God's promise to Abraham of a kingdom that would last forever. Longing for the political throne of David to be restored and foreign occupation to be ended, the people began looking for a savior, *mashiach* or messiah who would come in a blaze of political and military glory to restore their national identity.

But as they waited for centuries in the face of the seemingly irresistible and insurmountable power of the foreign occupiers, four main religious and political groups gradually evolved: the Sadducees, Pharisees, Essenes, and Zealots. These were not the only groups within Judaism in the first century, but they were the main groups as listed by Josephus, a first century Jewish historian, and they created four representative categories under which all the rest fell. Josephus called them the "four philosophies" of Israel, and they comprised the totality, the four cardinal directions of the social-political-religious ways in which the Jewish people, or any people, could respond to the harsh reality of their world...

...to yield, manipulate, exit, or destroy.

Yield.

The Sadducees, from the Hebrew, *saddiqim,* which means "righteous ones," was an aristocratic, Hellenized (Greek-influenced) group of Jews that controlled the Temple and its revenue stream and generally held the highest offices of the Jewish priesthood. Theologically, as they only accepted the first five books of the Hebrew bible or *Tanakh,* they rejected any later Jewish theological ideas or writings, including the Oral Law of the Pharisees. They questioned or rejected the existence of a human spirit, life after death, and the idea of a physical resurrection of the dead since none of these concepts are mentioned in the *Pentateuch,* the first five books. This theological stance explains the exchange between Sadducees and Yeshua recorded in Matthew's gospel in which they ridicule the notion of an afterlife only to be reprimanded by Yeshua for failing to understand the true nature of things.

They were the consummate insiders. Having come into political influence some two hundred years before the birth of Yeshua, They supported the successful Maccabean revolutionaries in the 160s BCE and became well entrenched in power with the Jewish Hasmonean kings who ruled until the Romans came to power in the 60s BCE. The Sadducees remained allied with political and religious power by staying closely linked to the Roman-appointed kings until the Jewish wars of 67-70 CE ended in the destruction of Jerusalem and the Temple.

The Sadducees were extremely unpopular with the common people from whom they remained aloof as they extracted their Temple taxes and fees. Their source of strength was the Temple itself, and with its destruction came the end of the Sadducees as well. To this day, the Sadducees have been largely erased from history, but where any mention of them survives, they are typically seen as worldly-minded aristocrats, primarily interested in maintaining their own privileged position.

The Sadducees represent the first way, the first philosophy for dealing with any overwhelming force against which a people may find themselves thrown. If you can't beat them, join them. If you can't remove an irresistible force, become that force itself—and profit from it. The Sadducees became indistinguishable from whatever force was in power in their world—at least from the perspective of the common people who found themselves exploited equally by the Romans, Jewish royalty, and the Sadducee temple authorities. The Sadducees answer to their world was to *yield*.

Manipulate.
The Pharisees were the largest and most influential of the four groups—at least from the standpoint of the common people. And since the source of their power was in the people themselves, as opposed to the Sadducees whose power was centered in the Temple, the Pharisees were the only group to survive the destruction of Jerusalem and the Temple in 70 CE. It was the Pharisees who, fleeing to the Judean coast after the Jewish war, to a city called Yavneh, reinvented Judaism as a synagogue and home-based religion rather than the Temple-based religion it would not be again for two thousand years and counting. The Pharisaical Rabbis virtually *became* Judaism for all intents and purposes, as all the diverse first century

Jewish groups and schools of thought whittled down to just one after the Temple fell.

Pharisee means "separated ones" from the Hebrew *perushim*, but since the Hebrew word *paroshim*, meaning "interpreters" also shares the same Hebrew roots as *perushim*, Pharisee could mean either the separated ones or the interpreters. And, in fact, they were both. The Pharisees were the Religious Right of their day, seeing themselves as the ones holding the line against the encroaching secularism of Greek influence. They were a lay society of brethren who created communities called *haburot* into which new members had to be accepted, trained, and initiated. Pharisees came from all walks of Jewish life and tended to be more middle class than aristocratic, and though there were differing schools of thought, all Pharisees saw themselves as the interpreters and keepers of the Law. They created hundreds of "fences," around the Law, called the Oral Law or Traditions—additional sets of rules that simultaneously interpreted the written code of Torah and guarded the people from breaking those codes. It was over these oral traditions that Yeshua and the Pharisees had their famous arguments, such as their disputes over the keeping of the Sabbath.

But the Pharisees were also very much the separated ones. They interpreted righteousness as being physically separated from anyone or anything that was unclean or unlawful. Every detail of a Pharisee's life was ordered to keep them separate: their clothes, their food, their daily routines, tithing, ritual bathing, even the color of the walls of their houses. They would have nothing to do with the *am ha'eretz*, literally the "people of the land," but meaning the common people who did not keep the ritual practices of the Law. Pharisees would walk along the innermost edges of the streets to avoid becoming unclean by even brushing the clothing of an unlawful one. For comic relief, there were the "bruised" Pharisees who would close their eyes as a woman passed to avoid looking at her lustfully and so were always bumping into things. This separation with the common people and those clearly on the margins of life such as tax gatherers and prostitutes bordered on the absurd and stood in stark contrast to Yeshua's willingness to sit at table and connect with any of these people, anytime.

Many, but not all Pharisees, as self-appointed keepers and interpreters of the Law, devolved into a legalistic attitude in which a keeping of the rules was all that mattered. Where the Sadducees exploited the people, the Pharisees burdened them with hundreds of their regulations while shunning those of whom they disapproved. And unlike the Sadducees who joined the power system, the Pharisees worked hard to stay separated from it while at the same time remaining within it. They looked to influence and manipulate the forces around them, to change the system from within and to hold the line in the meantime. Many Scribes were Pharisees, professionally working as the copyists of Scripture and the lawyers of Torah. Pharisees were members of influential groups such as the high court, the Sanhedrin, and other formal bodies as well, but it was with the people themselves that they had the most influence. The people saw them as their rabbis, teachers, and the preeminent experts on the Law. They listened to them, respected them, and obeyed them—and the Pharisees used this influence to try to remake the world in their image.

Where the Sadducees yielded, the Pharisees *manipulated*.

Exit.

The Essenes looked around at the world they had inherited and said in effect, "A pox on all your houses," and left the scene in disgust. Beginning in the second century BCE, again during the turmoil with the Greeks leading to the Maccabean Revolt, the Essenes reacted much as the Pharisees did as they saw the religious purity of their nation being polluted and watered down by the influence of Greek thought and culture. But unlike the Pharisees, they didn't see God as directing them to continue to live in the world in which he placed them, trying to remain pure as they worked to influence and manipulate it. They saw all contact with their world as corruption, and so they fled into the desert to create their own communities, which could be tightly controlled and kept ritually pure.

As they are not mentioned in the New Testament, all information about the Essenes comes from outside sources, most notably again from Josephus, who called them *Essaios*, a Greek word that means either "holiness" or "secret" or both. There is some scholarly debate on where the name comes from, but either of these meanings fits in the sense that the goal of the way of the Essenes was to remain pure, which meant to remain completely apart and set aside for God—the literal definition of the word holy. They believed that the high priest of the Temple was elected falsely, and that all forms of worship in the Temple and synagogue were corrupt, so they organized their own ritual practices in the desert wilderness of Judea, studying the scriptures, writing their own books and rules of living in justice and righteousness. They used a calendar that differed from the rest of Judaism, another example of their "pure" interpretation of the Law of Moses and saw themselves as the true priestly descendants of Zadok, the high priest in the time of David who established the priestly dynasty lasting through the time of the Maccabees.

Most scholars see the community at Qumran, the one responsible for writing and preserving the Dead Sea Scrolls, as having been an Essene community. If so, then the Essenes saw themselves as "children of light," following the "Teacher of Righteousness" as opposed to the "children of darkness" who followed the corrupt practices of mainstream Judaism. Living a simple and extremely disciplined life, the Essenes held theological beliefs somewhere between the Sadducees and Pharisees, but focused on the mystical, apocalyptic, messianic, and ascetic: that is, they believed in direct communication with God in their prayer life and prophetic utterances and visions; they expected God to directly intervene in human history in a dramatic way to reveal himself to the entire world and physically reestablish the Kingdom of David; they awaited a messiah, the Expected One, a great warrior-king who would arise to lead the people in God's plan of salvation for the nation of Israel; and in the meantime, they lived a life apart from the corruption and physical pleasures of the world. Many Essene communities were monastic, with brothers remaining celibate in order to better serve God and practicing rituals that now look quite Christian, including baptism by immersion and a common meal in which special blessings were given over bread and wine by a priest—all carried out in secret rituals and remote areas where only the initiated were eligible and acceptable.

So as the Sadducees exploited and the Pharisees burdened, the Essenes ignored the people of Israel. Cloistered in their desert communities, they worked to preserve a pure form of righteousness away from the corrupting influences of the people, awaiting the messiah and God's intervention in history for the moment when it was safe to reemerge and replant their righteousness in the reestablished kingdom of Israel. They waited and they watched from afar.

And so where the Sadducees yielded, and the Pharisees manipulated, the Essenes simply *exited*.

Destroy.

The Zealots were the terrorists of their day. A younger group than the other three that all rose in the turmoil preceding the Maccabean Revolt two hundred years before, the Zealots came into prominence much later—after the death of Herod the Great somewhere around 4 BCE. Josephus called them the "fourth philosophy" of Israel, the one to come on the scene when the other three were failing to effect any real change and patience was wearing thin. Zealots were militantly anti-Roman and activist defenders of "pure" Judaism and Torah as they saw it. Their movement can be traced from the revolt in 6 CE led by Judas the Galilean and Zadok the Pharisee...Pharisees could be all sorts of things besides Pharisees, including Zealots.

Judas instigated the revolt in response to a Roman census that was to be performed for tax purposes and apparently stormed a Roman garrison at Sepphoris, then the capital of the Galilee, only about four miles from Nazareth. Judas proclaimed Yahwey God as his only king and called for the institution of a complete theocracy as the law of Israel and complete freedom from Roman rule, urging the people not to pay Roman taxes or acknowledge the emperor as master. Naturally, the revolt was quickly crushed and Judas killed, at least according to a reference in Acts 5 of a reported speech by the Pharisee Gamaliel, which lists Judas as one of those who claimed the title *mashiach* or messiah of Israel.

But the followers of Judas scattered into the desert to reorganize as terrorist guerillas who fought the Roman occupation through assassinations and riots and disruptions of any kind. Seizing the Temple in 66 CE, they sparked the first Jewish-Roman War that ended with the destruction of Jerusalem and the Temple in 70 and the fall of Masada in 73. After holding off the Roman army for more than a year, almost 1,000 Zealots committed mass suicide in the desert stronghold of Masada, their last stand, rather than surrender to the Roman siege. But even in death they remained true to their beliefs: since Judaism strongly discourages suicide, the Zealots drew lots to choose men who would kill all the others down to the last man, who was the only one to actually die by his own hand. Two women and five children who hid in a cistern related the last moments of the Zealots to the Roman soldiers when they finally broke through the gates of the fortress.

And so the name Zealot is especially appropriate for this group as it refers to being filled with zeal or the passionate intensity to fight. It also carries the image of a fanatic, someone willing to go to the extreme. The Zealots were called *kanaim* in Aramaic, meaning "zealous ones," *sicarii* in Latin for the short daggers they used for assassination, and *lestai* in Greek, which literally means a robber or brigand. Yeshua was crucified between two *lestai* according to Mark 15, which suggests that the Romans possibly saw Yeshua in the same light, especially since Simon the Zealot is listed as one of Yeshua's apostles in Luke 6 and since Yeshua was linked at his Roman trial with Barabbas, who had led a recent insurrection against the Romans and was most likely a *lestai*.

The Zealots had a passion for liberty—that above all. Bringing nothing new to the religious table, they didn't try to create a new understanding of the Law as the Pharisees did; they simply wanted to enforce their traditional beliefs, make them the law of the land by any means necessary, including lethal force. They believed that Torah demanded they establish God's theocratic kingdom by rooting out paganism and foreign domination, separating in all ways from Gentiles, and raising up Israel as the chosen nation of God. With all their energy and identification focused on the physical kingdom of Israel, they could be considered the original Zionists, and as with all such movements that believe the ends justify the means, the Zealots lost all sense of the core beliefs they originally marched out to enforce: the spirit and intent of God's Law centered on healthy community and love for God and neighbor. And as with all such movements where the taking of human life is seen as noble, good, and even God-directed, the Zealots devolved into the destroyers of everything they swore to protect—Torah, Jerusalem, Temple, and the nation of Israel itself. They lost it all, including themselves as a group, in their mad dash into irony. The fact that they couldn't even see their own contradiction is also implied in their name: fanatics blinded by their tactics and the overwhelming force they opposed.

Where the Sadducees exploited, the Pharisees burdened, and the Essenes ignored the Judean people, the Zealots *terrorized* them. They considered anyone who continued to pay taxes to Rome cowards and treated those who would not fight with contempt. They swept their country against its wishes and better judgment into a disastrous war with a vast, unbeatable, and merciless Empire that left the people bereft of home, country, and religious practice.

The Sadducees yielded, the Pharisees manipulated, the Essenes exited, and the Zealots *destroyed*.

⊙ ⊘ ⊕ ⊕ ⊕

There had to be four. Four ways, four philosophies. It's as if the number is hardwired into the things of the earth, then and now. Just as there are only four cardinal directions in which we can move, there are only four ways in which we can react to life's adversity either individually or corporately. These four ways are the natural ways we use to cope with painful circumstances in our lives, unjust circumstances as we see them. Whether we see God as part of our lives or not, whether the struggle is being played out in spiritual or secular terms or a combination of both, the choices are the same. Neither good nor bad intrinsically, the Four Ways are simply the only tools we possess to move about the earth, to change things we wish to change. They are *necessary*.

When faced with difficult and intractable circumstances—the ones that just won't go away—we can give in or try to influence and manipulate. Those are always the first alternatives, the easiest choices, because they require the least amount of change and confrontation. If they are not sufficient to relieve the pain and stress, then the decision can be made to abandon the ship or to destroy it. Each of the four ways: yielding, manipulating, exiting, and destroying represents an escalation in the amount of change and confrontation a person or a group is willing to undergo to remake the circumstances of their world. As Thomas Jefferson wrote in the Declaration of Independence, *all experience has shown, that mankind are more disposed to suffer, while evils are sufferable, than to right themselves by abolishing the forms to which they are accustomed.* The pain and frustration has to be great enough or the principles and ideals of the people strong enough to take them to the next level.

Of course, these four ways don't normally exist in a pure state: just as the Sadducees and Zealots also engaged in manipulation and the Pharisees also yielded to power, there is usually a mixing of the four ways. There is north, south, east, and west, but also northeast and southwest. The compass provides 360 degrees to choose from at any given moment, but each degree is just one or a mixture of any two of the four cardinal directions. And so it is with the four ways. We can mix them into combinations, but there are still only four—and one will predominate.

>Something significant happened today. I realize now it was significant simply because it seemed so insignificant at the time. Small and simple. Yet it won't leave my mind. That's the significance.

>I took a break around noon and ventured out of my safe little apartment to get some lunch and decided on a Mexican take-out place down the street. Car battery is having energy problems and almost wouldn't turn the engine over, but it finally did. Walking up to the glass door, I saw a white paper flyer taped to it at eye level. Getting closer, I saw a picture of a child, a girl, and I knew it was a missing person flyer. They seem to be everywhere. Milk cartons, banners, posters, bumper stickers. A girl named Huber has been up on a banner off the freeway and on bumper stickers for almost three years.

>But this one was new. I don't remember her name, but I can still see her face. Dark hair, pretty, but in a plain sort of way so you'd never look twice at her in a crowded school yard. Twelve years old. Missing since August. $10,000 reward for whereabouts, $150,000 for return. Last seen somewhere on the east coast.

>I wasn't reading it all very clearly because I kept moving back to her face and thinking--east coast. She lived on the east coast and this flyer got all the way out here. $150,000. A lot of money, but how much compared to your daughter-- having her back in bed at night. And what did it say about those of us who would be motivated by all those zeros to put her there?

>I finally broke away and walked through the door; there was another flyer on the opposite entrance. I went up to it and looked at the back of it through the glass door and saw that it had been mailed directly to the restaurant, folded in half with

a computer-generated mailing label. They must have bought a list of public establishments, venues where there was foot traffic, and bulk-mailed flyers to them all. Nationwide. $150,000.

>What must they be feeling? How in the world do they get warm at night and pull the covers up knowing their baby is out there somewhere. Where? How does food taste good? How do you care if her brother wins his soccer game? How do you care about anything? How do you love God? I bought my burrito. I thought about you. How I would react with you suddenly gone. Helpless. With unknown monsters. Maybe cold. Maybe bleeding. Maybe starving. Maybe dead. And all I could do is sit in my living room and put a sticker on a flyer to George's Mexican restaurant in California.

>And pray. Maybe I'd think of that. Maybe I wouldn't hate God so much for letting that happen to my little girl that I wouldn't pray.

>And that's what was significant about today. As I was walking back to the car, it suddenly occurred to me to pray for that little girl. And I said, dear Father help this little girl. If she's dead, hold her tight. If she's still here, be with her, comfort her, make her strong. Be with her parents; don't let them despair. Help them trust in you. Help them learn to live with whatever they can't change, and to keep on loving and living no matter what. And Lord, reach out to whoever took this child. Soften his heart, if it's not too late, to bring her back safely; to not be cruel and scare or harm her anymore than she already has been. And if she's already dead, to bring him to full realization of what he's done and to make whatever amends ethics and society require.

>Other people react this way all the time. I see them. They run across something that moves them; they cross themselves if they're Catholic; they hold up their right hand and close their eyes if they're Evangelical. I suppose they may face East if they're their Muslim. But they pray. Spontaneously in reaction to the need before them. Not me. I am moved to pick up an earthworm twitching on a hot sidewalk and place it on

cool earth under a bush, but prayer is something I've always had to more or less try to sneak up on--quickly get into before I thought too much about how I wasn't probably doing it right and spoiled the moment.

>Just a few pages back I admitted I didn't understand prayer or its power. And today there was need and response. Automatic. A bright, obvious answer right there in my head where I never noticed it before. Showing me how simple the connection is. How significant. I still don't know if my prayer changed anything, but it doesn't matter. It has changed me.

>It's 2:30 AM on the east coast now. Do you think her parents are asleep? After two months. Endless phone calls and police reports and support groups and tears and missed days of work. And flyers.

>I don't know. I don't know if I would be. But I pray, with a new insight into what that means, that they are or will be soon. And that she is, and will have a chance to be a little girl again soon. And although I am sometimes ashamed to call myself human and be a part of the cruelty around me, I resolve to remind myself that there is still beauty everywhere that you put here in the beginning. And to learn, through my prayer, not to despair even in the face of that which takes the breath out of life.

Siren's Song

Yeshua practiced a Fifth Way, a Way that had nothing in common with the first four. But was he immune to the pull, the seduction of those first four? From birth? From some other point in his life? Ever?

The Four Ways are always calling us. Like Homer's Odysseus listening to the sirens' song, our boat is being lured toward the rocks by everything in us that's human and everything in us that hurts and everything in us that wants the hurting to stop...now.

Did the sirens call Yeshua too?

Wanting to hear the sirens' song, to see if he could withstand the pull of the creatures that had led countless mariners to their deaths, Odysseus had his crew plug their ears with wax and tie him securely to the mast of his boat. He gave orders that no matter what he said or did, they were not to untie him or take the wax out of their ears. Unprepared for the power of the sirens' call, Odysseus struggles and screams and curses and rants and raves at his crew to let him go to the sirens and his death until the boat finally drifts out of earshot. It's a striking image of just what we're up against. The Four Ways are an almost irresistible call to do everything in our power to fix what we see as broken in the circumstances of our lives.

At the end of Luke 2, Yeshua is described as growing in wisdom and maturity and graciousness both before and after the age of twelve. So common sense tells us that if he grew in these things, then there was a time in his life when he had less of them—room for growth. In other words, he had to learn.

After Yeshua is baptized in the Jordan River, he is driven by the Spirit of God into the wilderness where he is tempted for forty days. He is tempted three times and in three specific ways. From the number three, signifying completion and wholeness, we are meant to understand that these temptations encompass all the temptations and compulsions that Yeshua needed to face before he was ready to begin his public ministry.

And from the number forty, meaning an initiation or time of trial leading to rebirth in Hebrew symbology, we understand that the important truth being conveyed here is that this was the time in Yeshua's life when he learned to tie himself to the mast of his boat, to resist the temptation to follow the Four Ways that led to the rocks and not where he really wanted to go. Trial and rebirth is the primary concept to grasp in the number forty, not the timeframe; Yeshua's wilderness experience was almost certainly a very long time as opposed to a literal forty days. After all, there are at least eighteen years of Yeshua's life unaccounted for in the Gospels with no indication of the time span between his baptism and the beginning of his public tour through the Galilee and Judea.

Regardless of how long Yeshua faced his trials, Scripture is telling us that it was a long and hard fight. Yeshua was extended to the limits of his endurance and exhausted and hungry, it was by clinging to the mast of God's word and revelation as spoken directly to him and through the prophets before him that he prevailed.

But over what exactly did Yeshua prevail? What were those three temptations he faced that are meant to represent all the temptations each of us must face as well? Henri Nouwen has a deeply insightful way of describing them. He wrote in *The Way of the Heart* that Yeshua was dealing with the same basic human needs and compulsions that drive all of us every day.

When asked to turn stones into bread because he is hungry, Yeshua is being tempted to be *relevant*—to matter, to be worthwhile, needed, wanted, sought out, respected, liked, loved: to be the source of the basic necessities of life is the essence of relevance and would put any of us in a central role in the lives of others. When he is offered all the kingdoms of the world if he will bow down and worship the Adversary, he is being tempted to be *powerful*—to be influential, in control of circumstances and the lives of others. And when he is told to throw himself down from the pinnacle of the Temple in order to be buoyed up by angels, he is being tempted to be *spectacular*—to be noticed, astonishing, important, above the crowd, to make a difference, leave a legacy, *be* somebody.

Relevant, powerful, and spectacular. Henri is on to something here. Being relevant is just another way of stating our basic need for connection with each other. We need our lives to matter to others, to have them want us near. How far will we go to achieve that? Will we submerge our own principles and preferences, co-dependently yield to those of others in order to fit in and seem relevant to them? And conversely, if we can't find a clear path to relevance, will we simply leave and create new relationships and new opportunities to matter?

Being powerful is really just an expression of our need for security. How better to be able to control our circumstances, get the things we want and need than by being able to passively or aggressively control the lives of others, to make them do what we want them to do, to manipulate them or terrorize them into remaking our world for us.

And being spectacular is basically a search for meaning, an attempt to find meaning in our lives through the eyes of others. If others notice us, think we're amazing, and are willing to throw their spotlights on us, then there must be some meaning to our lives. The more people who think so, the more meaning we must have. What are we willing to do to be noticed? Are we willing to profit by joining the powers that be, to become powerful and influential in the process? Maybe we're not willing to exit, but how about to yield, manipulate, or destroy? Even suicide, as a form of both destruction and exit, is often a cry to be noticed.

The Four Ways allow us to indulge all the temptations we face, to constantly scratch at the itch of life's needs and compulsions in any way we can. To be relevant, powerful, and spectacular or in other words, to be connected, secure, and meaningful are the most basic human drives and the most powerful: big itches, driving compulsions that can draw lives onto the rocks. As a man, Yeshua was not immune; he had to learn to rise above them, learn that scratching alone would never soothe such an itch. Through the trials of his wilderness experience, he had to learn that none of the Four Ways could ever provide the answers to the real needs in life. They couldn't slake his thirst because the Four Ways are always focused outside, as if the answers to our need for connection, security, and meaning were "out there" somewhere, and not within, among, in our midst, moving from inside to outside.

Yeshua had to learn that the Four Ways are fundamentally in conflict with the Fifth Way of Spirit, because they are all moving in the wrong direction: from outside to inside. Transformation never occurs from outside in, only from inside out. Once this revelation was securely part of Yeshua's spirit, he spent the rest of his life trying to communicate it to others. But common sense also tells us that those most invested in any of the four ways will also have the most resistance to change, and they will do almost anything to protect whatever gains they've accrued in the process.

And so it was.

☉ ☽ ⊕ ⊕ ⊕

The Gospels are filled with Yeshua's conflicts with the four groups and philosophies of Israel. As he preached the Fifth Way of the Kingdom with its radical, inside-out approach, the four groups were initially curious, increasingly skeptical, and ultimately hostile. The Fifth way, if embraced by the people, would simultaneously weaken the grip the Sadducees held on Temple revenue, the sway the Pharisees held over the hearts and minds of the people themselves, the ritual and apocalyptic expectations of the Essenes, and the resolve of the people to follow the Zealots into battle against the Romans. All that they had gathered to themselves was at stake as Yeshua worked to connect the people directly to the presence of God already living in their midst.

Preserved in the Gospels are accounts of these confrontations between the Fifth Way and the first four—inquisitive testings and pokings initially, investigations into Yeshua's makeup and message that escalated into full-blown battles. Conflicts with the Sadducees were relatively few as they did not associate with the people as much as the Pharisees. We do see them from time to time, though, testing Yeshua by asking for signs from heaven or by trying to ridicule his belief in a resurrection through the absurd hypothetical in Matthew 22 of a woman who, in accordance with Hebrew law, married seven brothers in succession after each died without fathering children with her. Whose wife will she be in the resurrection, they want to know? "God is the God of the living and not the dead," Yeshua replies, demonstrating their non-understanding in such a way that they venture no more questions of him. But it is when Yeshua strikes at the heart of Sadducee power that the final cut comes. When Yeshua cleanses the Temple, overturns the tables of the moneylenders and merchants, and declares that his Father's house has been turned into a den of thieves, there is no turning back. The gauntlet has been thrown, and the Sadducees realize they are in a fight for the very source of their power: the monopoly they hold on the revenue stream from the Temple itself.

With the Pharisees, the conflicts centered on the external holiness and purity codes, the Oral Tradition that the Pharisees had developed over generations. Thousands of additional laws were forced on the people by the Pharisees, some of which actually subverted the original intent of the written Law itself. We see the sparring between Yeshua and the Pharisees over these points of the Oral Law in their questioning of his willingness to sit at table with those who were not clean and did not follow the Law or Traditions; over what it meant to keep the *Shabbat* or Sabbath and Yeshua's deliberate breaking of the oral code of *Shabbat* law in order to keep the spirit of *Shabbat* law; over fasting; over washing hands before eating; whether to pay taxes to the occupying Roman government; over the proper grounds for divorce and other issues.

But when Yeshua turns from academic discussion of the Law and attacks the Pharisees themselves for the damage they are doing to the people, it gets personal. Matthew 23 is the tipping point when Yeshua lays the Pharisees out as blind guides who heap burdens on the people but won't lift a finger to help them; who have fallen in love with their places of honor at banquets—their positions of influence and authority; who are as clean as whitewashed tombs on the outside but full of corruption within; hypocrites who devour widows homes by exacting their tithes; poisonous snakes who won't enter the Kingdom and won't allow anyone else to enter either. In this tirade and others like it, the Pharisees see *their* very source of power, their hold over the people, becoming precariously balanced—resolving to fight back as well.

Conflicts with the Zealots are indirect, but no less pointed. The Zealots would have been bitterly disappointed to hear Yeshua uphold the paying of taxes to Rome when he said to give to Caesar that which is Caesar's and to God that which is God's. Such a position was cowardly in their eyes and a refutation of their movement. If they had initially seen the possibility of *mashiach* in Yeshua, their disillusionment steadily grew as every time the mantle of power was offered to Yeshua, he pushed it away. He says to Pilate in John 18 that his Kingdom is not of this world. If it were, his followers would be fighting to free him, but as it wasn't, they weren't. Strike two. And in the Garden of Gethsemane at the time of his arrest, Simon Peter cuts off the ear of the servant of the high priest and is poised to fight. Yeshua stands him down saying that those who live by the sword will die by it, and then turns to heal the ear. Strike three. When it comes time to choose between Barabbas, a true warrior of Israel, and Yeshua, it's Barabbas for whom they cry. The Zealots couldn't afford their movement to be compromised by any message that weakened the resolve of the people to hate the Romans and fight them to the death.

Though the Essenes aren't mentioned specifically in the New Testament at all, it's with the Essenes, or at least with their way and mindset that a most telling and profound confrontation takes place. One rarely-discussed story in Matthew and Luke contains the essence of Yeshua's indictment of the Four Ways—and the difference he exposes between them and the Fifth Way. This story, seldom used in studies and sermons, remains largely unexplored because we really don't know what to do with it. It doesn't seem to make much sense on its face, and as it questions the faith of one of our most revered Scriptural characters, it's usually kept in a back room out of sight and mind.

But viewed in the light of the Four Ways of the earth and the Fifth Way of Yeshua, it makes perfect sense and springs to life and relevance both then and now.

>Decided not to run this morning. Still total darkness outside except for the path lights and various night lights scattered throughout the grounds and filtering through the trees. My desk lamp makes it look very black outside.

>This whole week has lacked reality, focus. Have not been able to fall into my routine that has been such a source of contact over the last few weeks, both in prayer and here in writing. Not sure why I make that distinction; they are often the same and always best when they are.

>The morning has become a magic time for me. I've always heard that it's darkest before dawn. I don't know about that. I think that might be more psychological, subjective, poetic than actual. But it *is* coldest before dawn. The whole surface of the planet cooling like a corpse until the last moment when suddenly life returns. Light striking across its face giving the first flush of color, letting temperature and eventually movement have their way.

>It's also cleanest before the dawn. The dirt and toxins we spend all day stirring up like a tractor in a dusty field settle and settle, become sealed over with a layer of protective dew. Harmless for the moment.

>Sunrises are so different from sunsets. Literally like day and night. Golden rather than red. Promising new treasures of possibility rather than turning in regret from the bloody field of daily realization.

>I can imagine that God loves the morning too. Remembers, relives the incredible sight of that first morning when the first light struck the face of nothing and defined it as such. Waiting patiently for something to warm. And those early mornings in

the Garden walking through the trees, fully present to a brand new world and a brand new man and woman.

>We come closest to all this in the morning. We awake from the oblivion and innocence of sleep not quite ourselves yet. Whatever that may be. Having been free and safe in the Garden for hours, now in that middle ground where, like the earth itself, the toxins of our lives that we inevitably stir up have settled somewhat, sealed over with sleep.

>This is the time to approach God. I am the most childlike and innocent I will ever be again in this life when I am asleep. When I first awake, I am greeted with the golden promise of fresh possibility at the exact time I am furthest from my last mistake. It is a magic time. It is a quiet time. It is when God speaks the loudest. Like right now. Thank you, Lord. I needed this moment more than anyone but you could know. I feel it's been so long since we've spoken. I feel your touch.

>The sky is lightening. It's time to go. Time to stir up the dust of my day with all the appointments and activities I am obligated to perform. But it's more all right today than it has been for many days.

>Because I reached out and found you as the darkness moved toward the light, I have the privilege of carrying you with me as my day and the world move back again toward night.

Blinded by Expectation

Biblical scholars have long speculated that John the Baptist, *Yochanan* in Hebrew, was an Essene. Naturally we don't know for sure, but we do know from the bits of evidence provided in the New Testament that he fit the profile of an Essene almost exactly while preaching and baptizing only a few miles from Qumran. And if John was in fact an Essene or someone with a similar mindset, it would explain very well why he expresses doubts about Yeshua and his ministry and identity in Matthew 11 and Luke 7.

At this moment in the Gospel story, John is in prison for standing up to Herod over the king's divorce and remarriage, and as he languishes there, he hears stories of Yeshua's ongoing ministry in Judea and the Galilee. Something drives him to send a few of his followers to ask Yeshua if he is the Expected One, or if they should *look for someone else*. Look for someone else? Is he serious?

John was the one who "jumped in his mother's womb" when Mary, *Miryam*, pregnant with Yeshua, came to visit. He was the one who, when he saw Yeshua approaching him in the river, said that he shouldn't be baptising Yeshua, but that Yeshua should be baptising him. He watched and listened as the Lord God spoke from the heavens over Yeshua in the river and later said that Yeshua must increase as he decreased—that he was unworthy even to untie Yeshua's sandals. If anyone should have known who Yeshua was, it was John. Yeshua himself said that John was the one who came in the spirit of Elijah to prepare the way for the Lord.

So...what happened to John? How do we explain his doubts after all he'd seen and heard? Was it just a natural reaction to the fear and misery he must have felt in the king's dungeon, of feeling abandoned there, sick about not being present to Yeshua and his work, wondering why God wasn't stepping in and setting him free? Was he sending his followers to question Yeshua not for himself, but for their own benefit, so they would hear the truth from Yeshua's lips with a spiritual impact that John felt they couldn't get from him?

Was he simply unsure whether the man he was hearing about was the same man he baptized in the river? A possible mistaken identity? All these have been floated as plausible explanations for John's apparent lack of faith. A lack and a lapse that no one wants to believe, that everyone wants to explain away.

But the scientific principle of Occam's Razor tells us that all things considered, the simplest explanation tends to be true: the one with fewest assumptions and complications is usually the right one. Any of the theories above could explain John's behavior, but most simply, it appears he was blinded by his expectations.

If John was looking at Yeshua as the "Expected One," the very title he uses in both Matthew and Luke, then he was looking at Yeshua as the Essene *mashiach* or the messiah who was to come in full political and military power. Did that describe what he was hearing of Yeshua through the prison grapevine? The consorting with tax gatherers and prostitutes, the time wasted in the backwater of the Galilee instead of taking his message to the centers of power? Where was God's mighty hand in reestablishing the throne of David in such activity? Of course John was disappointed, disillusioned, and confused, because he was following one of the Four Ways while Yeshua was following the Fifth Way and playing by entirely different rules.

Yeshua's response to John is characteristically indirect: he simply reminds John that the blind see, the lame walk, the lepers are cleansed, the deaf hear, the dead are raised, and the good news is preached to the poor. Is Yeshua dodging the question here? Not at all. He's trying to engage John in following his own path to truth.

In Hebrew thinking *shalom*, or *selama* in Aramaic, is much more than just "peace" understood as the absence of conflict. It is the greatest possible wholeness, completeness, and unity of all things: mind, body, spirit, relationship, community, nature, everything. Any diminishment of that wholeness, any separation from complete unity is *hataha*, sin. For a Jew in Yeshua's day, anything less than *shalom*, any illness or deformity or debility whether physical, financial, relational, or legal was the same as sin—*hataha*—not necessarily morally, but *functionally*. To be less than fully free was *hataha*; Israel was in *hataha* by being under the heel of Rome and not a free, independent nation. John himself was in *hataha* simply by being in prison and not free to be a fully-functioning part of the community.

Yeshua is saying two things to John. He's saying, look at my work and see how all things are being made whole, how *hataha* is being replaced by *shalom*, how God's unity and righteousness are being promoted and proclaimed to these people. What do you see and what does it mean to you? At the same time, he's reminding John of the words of Isaiah 61, which he is practically quoting here verbatim, and which he also had read from the scroll in the synagogue at Nazareth at the beginning of his ministry. It was his mission statement then, and he is reminding John now in a way he would not miss—as an Essene, as a dedicated student of the Scriptures—that the original intent of God's salvation was not political or military, but spiritual and personal. A relationship forged in *shalom*.

Yeshua is asking John to see that God's Way always seeks *shalom* first, as its own end. *Shalom* begets *shalom*. The Four Ways are content to seek *shalom* through something less than *shalom*, which is *hataha*, sin—*shalom* as ends justifying *hataha* as the means to get there. They do this because their vision of *shalom* is merely circumstantial, as if external circumstances alone can create *shalom*. But remembering that ultimately the quality of the means we use always matches the quality of the ends we produce, *hataha* can only and ever beget more *hataha* as like begets like.

Hataha can never beget *shalom*. Even when *hataha* is justified, as when force must be used to stop immediate abuse or aggression, something less than *shalom* will always result, because something less than all that *shalom* is can never produce *all* that *shalom* is. He who lives by the sword, dies by it: John's ability to see Yeshua's identity was dependent on his ability to see the Way to *shalom*. All this is present in Yeshua's terse reply.

And Yeshua doesn't stop there, but continues by first praising John as a great prophet but then adding that "among those born of women, there is no one greater than John; *yet he who is least in the Kingdom of God is greater than he*."

Yeshua is making a huge point here. One we must not miss.

☽ ☽ ⊕ ⊕ ⊕

111

There is a qualitative, quantum difference between the Four Ways—the ways of earth, of those "born of women"—and the Fifth Way, the way of the Kingdom of God. This difference is so vast that the greatest adherent of the Four Ways is still less than the least of the Fifth Way. A bad day fishing is still better than a good day at work... The four ways and philosophies of Israel have nothing in common with the Fifth Way. It's apples and oranges.

The Fifth Way is not merely a better way than the first four ways, a way that will simply get you to the Kingdom better and faster than the others. A jet plane will get you to New York better and faster than a car or a horse-drawn wagon, but how do you rate that jet plane as a way to get you to the moon or even a low orbit? Though the jet is the greatest way of travel over the earth, the least of any craft capable of reaching space is greater than the jet. It's not that the jet is just less desirable than the spacecraft, it's that the jet is *utterly incapable* of taking us where we want to go, if where we want to go is not of this world.

This is the reality that Yeshua is asking John and each of us to face...that any of the ways with which we are familiar—north, south, east, west, yield, manipulate, destroy, exit—have the ability to take us somewhere in *this* world, but no further. They are strategies we use to get the things we need and want by changing ourselves to match our circumstances, changing the circumstances to match ourselves, changing our mailing address, or by burning down the post office. But none of these have the power to get us even within sight of the gates to the Kingdom Yeshua is talking about.

Yield, manipulate, exit, destroy. The Sadducees exploited the people; the Pharisees burdened them; the Essenes ignored them; and the Zealots terrorized them in order to change their own circumstances, to secure their own personal *shalom* at the expense of the *shalom* of others. Everyone lost. *Hataha* simply bred more and more *hataha*, never *shalom*. From the perspective of the people of Judea, simply trying to live their lives and raise their families, each of these Four Ways in the hands of their elders was utterly unhelpful at best and a brick wall between them and their *shalom* more often than not.

>Tonight was great. Better than that. We couldn't find a movie we wanted to see, so we went to the pet store, or I should say the zoo. That's how you treat it. You have a little dwarf hamster that you talk about constantly and we found some tonight that look just like yours.

>Then we went to the grocery store, wrestling all the way across the parking lot to get apple juice, cheese, and bread for dinner along with mini-marshmallows and toothpicks. After our cheese sandwich feast with a side of Life cereal, we lit two candles, turned out the lights, and roasted the mini-marshmallows on the toothpicks. You were so excited you were talking very fast and very loud about just about everything.

>Then it was bath time and we watched Kung Fu together. I have no idea why you like that show so much, but it's one of your favorites. There was a funeral scene in the show tonight and you suddenly had a lot of questions about death. I tried to answer. What's a funeral? What's a ceremony? Really testing my ability to synonym. Why do you bury people? Why do they rot? The better word--decay--was a little beyond you. Well, do you remember when we carved the pumpkin last Halloween and after a few days it was gray and hairy inside and smelled bad? Yes. Everything that is alive, if it's a plant, an animal, or a person, dies. And after it does, it rots and starts to smell bad. Do they get scattered around when they rot? Well, that's why we bury them, so they won't get scattered around or smell...and to give them back to the earth.

>I guess you ran out of questions in that line after that. You were too shy to say prayers again tonight, so I said them for both of us. Thanks for your hamster, Raptor, and for Mommy, a host of friends, and all the fun we had this night. Also for

113

your victory over a fourth grade boy in kick back today--sort
of handball with your feet--for which you said you were very
proud of yourself.

>So nice to have you here, my little friend. You are a wel-
come breach in the silence I try to maintain. In a few minutes
I will spread out my own sleeping bag on the floor, turn out
the light, and take my place right next to you.
Then I will fall asleep to the deep and regular cadence of
your breathing.

In the Big Mirror

There is nothing new under the sun.

If Solomon could say that in Ecclesiastes three thousand years ago, has anything changed since? Apparently not. Religious and secular institutions, great movements, and individual people still flail away at the mountains in their paths using the Four Ways as clubs.

For the last fifty years or so, Christianity in the United States has been one of the combatants in an escalating culture war against an increasingly secular society. Just as the Pharisees in the second century BCE watched in horror as their traditional culture was being consumed whole by the politics, arts, architecture, religion, philosophy, and worldview of the occupying Greeks, many Christians in the U.S. today are having the same reaction to an alien culture "occupying" their land. From the all-powerful influence of the media; to legal challenges working to separate anything religious from the public marketplace; to the great social issues such as abortion, assisted suicide, same sex marriage, divorce, pornography, stem cell research—these Christians see their traditional values no longer in play in the culture around them. How are they reacting to the overwhelming force, the tsunami of the changing culture around them?

Predictably, in one of four ways...

One.
Before the 1960s, American culture largely mirrored traditional Judeo-Christian values for the most part. Parents raising their children in Christian homes could nominally rely on the institutions of their society—churches, schools, media, law enforcement, courts, local and state government—to reinforce the values they were trying to instill at home. But with the cultural revolution of the 60s,

everything began to change. The values of the institutions of society became increasingly humanistic, and relativistic, and increasingly at odds with more traditional values at home. No longer being reinforced by the institutions and culture around them, parents and churches soon found themselves actually having to fight those forces, trying to undo what was being done to the children, relationships, and ethics in their midst.

As the culture became increasingly alien to their values and forms of worship, traditional churches became increasingly irrelevant to younger generations saturated in that culture. The "Jesus Movement" of the 70s merged aspects of the youth-oriented culture of its time—music, language, hair and clothing styles, political and social beliefs, and sometimes the use of recreational drugs—with a focus on a personal relationship, as opposed to an institutional one, with Jesus, imagined as the original "hippie," preaching peace, love, and brotherhood. As the Jesus Movement gathered steam and numbers among American youth, some traditional churches realized an opportunity to reach younger generations again by simply meeting them where they were culturally, by adapting their styles and forms to the prevailing culture around them.

With that cultural model in hand, today's Christian music industry sells billions of dollars worth of products a year with state-of-the-art packaging, graphics, and marketing techniques...even its own awards ceremonies. Huge mega-churches, some with congregations of tens of thousands sometimes occupy former sports arenas or sprawling campuses that are virtual cities with administration centers, food venues, broadcast facilities, and audio/video production studios. Many of these churches continue to be "seeker sensitive," meaning culturally and theologically sensitive, in that they tailor their services and message to meet people where they are rather than risk trying to take them somewhere they may not yet want to go...the goal being to be sensitive enough not to shock or repel them as they come through the doors, to remove all barriers to their acceptance of church and faith.

Global Christian media networks broadcast twenty-four hours a day, seven days a week while Christian movies, books, and magazines are among the strongest sectors of their respective industries. Recently, with mega-churches as anchors, new cross-marketing techniques are greatly increasing the sales of Christian products by promoting and selling them at churches across the country, using newly-released books as seminar and small group study materials, and even buying blocks of Christian movie tickets for entire congregations. All this activity is not without its critics, especially from more conservative church voices who see it as "watering down the Gospel" or as having sold out to the secular culture.

Leaving the debate on the table as to whether the sum total of these mega-Christian industries have produced a positive or negative effect overall, the practice of yielding to an overwhelming force and obstacle, of becoming part of it and profiting from it is the hallmark of the first way, the way of the Sadducees. All this activity may or may not be a positive force in our society, but that's not the point. That all this activity is *social* and *cultural* and not *spiritual*...that's the point. No matter how well intentioned, no matter even that individuals may be personally benefiting spiritually, these industries are still engaged in social/cultural exchanges and not spiritual experiences.

There is no such thing as a "Christian company" or even a "Christian church," though there may be companies and churches of Christians.

As social institutions, companies and churches don't have the capacity to be spiritual, and neither do their products. Only people have that. And though the social and cultural exchanges companies and churches produce may also accompany genuine spiritual experiences between people and God, and though they may even foster such experiences, it's important to realize that they are not the spiritual experiences themselves.

Listening to Christian music may or may not accompany a spiritual experience; watching a Christian music award show rarely does. The activities of contemporary Christian industry, like the activities of the moneylenders and vendors of the ancient Temple, may serve necessary functions of the church, but in terms of serving our spiritual journey, they are tangential at best and a distraction more often than not. They blur the distinction between the emotional responses they elicit and the spiritual experiences they mask, and as an expression of the first of the four ways, these activities have nothing in common with the Fifth Way of Yeshua and can't take us where we really want to go.

Two.

Now it's not that conservative churches and voices have not also engaged in the first way—there are many conservative Christian books, movies, and media networks doing brisk business. Many conservative churches have grown to mega-church status or have planted chains of churches across the county and from humble non-denominational roots have become denominations themselves. But by virtue of being conservative, there is something that also keeps them at arm's length from the world. Just as with the Pharisees, there is a principled aversion to the secularization and permissiveness of society, and that aversion creates enough tension to keep them somewhat separate, but not enough to cause them to flee altogether...tension enough to see the necessity of attempting to influence and manipulate society for its own good.

The "Religious Right" as the media has dubbed it, has become a major voting and lobbying block in American politics. The clout of this block of conservative Christian voters has been growing since the 80s when it even fielded a Christian presidential candidate in 1988. Today, that candidate's organization, which includes a cable TV network and news program, continues to work in the political arena along with many other Christian groups, calling and lobbying for governmental policy change.

Another high profile and highly influential national Christian organization has shifted much of its focus from working for families at the psychological and relational level to the national political stage. The leader of this organization realized that families were increasingly at risk in terms of their ability to instill basic Judeo-Christian values in their children, threatened by what he saw as the concerted effort of secular forces to win the hearts and minds of American youth. Believing he needed to take the fight right to those institutions if Christian families were to have a chance, he and his organization have become a real force in American politics in the last decade or so with both the ability to help elect or unelect candidates in regional and even national contests.

A documentary film recently released to theatres nationwide follows children attending a Christian summer camp formed around a military model. Listen to the language the producers use on their website to describe this Christian group: "A growing number of Evangelical Christians believe there is a revival underway in America that requires Christian youth to assume leadership roles in advocating the causes of their religious movement. (This movie) follows a group of young children to (a summer camp) where kids are taught to become dedicated Christian soldiers in God's army and are schooled in how to take back America for Christ. The film is a first-ever look into an intense training ground that recruits born-again Christian children to become an active part of America's political future."

Christian colleges and universities such as Liberty University, Patrick Henry College, Baptist Cedarville University and others have long been focused on preparing young Christian men and women to take influential places in American society. A recent article in Newsweek, *Cut, Thrust, and Christ*, cites the ferocity with which these schools are now pursuing the art of debating, fielding nationally touring teams that have been giving such legendary schools as Harvard a run for their money. Debaters are being seen as the "new missionaries," "having realized they can save a lot more souls from a seat at the top—perhaps even on the highest court in the land," the article states. John Green, a senior fellow at the Pew Forum on Religion and Public Life is quoted as saying, "Evangelicals have always wanted to persuade people to the faith. The new thing is that evangelicals want to be more involved in the world now. Conservative Christian leaders would like to have a cadre of conservative Christian attorneys, who then become judges, politicians, and political appointees."

It's hard to imagine a more succinct expression of the second way, the way of the Pharisees who also rose to "seats at the top" in order to influence and manipulate their country's direction. But such activism is not confined solely to conservative circles. Mainline Protestant denominations, at least at the leadership level, have become so theologically, politically, and socially liberal as to be virtually synonymous with secular humanistic thinking. Positioned firmly left of the political center and pursuing social justice in society as the primary expression of the Gospel, such church denominations have allied themselves with political power even at global levels to attain social reforms. They also practice what they preach, reforming social structures within their own church bodies, often with devastating results as conservative and liberal wings fracture or secede from one another.

Here an important distinction needs to be made because in our culture today, the word "Pharisee" has become synonymous with "hypocrite," and no such connotation is being implied. For at least two centuries before Yeshua came on the scene, the Pharisees were the guardians and protectors of the traditional Jewish way of life, and if not for their influence through the Greek and Roman occupations, it is questionable whether Jews would exist today as a recognizable group. But power always corrupts, and over time passionate dedication to Torah gave way to pathological legalism and thirst for power. Following the second way of the Pharisees does not imply hypocrisy or pathology at all, just a genuine dedication to influencing adverse circumstances.

Debates can rage as to whether Christianity or any religion should insert itself into politics, but that also misses the point. Christians and any other religious group have as much right to engage the political process as any secular group, but we must be honest with ourselves and realize that as soon as we do, we are no longer being spiritual. We have shed our spiritual skin and have become one more political or social special-interest group acting in the secular arena. As soon as we believe that our faith can be expressed in political terms, we have lost the spiritual battle before we've begun.

We may be highly successful in changing public policy to match the moral and ethical purity codes of our choosing, but the mere following of codes and rules has nothing to do with true spirituality or the Fifth Way of Yeshua. And at what expense do we attain these political victories? How long do they last? The political process by definition is *hataha*—separation, division, polarization, and can never result in *shalom*.

The rule of the majority is not *shalom*, it is just the rule.

In politics, one person's *shalom* is always increased in direct proportion to someone else's decrease. This doesn't mean we don't passionately engage in political policy forums and activities, and it certainly doesn't mean that we never engage in activities that result in division or conflict—such activities are always going to be required in this life between heaven and earth. But it does mean that we realize that when we do, we've left the realm of "God's work," which is the pure creation of *shalom* from the inside out one person at a time, and have engaged in a limited process that at best can only create pockets of *shalom* at the expense of greater *hataha* elsewhere. As Winston Churchill said, "Democracy is the worst form of government ever devised by man. Except for all the other kinds." Our political process may be the best we can do for society as a whole, but as an expression of the second way it can't launch us even to *shalom's* lowest orbit.

Three.

When tension created by the aversion to contemporary culture and politics becomes too great, even the thought of remaining in touch with it enough to influence it becomes unbearable, and the urge to flee becomes irresistible. These are the separatists of our society, the ultra-conservative groups that head for the hills of Idaho or Montana and create mini-societies out of whole cloth with their own rules and way of life. For them, society is broken beyond repair, and government is the enemy forcing them to live an unclean life. Many of these groups are apocalyptic, just as were the Essenes, and are expecting to be the chosen remnant that will replant the earth after Armageddon and usher in the Millennium. David Koresh's Branch Davidians who set up their compound in Waco, Texas is an easy example, but many more exist. From rogue Mormon groups still practicing polygamy in Utah to the Amish in Pennsylvania, these groups are human time capsules buried in worlds of their own making until such time that the larger world is once again ready to receive them on their own terms.

Even those who are still trying to influence society can have a strong separatist streak as well. Many Christian organizations have moved to more remote locations, one moving its headquarters from its original offices in the Los Angeles area to create a virtual city in Colorado Springs that would better maintain the kind of living environment they desired. Christian universities, bible colleges, and the surging movement toward home schooling, especially strong among conservative Christians, are also an expression of the need to create enclaves away from an alien and increasingly hostile culture.

In a new and fascinating combination of the second and third ways, at least one group is attempting the ultimate separatist manipulation by trying to repopulate an entire state with their own members. The Christian Exodus is certainly thinking big, as their website states, "Christian Exodus is orchestrating the move of thousands of Christians (to South Carolina) to reacquire our Constitutional rights by electing State and local officials who will interpose on behalf of the people and refuse to enforce illegal federal acts.... Christians have actively tried to return the United States to its moral foundations for more than 30 years.... Attempts at reform have proven futile... Christian Exodus offers the opportunity to try a strategy not yet employed by Bible-believing Christians. Rather than spend resources in continued efforts to redirect the entire nation, we will redeem States one at a time. Millions of Christian conservatives are geographically spread out and diluted at the national level. Therefore, we must concentrate our numbers in a geographical region with a sovereign government we can influence through the electoral process."

Once again, it would be hard to write a more succinct portrayal of the escalation of the second way to the third—or at least of the second way on steroids—than this excerpt. As the tension and frustration over the inability to fight an overwhelming force take hold, the ante has to be continually upped to keep pace.

Four.
When the aversion and hostility to society gets so strong that even separation is not enough, the fourth way is invoked. Fortunately in American Christianity we don't see much of the fourth way, the way of destruction. Though many of the most militant separatists are also militarized and heavily armed, they tend to keep to themselves,

seeing their destructive power as more defensive than offensive, a protection against a tyrannical government in the mold of David Koresh who fought back in Waco only after being attacked by federal agents. Timothy McVeigh, the Oklahoma City bomber, fits all the profiles of a militant separatist extremist and chose the federal building as his target partly in revenge for the Waco siege, but any religious reasons for his terrorist attack are tenuous. On the other hand, in the name of stopping the killing of innocents, religious, anti-abortion extremists have resorted to the assassination of abortion doctors and terrorist bombings of abortion clinics, though virtually all Christian activist organizations disavow the use of violence to attain their goals even if radical members among them resort to it themselves.

But even if radical Christian use of the fourth way is limited today, it hasn't always been so, as any reading of church history will attest. From crusades to inquisitions to witch hunts, the church has not shied from the institutional use of the sword in the past, but now has ceded center stage to another group—as the way of destruction has become the way of choice for radical Islam. The 9/11 Twin Towers attack was only the most spectacular result of decades of institutionalized fourth way terrorism being practiced as part of a holy war against the overwhelming forces of the West. It's an interesting question as to why contemporary radical Christians have not turned in numbers to the fourth way, as have radical Muslims. Perhaps radical Christians have just not been pushed hard enough or deprived enough yet, or more hopefully, that the words of Yeshua himself restrain them, but for whatever reason, the fact of the fourth way exists and the promise of its continued and increased use exists as well.

The fourth way is the last stage of increasing desperation, and as with the Zealots who lost it all the moment they sank to the place where terror and murder looked to them like the will of God, so too will these modern-day Zealots. All will be lost and all will lose. Victory will be fleeting and loss will be permanent until the Four Ways are seen for what they really are.

>Rain last night. Started about 10:30. Working at the keyboard in a quiet moment, I was suddenly aware of white noise outside my window. Been a long time since I've heard that. Too long between rains in Southern California. Went out to the balcony to drink it in. Not literally; it is covered. A few flashes of very distant lightning--the weak thunder only barely arriving like an afterthought many seconds later.

>I stood in the cool dark looking up and listening to millions of drops hitting millions of leaves and making that sound-- exactly like bacon frying in a pan...without the aroma.

>This morning running around puddles and trying to avoid mud in the dark. Washing it off in the puddles when I didn't. It's light now. When I sat down here fifteen minutes ago, there was barely enough light to see the pages as I reread the last entry. Now it's full morning, overcast, but bright. I seem to be so aware of the passage of time lately. How high the sun gets in the sky only an hour and a half past sunrise. That I can practically see the movement of shadows across the sidewalk. Time. I'm so tired of its tyranny over my life. The urgencies it creates. The false importance it places on those urgencies, simply by virtue of their urgency--the urgency that someone has arbitrarily created, usually for some financial reason.

>The truly important things of life are relational--not temporal. Like God, they exist out of time, at least in the sense that they are open-ended. Not like a temporal urgency with its little segment end points: project start and deadline stop. Human relationships, unlike God, do have a starting point, but usually no perceived ending point. That lack of perceived deadline is what takes them out of the realm of the urgent.

>And since we've all learned to place importance on what is urgent, we tend to place the non-urgent in a subservient posi-

tion. To always do the urgent first. Problem is, there is no lack of urgencies. There will always be another dirty table to clean, another transaction to complete. Most people spend entire lives running from urgency to urgency, trying to keep up, thinking that as soon as this job is done, they can do that other thing that they know beyond conscious knowing is calling their spirit. Relationship. With God. With their own spirit. With spouses. Children. Friends. People.

>But there is never time for such things. These are things of being rather than things of completion. If you sell your soul to the god of accomplishment, he will answer your prayers and supply you with a never-ending stream of deadlines to work against. Keep your mind so busy and cluttered that you simply run headlong through your life, bursting through deadline after deadline like the paper signs football players run through at high school games, until you flatten yourself against the brick wall of your final deadline. The one you never saw coming beyond the paper ones.

>And this is the tragedy. That our human relationships, our very lives, have deadlines too. We just don't see them. We don't want to. We don't want to think of separation. We don't want to think of death. But by removing the deadlines from the relational, we remove the perceived importance also. Now we're free to neglect our wives, to distance ourselves from husbands, to miss whole feet and inches of our children's childhood, to miss God completely, to have that worst of all experiences: to hit the deadline before the project was ever begun.

>Our whole life is an urgency, but only a very few of us know our deadlines--even approximately. Maybe that's what's happening to me. The Lord is making me aware of the passage of time in order to appreciate the moments of my life. And once appreciated, to move beyond that temporal tyranny into simple being-becoming. Watching the shadows move, never forgetting that that movement is defining my span, taking me closer the deadline I can't see--but liberated from the urgency.

>In the hands of All-Being, there is no urgency. In the light of eternity, urgency has no definition. Urgency is a figment in the imagination of the creatures of time. It has no kinship with us, with who we really are.

>Let's all see urgency for what it really is. A necessary evil, perhaps. But an evil nonetheless.

Little Mirrors

But the Four Ways don't just stop at the shores of national policy and politics. They are used every day within every human subgroup by people confronted with painful circumstances they can't seem to overcome. Consider behavior in our churches. After all, what is a thoughtless conversion to faith—one based only in the fear of damnation or in the syllables of a prayer from an urgent evangelist—but an ultimate yielding to the pressures of life and fear of the unknown? Such movement from outside in and not inside out is always one of the four ways in spite of its religious trappings.

And once safely inside the walls of our church, how much are we willing to yield to become just what is expected or needed in order to gain the acceptance and attention we crave? We say "prayer changes things" and "you can't out-give God," but what do we really mean if we're just hoping against hope that our prayers and good works will manipulate or influence God and others to change the things in our lives that hurt? We exit one church and join another when differences arise, or we convene church councils to stamp out (destroy) the differences themselves, often along with the people who are different.

The four ways operate in our homes as well, of course. Think of two people in a difficult marriage. How to cope? To keep the peace, one spouse may yield to the other, co-dependently submerge his or her own feelings and preferences, become a doormat or an enabler or both. One may try to dominate the other either by passively or aggressively manipulating decisions and circumstances to advantage. Such domination can escalate to outright abuse, either emotional or physical, as one spouse uses destructive tactics that can be as mild as criticizing or ridiculing the other privately or in public or as devastating as physical beatings, rape, and murder. And of course, everywhere in the mix lies the option to simply leave—to exit physically or metaphorically into the addiction of drugs, alcohol, adultery, emotional affairs, gambling, pornography, or any activity that removes the immediacy of the pain.

In all our relationships, whether centered in the family, the street, workplace, school, church, or any other social grouping, people are yielding to stronger personalities and groups either for profit or out of convenience or desperation, manipulating others for principle or personal gain, leaving painful relationships and circumstances, and seeking to destroy them.

In describing the effects of the Four Ways used harmfully in fear, we can't forget that as the Four Ways are the only tools we have for advancing physical journeys, they must be used helpfully in love as well. The flip side of yielding is compromise—the essential ingredient of any relationship or group. Manipulation is typically self-serving in connotation, but influence can be positive, necessary for the greater good. We do need to exit abusive situations and relationships that we can't change, and to absolutely rule out the use of force is to abdicate our human roles as protector and defender.

As something less than Kingdom, the Four Ways can never produce Kingdom, but they are a necessary part of life among non-Kingdom residents. It's when we deceive ourselves into thinking we can advance spiritual journeys through non-spiritual means that we defeat our purpose before we begin.

When will we as people of faith, in our institutions of faith, see that the Four Ways are the ways only of the earth and are incompatible with the Way of God? That their use under a spiritual banner does nothing to change this fact. That in fact, it is *we* who are changed as we use them—from spirit to dust, we hand back our wings and strand ourselves on earth. Marooned. Grounded. Telling ourselves that we really are doing God's will, praying that the ends really do justify the means, we press on, doggedly trudging our way to heaven...having forgotten that our job wasn't to get to heaven, but to bring heaven to earth. In our own hearts. Without a shot fired.

God's will never includes consciously leaving a relationship worse than we found it, and Yeshua is always reminding us that though we may be the greatest of those born of woman, the least of the Kingdom is still greater than that.

Then suddenly there was Marian.

>With auburn hair and impossibly big eyes, she lit up rooms that had been dark so long, I'd simply learned not to move the furniture around—safe inside familiar tracks in the carpet. And just as suddenly it seemed that life was finally beginning to give back what it had always been taking. I brought Marian to the warehouse and watched the same collision on her face between this Jesus and the memories of her own Catholic childhood. But she didn't run, and in a breath and a half I had a new best friend. I still rode my bicycle, but it was just a bicycle after all, leaning unhallowed against the wall of an increasingly unseen apartment.

>Religion and spirituality are very different things.

>The friends, the music, bible studies and Sunday mornings with Marian at my side, my growing role as musician and leader flowed in and filled my spaces. It all felt like truth, like meaning and purpose, and it overwhelmed the agonized questions I'd been asking the way the sun overwhelms all other stars at dawn. But like the stars, questions remained undimmed behind the blue curtain patiently waiting for dusk.

>And dusk fell two years later when Marian and I ran like children up to Papa Pastor to ask him to marry us. Without the slightest cloud on the horizon, we were completely unprepared to hear that he wasn't sure he could marry us since we'd both been married before. He didn't know if we had biblical grounds for divorce of which there was only one, adultery, and without which remarriage would be the same as adultery itself. I would be disqualified as a leader in the church because leaders had to be the husband of just one wife, which was interpreted as one wife in a series, not at the same time... It was all right there in the book.

131

>There was a beat, a staring silence, which he quickly filled saying he'd have to talk with the rest of the pastors and elders for a decision. As I watched night fall in Marian's eyes, all my big questions lit back up against the darkness there: these men didn't know the details of our first marriages, didn't know that Marian's husband was an alcoholic and what sort of pain it was that ended with their marriage those years ago; it didn't seem to matter. It was all in the book...

>No grounds for divorce except infidelity. Divorce without adultery, even to escape abuse or neglect or abandonment, meant remarriage itself was adultery. Forever? Without the possibility of pardon or parole? Without the possibility of any position of leadership within the church? Ever?

The drummer who played alongside me on Sundays had become one of my best friends: a recovering heroin addict who had lived on the street, eating out of dumpsters, stealing and prostituting himself for his next fix, sliding in and out of jail. He would give his testimony at the pulpit from time to time on Sunday mornings as we applauded and praised God for his recovery, asking him to teach our Sunday school children about the dangers of drugs and how to avoid the life he had led...because he had been saved, because he was recovered, because he was a living example of God's forgiveness and healing...because he wasn't divorced.

>If divorce was an unforgivable sin, if common sense was the enemy of faith and the Bible, if Jesus and his Father wanted people to remain in abusive marriages or alone for the rest of their lives if they didn't, then maybe I couldn't follow them, maybe I shouldn't follow them; if this was Christianity, then maybe I wasn't Christian after all.

The Fifth Way

As far as the east is from the west...

DAVID SINGS IN PSALM 103 THAT THIS IS HOW FAR GOD HAS removed us from the separation of our sin. For David nothing was farther apart than sunrise and sunset, which appeared at opposite ends of heaven and earth, at opposite ends of day and night. Go far enough north, and eventually you'll end up going south; go south long enough, and you'll find yourself going north. But go east, and you will forever be going east, or forever west. East and west never meet.

David was singing about the distance God puts between the separation our choices create and the unity he longs to have with us, which is exactly the same distance between the Fifth Way and the Four Ways, between the Way of Unity and the ways of separation...and for the same reason. They never meet, as east and west never meet. The Fifth Way, the Way of Kingdom, is always heading in a completely different direction than any the Four Ways may travel. They are diametrically and unalterably unaligned because true change always comes from the opposite direction the earth would have us believe. *Always*. Anything else is not the Fifth Way.

Having used the Four Ways all our lives, the Fifth Way is maddeningly elusive. Yeshua never approached it directly, but snuck up on it through parable, metaphor, and the action of his life. It's the only way; straight lines won't take us there.

No one has ever seen electricity. No one really knows exactly how it works. We know how to make it, and we know how to use it, and when the light goes on as we flick the switch, we see its effect, and we know it's there. Yeshua said to Nicodemus in John 3 that, "The wind blows where it wishes and you hear the sound of it, but do not know where it comes from and where it is going; so is everyone who is born of the Spirit."

And so it is with the Fifth Way.

We can't see the Way; we see its effect.

Yeshua's language reflects this as he tries to bend our hearts and minds around a new concept: that while the Four Ways are always working to make us relevant, powerful, and spectacular in order to find meaning in life...

...the Fifth Way simply makes life meaningful, which in turn makes us relevant, powerful, and spectacular.

It makes life meaningful by making God's presence real in our lives. Yeshua encouraged us to seek first the Kingdom and all else would be added. The Fifth Way directly seeks the source of the stream high in the mountains and so deals in one thing, Unity. Flowing effortlessly into the valley as the stream becomes a great river branching off in many directions, the Way of Yeshua continues to see Unity in the river's diversity because it flows with it. Conversely, the Four Ways try to harness the power of the downstream tributaries, and so deal in many things: complexity, separateness, disunity, and can never flow back upstream to the Unity at the source.

The Fifth Way literally stands the four ways on their heads. Think about the wild language of Yeshua's difficult sayings as he tries to help us see that compared to the Four Ways, the Fifth Way is...

...inside out, downside up, and backside front.

☉ ☽ ⊕ ⊕ ⊕

Inside Out.

The Four Ways teach us to try to become relevant by looking for something outside ourselves—like turning stones into bread— to complete us, to change our circumstances, to make the hurting stop. Whether another person, a marriage, a divorce, a move to another place, a different church or pastor, a mentor, to have children, to get rid of the children we have, a job, better health, better looks, better finances, to be older, to be young again, more friends and activity or less...it doesn't really matter; it's all equally useless. Some things in life are not transferable. Nothing out there will "complete us" because true change or transformation doesn't come from the outside in, but from the inside out.

Yeshua said in Luke 17, "the Kingdom is not coming with signs to be observed; nor will they say, 'Look, here it is!' or, 'There it is!' For the Kingdom of God is within you." As the Greek word *entos* here means within, among, and in the midst of all at the same time— all are relevant. And more dramatically, the Aramaic behind the Greek is *legau men*, meaning moving dynamically from inside to outside. Yeshua could hardly be more specific.

At Mark 7, "Are you so lacking in understanding also? Do you not understand that whatever goes into the man from outside cannot defile him, because it does not go into his heart, but into his stomach, and is eliminated? ...That which proceeds out of the man, that is what defiles the man." This inside out principle, stated in the negative here, also works in the positive where the external purity codes of the Pharisees were shown by Yeshua to be spiritually useless in Matthew 5: "If you are presenting your offering at the altar, and there remember that your brother has something against you, leave your offering there before the altar and go; first be reconciled to your brother, and then come and present your offering." No religious ritual or spiritual practice can transfer anything of real value to us; only the yearning for true relationship from deep inside makes that happen. Our rituals and religious practices are external symbols of that deep yearning or nothing at all.

And if we're still thinking we can be relevant from the outside in, by doing all the "right" things, the expected things we do to be liked or loved by others, Yeshua dispels that notion in one of his most difficult sayings at Luke 14: "If anyone comes to me, and does not hate his own father and mother and wife and children and brothers and sisters, yes, and even his own life, he cannot be my disciple." Even understanding that the Aramaic word for hate, *sena*, doesn't mean here to hate in a malicious way, but merely to prefer less, this is still a hard saying. Like a slap across the face, Yeshua is trying to wake us to the notion that clinging to any of the external social conventions of the Four Ways will not take us any closer to the Fifth Way. Even though love precludes us from neglecting any of the personal relationships in our lives, there must at some point be a clean break with those conventions that have become security blankets—a radical break, a quantum shift in our approach.

Yeshua asks a man to follow him in Luke 9, but the man replies, "Lord, permit me first to go and bury my father." Yeshua spins him around saying, "Let the dead bury the dead; but as for you, go and proclaim everywhere the Kingdom of God." This saying is also softened somewhat by understanding that in first century Judea "burying my father" could mean anything from waiting up to a period of a year to perform the ritual second burial of a corpse to continuing to live with and care for parents until they died. Still, Yeshua is recognizing the man's reply for what it is—an excuse, a procrastination, a kicking the can down the road—and is clear that the Fifth Way is not for the faint-hearted or the conventional: "The foxes have holes and birds of the air have nests, but the son of man has nowhere to lay his head."

Following the Four Ways, working from the outside in, through existing systems is a burying of the dead, and we the "dead" must tend the physical details of life, of course. But what is required if we want to also be counted among the living? Yeshua knows we don't literally have to choose between burying our fathers—taking care of the personal relationships in our lives—and following our spiritual journeys. We do both at the same time; we can follow Yeshua without ever leaving home, and "proclaiming everywhere the Kingdom of God" is always at its loudest and most eloquent when no words are used at all. But there is also a radical departure in mind and heart that must be made, and we must know the difference. Yeshua is leaving a trail of breadcrumbs through the New Testament, shovelful by shovelful, to point us in the right direction. "Come follow me," Yeshua says, and no excuse will do, no half-measures will suffice. It's full extension, full commitment, or nothing further.

Downside Up.
The second great temptation is the one that seduces by making us believe that if we just had enough power, we could really change things, better our circumstances, everyone's circumstances. Along with every beauty contestant, we really do want world peace, and we look for great leaders or a messiah to ride to the rescue and fix what's broken in our world, our communities, our lives. We field or support candidates for office, form new groups and committees, or work through existing organizations to lobby for change in policies, laws, and administration. We send emails and letters rallying people to our causes while, closer to home, we jockey for the best, most visible, most influential positions in the workplace, the church, and the home. Some of us seek power for ourselves and others are content to share in the power of others, but regardless, the quest for power consumes, and once gained, corrupts—and the more things change, the more they remain the same. True change never comes from the top down, from a few dictating to the many, but from the bottom up, from a grassroots sea change in the hearts of the many, affecting the entire community all the way to the top.

"Who is the greatest in the Kingdom?" Yeshua's followers ask in Matthew 18, and Yeshua brings over a child as model to follow; there is a letting go of control, not a consuming quest for it, that takes us to new heights. A fight breaks out in Matthew 20 when two of the Twelve lobby Yeshua, through their mother, for the seats at the top in the Kingdom—at Yeshua's right and left hand. There are only 28 chapters in the Gospel of Matthew, and even by the end of chapter 20, the Twelve, those closest to Yeshua, still don't understand. Yeshua patiently explains yet again, "You know that the rulers of the Gentiles lord it over them, and their great men exercise authority over them. It is not this way among you, but whoever wishes to become great among you shall be your servant, and whoever wishes to be first among you shall be your slave..."

Should we pay our taxes, our tribute to the government that oppresses us or refuse and find ways to take that power back? "Give back to Caesar the things that are Caesar's, and to God the things that are God's." Yeshua is carefully keeping the Four Ways and the Fifth Way separate. He's not saying there is never a time to oppose oppression and cruelty through one of the Four Ways, but in doing so, don't suppose you're giving anything back to God. Do your four ways work and deal with the Caesar du jour as you see fit; just don't pin God's name on it. It's not "God's work" you do, even if it's through God that you do it.

By the time he was re-elected, Abraham Lincoln understood this message possibly better than anyone alive, which allowed him to express it so poignantly in his magnificent Second Inaugural Address. As he ascended the platform in front of the new Capitol building that Saturday morning, the Civil War was all but over, and the unthinkable toll the war had taken on the Union was sinking in. "With malice toward none and charity for all," the President turned his attention toward "binding up the nation's wounds" with the realization that both sides sought different ends through the same means—that North and South "Both read the same Bible and pray to the same God, and each invokes His aid against the other. It may seem strange that any men should dare to ask a just God's assistance in wringing their bread from the sweat of other men's faces, but let us judge not, that we be not judged. The prayers of both could not be answered. That of neither has been answered fully. The Almighty has His own purposes."

I wonder if God knows how many good causes he supports?

Yeshua is telling us not to suppose he supports any at all. The things we give to or try to take from Caesar have nothing to do with God's Way; the things of God are of a different order and can only be expressed from the downside up and with just the power that can be mustered by a child or a slave. Maybe the next time we inevitably drift back to the halls of power to fight God's fight and defend the faith, we'll hear Yeshua reminding us, "My Kingdom is not of this world. If my Kingdom were of this world, then my officers would be fighting (for me); but as it is, my Kingdom is not of this world." John 18.

Backside Front.

To throw yourself down from the great height only to be borne up by angels in flight, to be spectacular, known, admired, adored, to be famous and remembered—to be on TV—is a very strong pull. As this media-obsessed culture runs headlong, making people feel more and more disconnected and overlooked, the need for attention becomes irresistible. Like petulant children, any attention is better than none, and there seems to be nothing people won't do to grab the spotlight even for just the fabled fifteen minutes. Whether in the media, the workplace, the church, or even the family, to be noticed and attended becomes the only validation and meaning most of us recognize. Maybe we know somewhere down deep that we can never get enough, that the thirst will never be slaked, but then maybe we don't—and regardless, the beat goes on.

And the words of Yeshua calling from a great distance bounce off our personal force fields and fall away, but if we could only hear... As we look for meaning in the eyes of others, Yeshua is trying to tell us that we already have God's full attention, full-time. Ironically, for all our searching, God's attention is all that can ever really bring us meaning, and there is nothing we can do to turn his spotlight up any hotter than it already is. In Yeshua's story of the prodigal son in Luke 15, the father tries to coax his elder son into celebrating his brother's return, tries to make him understand that he hasn't lost anything because his brother is having a party thrown for him. "All I have is yours," the father tells his elder son—there is nothing more I can give you than everything I have, and not to celebrate your brother's return would only diminish my love for you by diminishing me.

We don't get to see the elder brother's reaction, but if we didn't get the point, Yeshua tells another story in Matthew 20 of groups of laborers who come to work, early in the day, at midday, and late in the afternoon. When all the workers are paid the same wages at day's end, the ones who came early and did the most work are outraged, feeling cheated: perfect four-ways reasoning. But when we are already getting all there is to get, what more can be gained? How can we be cheated? All the Father has is already ours. To seek more than everything is pointless, absurd, and to try to diminish someone else's share does not increase our own. There is no hierarchy with God; we all are "paid" the same, all the time.

And so he tells us he'll leave ninety-nine sheep in the fold to go looking for just the one that is lost. And that "anyone who exalts himself shall be humbled, and those who humble themselves will be exalted." But how many of us are free enough to really believe that moving to the back, taking the last place at the table will result in getting the promotion, the deal, the seat at the top? Like the elder brother, we are scandalized and outraged when someone else gets a party, because we think there are only so many parties to go around. If someone else gets one, that's one less chance for us. Zero sum game. But Yeshua is trying to tell us we all are having parties in God's eyes, that there's always one more party in God's pocket.

In our desire to be significant, we are driven to be *different*—to stand apart, head and shoulders above the crowd. We think we have to be different to be significant, but everything the Father has is already ours and as long as we show up, we all get paid the same, and in the face of a perfect love that has no degree...

> ...we are not significant because we're different,
> we're significant because we are the same.

If we can see past the Four Ways for just a moment, we will see that the compulsion to get that top spot is only an exhausting search to get what we already have. We are all first with God. We are all his favorites. He has the capacity to do that—to have an infinite number of best friends. "The last shall be first and the first last," because in the end, those who seek to be first, miss the Way completely, laboring on for what they already possess, and those who are content to be last, are still always first—without all the sleepless nights and sweaty work.

� � � � �

So to what does it all come? In terms of our choices, what does this Fifth Way look like? Well, at the risk of sounding like a greeting card or a song lyric, it looks like love.

We use the Four Ways to make ourselves relevant in order to feel loved and needed and connected; to make ourselves powerful in order to feel in control of our lives and secure; to make ourselves spectacular in order to be noticed and important and to live on in the minds of our descendants. We search for worthiness and personal meaning through all these means, but our four ways search is always vampire-like, trying to suck our meaning from the lives of others, diminishing their *shalom* in a vain effort to increase our own. Diminishing anyone else's *shalom* only diminishes ours as well, and most importantly, the Fifth Way shows us that the converse is also true: increasing another's *shalom* increases ours as well— and is the *only way* to increase it.

Yeshua said if you try to save your life, you'll lose it, but if you're willing to lose your life, you'll find it.

If you want to be relevant in life, *give relevance away*. If you want to feel worthwhile and valuable, put value and worth into another person's life. If you want to be loved, be a lover and see how that makes you feel. If you want to be powerful, *give power away* by empowering others through your teaching and mentorship. If you want to be spectacular, *give attention away* by being the listener and the encourager. Nothing will focus someone's attention on you faster than really listening in a world full of noise.

This is not a quid pro quo or mutual back scratching, but just a statement of what is. If we give only to receive back, we've re-entered the second way of manipulation and have received our reward in full. But if we give because we've lost our awareness of ourselves for a moment, because we've really seen the person standing in front of us and know in this moment the gift we have to give is what he or she really needs, that moment is a Kingdom moment along the Fifth Way—and the best definition of love imaginable.

The only way we can freely give something away is if we already possess it in the first place. And the only way we know for sure whether we possess a thing is if we can freely give it away. No strings attached.

Whether relevance, power, or spectacular meaning, we'll know it is really ours, that it really exists within us, when we can see its effect existing in the life of another, when it becomes as solidly real as Scarecrow, Tin Man, and Lion dancing and singing with us along the Way. And of course such free gifts never diminish us any more than they diminish the father of the prodigal son or our Father in heaven.

There is always one more party in our pockets too.

>I started attending a "Parapastor" program at church Wednesday night. It's a program designed to prepare men for ordination. Women aren't allowed--Bible seems to prohibit that--at least in most Christian interpretations. Not sure why. Makes me uncomfortable, but there it is. I'm in no theological or moral position to argue yet. And who said it was supposed to be comfortable anyway?

>For that matter, I may not be eligible for ordination either because of my marital status. Divorced. Makes me an honorary woman, I guess. It amazes me and saddens me how all the decisions and mistakes of my life continue to limit the scope of my potential usefulness, if not in reality, at least in the eyes of some. At the same time they have all conspired to make me what I am. And since right now that is a person who loves God and even is occasionally aware of his presence, how can I regret? Well, I do. Somewhat.

>Maybe there was an easier way, straighter way, earlier way to get to this place without all the damaging detours that have permanently rearranged my life. I don't dwell on this, thankfully, but it does occur to me at regular intervals.

>So I sat in the Parapastor meeting wondering, at considerably shorter regular intervals, if I belonged there at all. I don't know how much I have in common with the others; they're all pretty young and thinking along apparently different lines from me. They asked me why I was there. Much of what I was thinking came out. Because it wasn't just those in that room I was feeling apart from. It's been most everyone and everything at the church. The more I begin to understand what a relationship with God really means, the more I realize it's nothing like I ever imagined--more profound, more beautiful,

more difficult, more changing, more consuming, more solitary.
And the more apart I feel.

>I wasn't prepared for this apartness . Who can I talk to about
the latest treasure I've uncovered? There are some, but most
are politely uninterested. I think they think I'm regressive, that
we should have evolved beyond such things. Naturally I didn't
say all of this at the meeting, but I said enough. I thought it
was interesting that everyone wanted to help me. They started sharing how they overcame difficulties and problems in
their lives. Offered advice, encouragement, consolation.

>But they all missed the point that there is nothing to fix.
There is nothing wrong. I wouldn't change anything if I could,
though I can't. I couldn't go back now if I wanted to. But I
listened quietly to the suggestions, tried to gently redirect the
conversation where possible. Only the pastor in charge
seemed to understand. He said several times that they had no
answers for me. But I don't think even he understood that I
wasn't asking any questions. I was simply answering theirs--
why I was there. What brought me to where I am. I must have
sounded plaintive. I didn't mean to. Or maybe we all just have
a need to try to fix things we can't understand or categorize.
Without stopping to consider that a thing may be just as it
ought to be, we start whittling off corners to make it fit the
niche we have prepared for it in our minds.

>I've heard that women are often driven at least partially in-
sane by men who try to solve their problems for them with
methodical and logical advice, when all they really want is to
be held. I've always acknowledged that with a chuckle, but
now I think I understand.

Barest Beginning

In the midst of the Second World War, but after the worst of the blitz of England, Winston Churchill said, "This is not the end. It is not even the beginning of the end. But it is, perhaps, the end of the beginning."

And so now in the midst of all these pages, everything that has been said so far is not even the beginning of the beginning. Anything merely said about the Way and not acted upon, leaves it not yet even begun. We can't deceive ourselves if we want to follow the Way. There are no shortcuts, no work-arounds. If we can think it all through and diagram it out, then it's not the Fifth Way; it's one of the other four. If we can explain it to another, it's not the Fifth Way. The Fifth Way can't be thought through, it must be lived through. You can't know the Way until you're on the Way. And like electricity, you'll only know you're on the Way, when you throw the switch and the light burns—when your life lights up and fear and discontent begin to fade to white. When you suddenly realize that more often than not, you are content, when more often than not, your smile and laughter characterize you, then you will know you're on the Way and that you know something of it.

The Fifth Way is a process, a way of living life, an attitude by which you move from moment to moment, and which only exists in real time—in those moments. It can't be extracted, bottled, theorized, categorized, formalized, ritualized, doctrinalized, creedalized, or in any way removed from the experience of each moment without changing it into something else. As soon as electricity stops flowing, stops doing work, it ceases to exist as itself. The Fifth Way, like the faith that precedes it, is the same. It only exists as long as it is moving—flowing through us and creating effects in our lives that can warm those nearby or help them see more clearly in the dark. They will see it as love; we will experience it as following the Way.

Then why are we still talking here? Why are there still so many pages under your right hand?

Yeshua reserved most of his anger for the Pharisees and Scribes, and the most telling of his accusations against them was that they burdened the people, but wouldn't lift a finger to help them, that they wouldn't enter the Kingdom and wouldn't allow anyone else to enter either. Their way of thought, their legalistic attitude, and their thousands of rules blocked them and anyone who followed them from even recognizing the existence of the Way to life toward which Yeshua was pointing. It was not that they didn't want life, it wasn't even that they were necessarily trying to keep the people from that life; it was that they had lived so long in the bottom of their well that they had completely forgotten there was a wide ocean outside it. The Gate to the Way had been so long unused, so completely grown over with vegetation that it simply ceased to exist in their minds.

We are no different. Our churches, for the most part, don't teach or preach the Fifth Way of Yeshua. They teach and follow the Four Ways of man and earth. It has always been so. From the first generations after Yeshua, people gathered in groups to follow the Way, wrote it down, made rules, and changed it into something else. The moment the church believed that the Way to life was through the church and not the Way itself, it lost its Way. As soon as the church believed it could confer life or salvation through its creeds and doctrines and rituals, it gained immense physical power over people's lives, but lost all spiritual authority. Just like the Pharisees and Scribes, the leaders of the church also forgot about the existence of the Way and stopped living it, then seduced and corrupted by the material promises of the Four Ways, would not let anyone else live it either.

As an institution, this is the church we always inherit, and why we're still talking. The message of Yeshua and his accusations against the Pharisees are as pointed and applicable today as they were then, and to every generation in between. We as humans, left to our own devices, will always turn to the Four Ways—it's what we do. Only through the action of God in our lives is the Fifth Way possible. But God doesn't act unilaterally. Yeshua poked and prodded and exhausted himself telling stories that pointed, but never coerced. We are partners with God along the Way, or we're not on the Way at all.

When at last we're ready, we simply pick up our feet and put them down again, making tracks in some direction as we watch the scenery go by. It won't be all figured out before we embark, because the Way doesn't even exist until we're on it. We try to define it, strain to see its shape, but it's as if the Way materializes beneath our feet with each step we take: growing with us as we move, remaining blank and empty before us if we stop—nothing in front of our toes. We crave clarity, but all we really need is trust. Trust enough that the Way will really be there to hold us up each and every time we put one foot down in front of the other.

This is the nature of it. This is what Yeshua was trying to tell us with his beautiful stories. But as captives of our Western language and thoughtforms and of the institutional church we have inherited, we have a lot to unlearn. And that's what we've been doing all these pages—unlearning what church, society, culture, and our own experience have taught us about life and the living of it.

If you're on a recognizable path, a familiar path, you're most likely not on the Fifth Way, but one of the other four. We know the Four Ways best and will always revert to them when we let our guard down or when we get tired or fearful. *Always.* The Fifth Way will forever be new and different, never really familiar and certainly never boring. You won't see it stretching out before you, but materializing under your feet. It will be unsettling, even frightening at first, until you learn to trust it.

But also remember, as the ancient Jews conceived it, we live between heaven and earth, between *shemaya* and *a'ra*, which means that we really will always be on one or a combination of the Four Ways at the same time we're on the Fifth Way. The Fifth Way always points God-ward and is not very effective for getting somewhere on earth. As long as we're breathing, we need to feed, clothe, and shelter ourselves—and be responsible for those we love, which means we need to work and plan and chart definable courses upon which our children can depend. We will always be on one of the Four Ways as long as we are breathing in community with one other person or a million.

For the good of everyone around us, we are to bring heaven to earth and earth to heaven in such a way that we live our personal lives in the micro by following the Fifth Way—seeing our lives and all life through that lens of unity and connectedness—even as we practice the Four Ways as necessary in the macro for the good of those in our home and community. The Fifth Way, the Way of Spirit and Kingdom, will bring meaning to our lives and will temper our use of the Four Ways so that *shalom* is always maximized in the lives of everyone around us.

While on the Fifth Way, we will never try to maximize our *shalom* at the expense of another, but will realize that the *shalom* experienced by our neighbor is really all the *shalom* we can ever have or experience ourselves.

○ ① ⊕ ⊕ ⊗

As he lived and taught, did Yeshua actually have a concept in mind of his Way as the *Fifth Way*? If he did, he never expressed it as such, but he spoke of himself as the Way and taught about life along the Way and confronted the worldview of the Four Ways throughout his public life. His first Jewish followers never called themselves Christians, that name came later, attached by Gentiles trying to distinguish Yeshua's followers from the Jewish faith from which they sprang. They called themselves *talmidim orha*, Followers of the Way. Which Way? Yeshua's Way: something other than and beyond the four ways and philosophies of Israel.

Looking at the Way of Yeshua as the Fifth Way is a tool for us herenow. Implied by the Scriptures and the symbolic use of numbers in the ancient world, the Fifth Way hopefully gives us here today a concept with teeth and traction. For us, deep in our modern or postmodern Western wells, so removed in space and time from the ancient Eastern mindset of Yeshua's world, it is nearly impossible to suspend enough of who we think we are to really enter that world and live what the first Followers of the Way were living. The concept of the Fifth Way is a lever to help us pry up the veneer of our own worldview and see another Way in the lives of a far-off people. But though the people may be far off, the Way they followed is as near and real as our next breath.

And nearly impossible is still not impossible. To touch the essence of Yeshua's message, the rest of these pages will not be describing the Fifth Way so much as they will be pointing toward it, describing its effects—which do have discernible shape—and removing obstacles that obstruct our view. And each chapter and each image can be another shovelful of dirt dropped onto the floor of our wells that may lift us a bit higher each time, if we let it.

Now that hopefully the hard-packed ground of our entrenched worldview has been broken up and turned a bit, we'll next try to peer behind the Aramaic words of Yeshua—plant some Aramaic seeds in our prepared soil by entering the Aramaic Agreement between Yeshua and his first listeners that gave his words their meaning. We'll try to undo what our ignorance of the ancients and the actions of well-meaning Pharisees, both ancient and modern, have done to obscure both Gate and Way. Then we'll tend the first shoots of our Aramaic plantings by looking at how the truth of Yeshua's words applies to the life we can have along the Way.

But even here, don't confuse the concepts or mental constructs in these pages with the acting out of the Way in your own life. If these pages help clear the overgrowth around the Gate or help lift your eyes over the edge of your well to the ocean beyond, then keep reading. If not, then put them down now and go your own Way.

No book is the Way itself.

THE TRUTH

THE TERMS OF THE WAY

>Before I go completely numb, I must write this. A friend called today to tell me she was getting a divorce. And that she has rededicated her life to the Lord. Good news, bad news, I guess.

>What thoughts and emotions went through me. I understood better than she probably realized, but I wanted to scream--No! You don't understand what you're doing. And I don't think she does, even if she says so. But then I don't think anyone can be prepared for what comes out of broken relationships, the widening circles of fragmentation that break down everyone near like shock waves from a blast. How long it lasts. How permanent the condition of debilitation. Well, they have no children, maybe they will heal quicker. At any rate, she says she won't allow herself to live in unhappiness the way I have. And that I should stop.

>It's hard not to agree with a statement like that, but although it's perfectly clear what it means to her, it's not at all clear what it means to me. How it could possibly penetrate my life, affect me and those who've suffered with me.

>I talked to her for awhile, but my heart wasn't in it. She was adamant, militant even, throwing statements out like a glove across the face. I calmly and weakly tried to deflect some, but there wasn't much to say. I didn't create the situation and I couldn't fix it. She wasn't asking me to anyway. I could understand, but I couldn't condone. Sympathize, but not console. So we said we needed to get together and hung up.

>Then I called her husband. He was at work. He tried not to cry and succeeded mostly. We weren't close, no common interests. I told him so, he agreed. But I told him I was his brother anyway and even if we weren't close, I was there for him. It was also weak, but sincere. I hope he realized that.

>He asked a few questions about his wife. Did she tell me when she was moving out, because he didn't know. And then I almost cried because I recognized that deep agony, that wail that comes out of your soul when the separateness sets in and you just hunger for any scraps you can get about the one you love. How many times have I felt that wail coming up? How many times have I caused it to come up in others?

>So how do I not allow myself to be unhappy? I don't know. I think I am learning more about contentment, but happiness and joy continue to elude. Except sometimes when you say something really funny, or when the sunlight comes through the trees just right, and I smile right out loud before I can even think about it.

The Aramaic Agreement

Words are fluid things.

LIKE MUSIC, THEY EXIST FOR AN INSTANT AS VIBRATIONS, SOUNDS IN air, and then they are gone. But as mere sounds, they have no meaning, no value of their own. They are not connected to anything solid and only mean what we agree they mean. Their only value is in the mutual agreement between two minds that allows the same image to arise simultaneously when a particular sound is uttered by one, travels through the air, and is received by the other.

Paper currency has no value of its own beyond the value of the paper and ink. We simply agree that this piece of paper with "100" printed on it is much more desirable than that one with "1" printed on it—and it is so. And before *that* agreement is possible, we have to agree on what the word "hundred" and the word "one" mean in the first place.

It's only the Agreement that gives a word value—and the greater the number of people who agree, the greater the value and the power of the word. The more it can be used to create desired effects.

This is where it gets tricky.

In order to understand each other's meanings, we often have to translate from one language to another. But this is not a straight-forward process, because each language doesn't exist in isolation: it's a product of its Agreement—the culture of people who live together and have agreed on their shared experiences, their conception of how the world works, their slang, and their peculiar, idiomatic expressions that can't be understood at all from the meanings of the words alone. All these components are as agreed-upon as the words themselves; they are a part of both language and Agreement and are unique to the people who created them.

So when we translate from one language to another, we also have to translate from one *Agreement* to another—every agreed-upon thing that contributes to the *intended meaning* lying beyond the dictionary meaning of each word—or the wrong image will be painted in the mind of the hearer. To do this, we must understand something about the people, their culture, and their worldview in order to know what the intended meaning is. This is not terribly difficult with living languages, especially in a world becoming increasingly globalized—we can simply ask people what they meant by such and such an expression, or go live with the people and find out for ourselves.

But dead languages were created by dead cultures; the people and their culture no longer exist. And if the gulf of time is very great, understanding the people and culture from which a language came can become quite a forensic exercise. Understanding this difficulty is one thing, but not even realizing that it is an issue creates huge barriers to the understanding of agreed-upon meaning.

$$\odot \ \oslash \ \oplus \ \oplus \ \oplus$$

And so it is with the reading of ancient Scripture. The books of the Judeo-Christian Bible were written in Hebrew, Aramaic, and Greek—three ancient languages, while not dead technically, have been altered enough in their modern versions to make them, if not completely separate languages, then separate dialects at least. Even if the ancient and modern versions of these languages are still similar, the cultures that produced them from a distance of two to four thousand years are now from different planets. If we are to understand the meaning a Hebrew scribe was originally intending when he wrote a book or a passage three thousand years ago, we have to understand something about his language, culture, and worldview.

Now why spend so much time developing these ideas, which may seem so painfully fundamental? Because our theological beliefs often and inevitably muddle our common sense if we're not careful.

Sometimes what we believe about Scripture makes it hard to remember that Scripture is made of language, and language is made of its Agreement, and if we don't understand the Agreement, we'll never understand Scripture. We'll never understand the Aramaic message of Yeshua if we don't understand the ground from which the Agreement of the ancient Jews sprang.

It was an ancient Jewish Agreement that produced both the Old and New Testaments, but when it comes to our reading of Scripture, much of this logic is suspended or missed altogether. Consciously or subconsciously, our theological understanding of Scripture as being inspired by God, being the word of God and therefore "infallible," tends to create in us the idea that the "simple meaning" is all we need. And by that we mean that we can read the Biblical text as if it were written yesterday in our own language, and God's Spirit will impart just the knowledge he wants us to have as we read our modern translations of ancient texts. If that were so, then all sincere readers would eventually come to the same understanding or interpretation of what Scripture means. But they have not ever yet and don't look likely to anytime soon.

Scholars still widely disagree on the mechanics of just how Scripture is inspired, but most have come to the conclusion that God-inspired human authors wrote texts with their own levels of writing ability and knowledge of grammar and syntax; they wrote through the lens of their own beliefs about life and God and the physical world. Most importantly, they wrote not for posterity, for distant readers thousands of years later, but for the people in whose eyes they looked each day. They wrote for each other, to bring God's message home to the people they knew and loved, to make their lives better as a result. And so they wrote to be understood by people who were part of their Agreement—those who shared their agreed-upon language, common experience, culture, and worldview.

The burden is not on the Ancients as writers to help us understand their intended meaning, nor is it on God to super-naturally flow that meaning into us. It's our responsibility to dig in and learn how to understand, to take the necessary steps toward entering an ancient Agreement, creating a new Agreement between us and the writers of Scripture across a gulf of time.

Having said all that, one of the beauties of our personal relationship with God is that such an Agreement is not necessary to the relationship at all. At a non-theological level, if we're ready to hear, God speaks to us directly and communicates from a place beyond all Agreements and in such a way that the least literate among us may actually become the closest in spirit to the Kingdom. After all, Yeshua said that the last would be first and the first last. He said at Matthew 18, that unless we were changed and became as a child, we could not enter the Kingdom at all. But the Aramaic word he used here, *talya*, actually means both child *and* house servant or slave, so by combining the innocence, naiveté, utter dependence, and sense of joy and wonderment of the child with the submission, humility, and service of the house slave, Yeshua's picture of the qualities of Kingdom living becomes complete.

This is a wonderful example of how the Aramaic Agreement conveys a deeper meaning than the Greek translation can convey. Though *talya* means both child and servant at the same time, from the context, the ancient Greek translator chooses "child" as the probable primary meaning. But neither child nor servant carries the whole meaning Yeshua is trying to convey; it's both of these together that bring the fullness of the meaning of Kingdom relationships to life. The volitional submission of the servant tempers the naiveté of the child creating a relationship based on choice and not just dependence. Neither servant nor child necessarily know or need to understand the Master's/Father's business, but the submission and humility of the servant and the dependence and joy of the child make those relationships secure without the need for such understanding.

And that is exactly what Yeshua is trying to communicate: a partnership between God and man based on conscious choice and shared desire but not complete understanding. Whatever we understand or think we understand about our Father's house and business as child and servant does not have any bearing on our relationship with God as our Father and Master. The role of our relationship is the central fact; if our understanding enhances that relationship, then it is useful, if not, it's just in the way.

But even though a degree in literature or theology is not one of Yeshua's requirements for relationship, clearing up any misunderstanding of Yeshua's words can greatly enhance the meaning and experience of our relationship with the Father. And more urgently, if we believe that Scripture is the main source of our communication with God and should be taken as literally as possible, if we're willing to give authority to Scripture that as it's enforced will have real-world effects over the lives of people in our homes and churches, then entering the ancient Agreement becomes essential.

If we want to take Scripture literally and live by it literally while encouraging others to do so as well, then we must translate both the language and its Agreement to avoid any possibility of getting utterly wrong, even abusive, impressions by reading ancient communication through modern eyes, culture, and viewpoints.

>Strange morning. Santa Ana winds blowing. Almost due west. Right now making white noise out of what's left of the brown October leaves outside the half-opened window. Bringing unfamiliar, warm desert smells with them as they flow around the mountains and through the passes toward the sea. And this time bringing smoke.

>I smelled the smoke as soon as I stood up this morning. Dozens of brush fires burning. Thousand Oaks. Santa Susanna. Riverside. San Bernardino. Must be at least sixty miles from the closest, but smelled like the chimney next door.

>Going out to run at 5:30, stepping into the swirling warm air--just yesterday morning cold and fogged in, today fifteen degrees warmer--with Orion twinkling bravely overhead. Not as bright as I expected. The gray smear of smoke to the north lit up underneath by the lights of L.A. did much to burn out the southern sky.

>I ran to the darkest part of the college lot, trying to clear my head. Useless. So much going on, so many projects, thoughts. I want to pound on my skull to quiet it. Tried to focus on prayer; I can't keep a focused line of thought for more than a few seconds. Thoughts pop up like ducks in a shooting gallery, parade across my consciousness, and flip down the other side.

>This is the most focused I am--writing. Takes a certain amount of concentration just to keep the pen moving. But still I stopped to note nine phone calls I have to make this morning. Where does it end? To what end do I do all this? I pray for peace and silence and only get more noise and activity. It's true that I seem to be growing into the task. My mind is clear in action--seems to suddenly be able to analyze, synthesize quickly, formulate response. I can only move with it for now. Accept what seems to be my path.

>Lord, I hope you are in the wind that blows warm and strange smells into my life. It comes from places I've never seen on the other side of the mountains to the north and fans the fires that burn all around me. I'll burn for you as long as I can. I'll burn out burning for you. But let me know it's you in the wind, blowing on me, making the fire hot, uncontained, burning a path to the sea.

The Red Letters

There is a tension in the New Testament.

Not so much within the New Testament itself, as between it and us. And not so much between us and all the New Testament, as specifically between us and the red letters—the words of Yeshua sometimes printed in red ink. Those words create tension because we don't really know what to do with them. And neither does the church for that matter.

When I was teaching grade school English a lifetime ago, if a student failed a spelling test, I decided he or she had to keep a dictionary on the upper right hand corner of his or her desk as a reminder to look up unknown words. The dictionary stayed on the desk the whole day, every day until the next weekly test was passed. One girl, I still remember her name, had a dictionary on her desk for over a month. It became a running joke with the class, and I worried over dropping the policy for her sake, but you should have heard the cheers and seen the smile on her face when after passing her first test, she walked across the room to put that dictionary back on the shelf...a very good moment.

What do we do when we encounter words we don't understand? Do we really take the time to look them up? Most often we pass lightly over them, gleaning from the overall context and flow of the passage what the meaning must be. Like missing a line of dialog from a movie with no way to get it back, we mentally stitch the edges of received meaning together over the hole and make sense the best we can. And if there are too many of those stitched holes across our understanding, if it takes too much work trying to keep up, we simply move on to something else—another passage, another book, another movie.

A man comes up to me after I spoke to his group recently saying he's new to the faith and wants to know where he should begin reading in the Bible. I hesitate, as I always do when asked such a question especially from someone I don't know anything about.

Someone nearby has overheard and automatically throws out, "The Gospel of John," and I suppose that's as good a place as any, and after giving a few more suggestions, I encourage the man to get into a directed study as well, because I know what will happen when he hits all those unknown words. David Bivin states it well in his book *Understanding the Difficult Words of Jesus*:

"I began my Bible reading as a teenager. My greatest difficulty was trying to understand the words of Jesus. I would note sayings of Jesus such as 'For if they do these things in a green tree, what shall be done in the dry?' (Lk 23:31), or, '...from the days of John the Baptist until now the Kingdom of Heaven suffers violence, and the violent take it by force." (Mt 11:12) Picture a teenager trying to make sense out of such good King James English as, 'I am come to send fire on the earth; and what will I, if it be already kindled? But I have a baptism to be baptized with; and how am I straitened till it be accomplished!' (Lk 12:49-50) I would question my pastor or teachers or visiting seminary professors as to the meaning of such passages and would invariably receive the common response: 'Just keep reading, son, the Bible will interpret itself.' The truth is that one can keep reading the Bible forever, and the Bible will not tell him the meaning of these difficult passages. They can only be understood when translated back into Hebrew."

We think because the Bible in our hands is in English, that it's in our language, but it's not. The language of the Bible, however translated, is still its own and not ours, and unfortunately, there is no dictionary we can put on our desks to bridge the gap. Knowing the meaning of individual Hebrew, Aramaic, or Greek words is only a first step, and reading the Bible as if we understand the English words we encounter on the page is like watching a movie and missing every third or fourth line of dialog. We think we can retain an overall sense of meaning and flow, but key passages we miss are foundations for other passages we now can't hope to understand, and entire foundational concepts are not even presented in the text, since it was common knowledge at the time, part of the Agreement. Thomas Merton has some insight here from his book *Opening the Bible*:

"It is the very nature of the Bible to affront, perplex, and astonish the human mind. Hence the reader who opens the Bible must be prepared for disorientations, confusion, incomprehension, perhaps outrage. The Bible is without question one of the most unsatisfying books ever written—at least until the reader has come to terms with it in a very special way. But it is a difficult book to come to terms with. Far easier, perhaps, if one just *pretends* the question is all settled in advance: one hears from others that this is a 'Sacred Book,' and takes their word for it..."

And that is exactly what we do. We pretend we understand what we're reading, taking any incomprehension as a sign of spiritual immaturity or lack of faith, taking the word of others over the words actually preserved in Scripture, and finally taking sheer familiarity as a substitute for comprehension—if we can't understand something, we can at least be so familiar with it that it ceases to shock us anymore or present any logical problems. At this point, we've not only stitched the edges of the holes in meaning together, but we've forgotten entirely where the holes were in the first place. But remember, Yeshua's entire method of teaching was built on the use of his wild words to shock us out of our normal Four Ways of thinking and living and over to the Fifth Way. So as we settle for mere familiarity, we drain the life-transforming power out of Yeshua's message and leave our spiritual common sense in critical condition on the operating table. Then we simply move on to those parts or passages of the Bible that make more sense to us.

It's ironic that we print the words of Yeshua in red, signifying their special importance, and then give them much less attention than the black letters...

☉ ☽ ⊕ ⊕ ⊕

Have you ever noticed how the contemporary Church spends much more time studying and discussing the epistles of the New Testament, especially those of Paul, than it does the Gospels and the words of Yeshua? I only have subjective data for this, but tune in to any radio broadcast or Sunday sermon or Bible study, and I trust you'll bear it out. And Paul himself, not having met Yeshua face to face and writing well before the Gospels were composed, never quotes Yeshua or discusses his words directly in any of his writings in the New Testament, further separating us from the

Hebrew/Aramaic source. We as Westerners gravitate naturally to the language and thought processes of the Greek epistles and to the Greek Gospel of John, rather than the "synoptic" Gospels of Matthew, Mark, and Luke—the Gospels whose sources most scholars now believe were first communicated in Hebrew/Aramaic and later composed in Greek. Why do we focus more on the "Greek" books? Because they speak so much more clearly to our Western minds and worldviews.

The truth is, the red letters, the words of Yeshua just don't make that much sense to us. We pass over them, acknowledging a kind of poetic beauty and a general direction of thought, but the real meat, the bottom line for us, is the good, hard nut of a logical, Pauline argument: something to really get our teeth into and hang a church upon. When you get right down to it, Yeshua didn't give us a theology at all—he gave us a way of living life. He didn't give us a framework for the infrastructure of a church either, but Paul gives us both in detail. And so Yeshua and his enigmatic words remain either at arm's length or papered over with the faux comprehension of familiarity as he speaks to us from his distant Eastern well—as we subconsciously bypass him in favor of Paul who stands, if not in our own well, at least in one we can imagine we understand.

It is this imagined understanding that is even more destructive than conscious incomprehension, because what is Paul's message if not built on that of Yeshua? If we don't understand Yeshua, how is it we think we understand Paul?

It all comes down to Yeshua—Yeshua and his Aramaic message.

>It all begins to sort itself out. Slowly. So slowly, like the hands of a clock, that I am not aware of progression as long as I stare and try to see. But if I look away long enough and then turn back... there it is--elapsed time, perceived progression. It's uncanny, almost diabolical, how difficult it is to grasp this concept, and once grasped, to hold on and not fall back on old ways. To really become one with the realization that the very effort applied to the task is proof that the essential revelation has not even been addressed.

>Because the thought, the realization, the revelation, is that there is nothing to do.

>Nothing that has to be done. Nothing I could do if I tried that would make any essential difference to God. In fact, all my efforts are irrelevant at best, maybe an insult at worst. Acts of ignorant arrogance.

>But, but, but... All the buts coming popping up in my resistant, conditioned mind. How can this possibly be? In a life and world and philosophy so geared toward action, accomplishment? My whole life has been based on activity. What I can do. I identify myself with my talents and accomplishments. They are who I am, or was. Now in the church, I hear that it's all about grace, that I must die to myself, let Christ live in me. But no one tells me what these mean.

>At the same time, the church says that faith without works is dead. There are all those lists of dos and don'ts and eternal fire promised for the don'ters. Good cop, bad cop. But the bad cop I can understand and accept. These rules, these things to do, keep my pride and self-worth intact, because they imply that I am still at least partially in control. There are things with which to comply and I will be rewarded or punished according to my performance. And I look around and

167

see two thousand years of Christian tradition largely based on this premise.

>And yet when all the brush is cleared away, this truth alone is left standing. There is nothing to do. Am I making way too much of this? Maybe. But just like the scientific theories of chaos, very small differences in input yield huge differences in output. In this case, the difference between living fully in God's presence and merely coming in twice a week to sweep the floor around his feet.

>There is nothing to do. I am beginning to see. All is complete. I simply identify myself with the truth or I do not. There is no middle ground. All my well-intentioned activity only pulls me away from the center, the place of silence and truth. All my activity feeds the self-awareness and self-consciousness that identifies me with something other than God. The effort itself is prideful, distracting, and arrogant until...

>Until it is effortless. Until my all my efforts flow effortlessly out of my silence, God's silence, they are something less than worthless. Until all my activity is the result of God's presence and not the proof of its purchase, it's a gathering of the wind. The clanging gong. The crashing cymbal.

>Let my measurement of unexpended effort be my guide toward the center. Let my lack of self-consciousness be the compass pointing toward full identification with you. Let nothing come between us—not even faith.

>For as soon as I believe in faith, I no longer believe in you. As soon as my works determine the measure of my faith, I believe in myself.

>Sympathy, compassion, fortitude, perseverance, dedication are not synonyms for Kingdom. They are the results of its realization in my life. There is no other Way. I go to the Father through the Son.

>And his yoke is easy and his burden light. I never realized how light. It's getting lighter all the time.

An Aramaic Yeshua

When I speak about the Aramaic message of Yeshua, people often ask where they can get a translation of the Aramaic text of the New Testament. I tell them that they can certainly go out and get one at the nearest bookstore, but they'll be disappointed because, with just a few surprises, it will read in English much like any translation of Greek texts. It's not the words themselves that are the problem; for the most part, we've got the right words whether in Greek or Aramaic. It's our non-understanding of what those words originally meant to speaker and listener, the Agreement behind them, that is the problem—and no word-for-word translation can bridge that gap.

Like a coded message, getting an accurate transmission of the code is only the first step; to make sense of the message, the code must then be deciphered through some key. For us, the key to the literal meaning of the words of Yeshua's message is the Aramaic Agreement itself.

Why Aramaic? Did Yeshua really speak Aramaic? Think in Aramaic? Most scholars believe so—most, but not all. There is a loud and growing minority with a persuasive argument that he would have spoken Hebrew, at least as a second language if not the primary language with which he communicated. Truth is, we can't know for sure, but since we're going to use Aramaic as the foundation for establishing Yeshua's intended message, why is a valid question.

☉ ⊕ ⊕ ⊕ ⊕

History shows us that the Jewish people in Judea primarily spoke Aramaic, the language of the Babylonian empire, after spending two to three generations there in forced exile after Babylon conquered the southern Kingdom of Judah in the 6th century BCE. Hebrew was still spoken, but used mainly for religious purposes, and the Hebrew scriptures had to be translated into Aramaic for the people's use. We know the Jews of Yeshua's first century Judea and Galilee still spoke

169

Aramaic and Hebrew because of evidence preserved in the books of the New Testament and other contemporary documents such as the Dead Sea Scrolls, which are written in both languages.

The Gospels, written in Greek decades after the crucifixion, were compiled from oral stories, written catalogs of sayings and signs, and eyewitness accounts—source information that was remembered and written in Aramaic and Hebrew. Scholars know this because the Greek of the Gospels, especially the first three "synoptic" Gospels of Matthew, Mark, and Luke contain so many Hebrew and Aramaic idiomatic expressions and untranslated words and phrases as to make the Greek very unnatural in many places. In other words, the Gospels are obvious translations of original Aramaic/Hebrew sources.

Did Yeshua speak Aramaic or Hebrew or both? For the purposes of understanding Yeshua's intended message, the question is less important than you would imagine. Aramaic and Hebrew are sister languages descended from a mother tongue or tongues, sharing the same alphabet and much the same word roots—the building blocks from which words are constructed and meaning is derived in Semitic languages. And of absolute overriding importance, both languages share the same *Agreement*: Eastern/Hebrew worldview, culture, and history.

Word meaning, idiomatic expression, and cultural understanding flow seamlessly between Aramaic and Hebrew without loss in translation. This stands in sharp contrast to a translation into a Western language like Greek that has a different Agreement and no such linguistic similarities. Once a thoughtform is moved from Aramaic or Hebrew into Greek, the translator has many decisions to make about how to translate alien thoughtforms into each other—decisions that always affect meaning and understanding.

Without trying to settle the debate over whether Yeshua spoke Aramaic or Hebrew, the Aramaic message of Yeshua has one distinct advantage over the Hebrew...it actually exists in printed form. While we have no surviving copies of any Hebrew texts of the New Testament, we do have Aramaic manuscripts, and in particular, we have the *Peshitta*: complete Aramaic bibles written in a dialect called Syriac that originated in northern Mesopotamia (present day Syria). *Peshitta* manuscripts containing both Old and New Testaments date to the fifth century CE, but are believed by the Eastern Orthodox Church and some scholars to be copies of much earlier Aramaic texts. *Peshitta* is itself an Aramaic word that means simple, straight, or true—conveying the belief of the Eastern Church that it contains the accurate and original words of the Scriptures.

So which version of the Gospels came first, Greek or Aramaic? It's sort of a trick question because if you're talking about the surviving manuscripts themselves, then overwhelmingly, scholars agree (especially those in the West) that the Greek came first and the Aramaic/Syriac was a translation of the Greek. But if you're talking about the message and thoughtforms of Yeshua as originally communicated, then it's the other way around. What we likely have in the Peshitta are original Aramaic/Hebrew source documents and oral stories that were compiled, translated, and composed as Greek books and then translated back into Aramaic/Syriac.

The obvious question then is whether the Aramaic/Syriac version is really of any help to us in entering the Aramaic Agreement and approaching Yeshua's original intent. If the Aramaic/Syriac versions we have are only translations of the Greek, then isn't the Greek just as good? Better even, since it's a generation earlier?

It's all about the content and the container. Sometimes content created for a specific container just won't work right in another. Language is like this: thoughtforms/content are created in and for one language/container and exist in their pure state in their native Agreement. Translate them into another Agreement, and the message changes the way a painting can appear changed in a different frame. But if the translation has been accurate, the thoughtforms can be moved back into their original Agreement and restored.

This is exactly what happens when we "translate" the Greek back into Aramaic by studying the *Peshitta*. The thoughtforms and message of Yeshua spring back to life as peculiar idiomatic expressions can be recognized and understood as such, possible mistranslations can be identified, puns and plays on words that give new insight into meaning are revealed, and the roots of words can be reestablished, bringing great depth of meaning to even the simplest passages.

Ancient Aramaic and Hebrew have relatively small vocabularies as compared with a Western language like Greek. This means that words in ancient Aramaic have to work harder, containing multiple meanings and layers of simultaneous meaning. It also means there are fewer word choices to make when translating from Greek back into Aramaic—fewer choices mean fewer chances of error and more likelihood the original construction has been recreated, especially considering the fluency of the ancient, native-speaking Aramaic translators of the *Peshitta*—a translation that some believe dates back as far as the second century CE. Once a passage is restored to Aramaic or Hebrew, these rich layers of meaning are restored as well.

Just as importantly, the text, back in its native Aramaic/Hebrew Agreement, can be tied to its native culture and historical setting as closely as possible—comparing it to the vast library, both sacred and secular, of other Aramaic and Hebrew writings of the same time period, especially the writings of the ancient Jewish Rabbis. This is why the Dead Sea Scrolls have been so crucial in helping us better understand Christian origins even though no books of the New Testament were discovered among the caves at Qumran. The documents discovered there were another source of Aramaic/Hebrew writings from the same period, which when compared and contrasted to the books of the New Testament, shed much light on the lives and worldview of first century Jews, and thereby on the meaning of our Scriptures and the words of Yeshua.

As we prepare to enter the Aramaic Agreement and hear Yeshua's message again for the very first time with Aramaic ears, it will be the result of this method of study that will take us there. But before we set off, there's one more turn to negotiate.

>There will be no poetry tonight. No beautifully flowing words. Just the rough, grating sounds I make as I draw my spirit across my self-recrimination. Not because I haven't written. You don't need my words. Not because I haven't run or greeted your dawn in days. You have managed to turn the globe without me. But because once again I have allowed myself to lose the joy in these things, which has allowed me to cease them altogether. That's worth a grate or two.

>There will be no gracefulness tonight. Only a beginning and a cessation. But still I pray somehow there will be grace. How often do I have to be reminded there is nothing in me but the natural tendency to return to just this place of despair and re-crimination? How many times do I have to be reminded that it is only the covering of your grace that takes me anywhere else, makes me look anyway else?

>How many times do I have to be reminded that I have to be reminded every day?

>Every day.

>Every day to get up with you in my thoughts. Every day to move out into your creation and experience enough of it to begin to feel those first few stirrings of thankfulness. Every day to give utterance to those stirrings in thoughts or sounds or songs or smiles or laughter or silent awe. Every day to ask you to run with me, to be close. To keep me close to you.

>Every day.

>Because I will never change on my own.

>On my own, I can't change who you created me to be and life amended. And worse, I can't believe I can't. At least not for long. Not for more than a day. So every day I have to stop

173

trying and ask you to change me. Every day I have to look for you. In these pages. In your pages. In the faces of each person you place in my path.

>Every day. Every day. Every day. Every day. Is this clear? Every day. Without cessation. Every day. Because of the sheer joy of it all and for no other reason.

>Every day.

Reading the Silence

Yeshua spoke Aramaic/Hebrew and lived and breathed the common experience of his people that the culture and realities of first century Judea and the Galilee afforded. Although immersed in his own culture and times, many of us believe that Yeshua also had knowledge and understanding that far exceeded the collective experience of his people, even up to the point of omniscience, by virtue of his standing as prophet and Son of God.

But whatever you believe about what Yeshua knew and when he knew it, consider this: regardless of what other knowledge he possessed, Yeshua spoke to the people of his world using *their agreed-upon system of language and worldview*. He used words such as *malkutha, shemaya, torah, talmid, haimanuta, taba, bisha, hataha, Gehenna,* and others that when translated into our language as "kingdom," "heaven," "law," "follower," "faith," "good," "evil," "sin," "hell," have specific meanings that we as modern Westerners have all agreed upon, and which paint common images in our minds. But are they the same images that were painted in the minds of his first hearers? Did anything change from Yeshua's lips to our ears?

When we read Yeshua's words, we need to know what images he was painting in the minds of his *first* hearers, those from his own world—those with whom he was directly communicating through their Agreement. In other words...

We don't need to know what Yeshua knew, we just need to know what his first hearers knew—what they would have understood from Yeshua's lips.

Yeshua knew how his followers would understand the words he used to convey his message, and just as importantly, he knew exactly how they would understand what he *didn't say*. All throughout Scripture, concepts generally understood by the people are not discussed or defined at all: they are part of the Agreement, assumed to be sufficiently understood and needing no further explanation. We do the same today. We don't bother to explain what everyone already understands, but what is not stated is just as critical to intended meaning as what is.

This means we literally need to "read the silence" surrounding undefined and missing words in Scripture as much as the words themselves. We need to step into the sandals of those first hearers of Yeshua's message and see whether the images that appeared in their minds are the same ones appearing in ours.

☉ ☽ ⊕ ⊕ ⊕

In our culture, we can ask a question like, "Is it lawful for a person under the age of twenty-one to drink in this state," and everyone understands what actually is a nonsensical question. Is it lawful to drink what, water? We supply the missing words, "alcoholic beverages" automatically as part of our Agreement. But when Pharisees come to ask Yeshua in Mark 10 "whether it was lawful for a man to divorce a wife," we miss the context of the question entirely because of missing, silent words. In the parallel passage at Matthew 19 we get the missing words when the Pharisees ask, "Is it lawful for a man to divorce his wife *for any matter*," but if we don't know that "for any matter" was a legal term distinguishing between two first century BCE Jewish schools of thought and generations of debate on divorce and remarriage, we still miss the entire context of the question.

The Pharisees were asking whether Yeshua sided with one school of thought or the other, that of Hillel or Shammai, and not whether divorce was acceptable at all. Of *course* divorce was acceptable: everyone in the Jewish Agreement knew that there were really at least five grounds for divorce allowable under Torah, so those grounds are not mentioned in the passage either; they are understood. To ask a first century Jew whether divorce was lawful without adding the words "for any matter" was as nonsensical as asking us today whether drinking is lawful without adding the words "alcoholic beverages."

In characteristic response, Yeshua, knowing the question is misplaced and the "students" are not ready, answers question with question trying to redirect back to God's original intent for marriage as a beautiful, monogamous, life-long commitment. Only when pressed further, does he reply that divorce was only acceptable for *a matter of indecency*. If we don't know that a "matter of indecency" was the precise legal term used by one of the schools, that of Shammai, to define their position, then we won't realize that Yeshua is merely siding with the Shammaites (who still agreed with the five grounds for divorce allowable under Torah) over the followers of Hillel (who believed that divorce was acceptable "for any matter" up to and including the spoiling of a husband's dinner).

Yeshua was not making a new, sweeping statement about divorce law; he was upholding the existing Law—as were the Shammaites—against a new "no fault" system proposed by the Hillelites, which was responsible for an increase in the numbers of divorces for frivolous reasons and for Jews actually "shopping" for Hillelite judges who would give them the divorces they sought.

But Yeshua has more to say in Luke's Gospel: "Everyone who divorces his wife and marries another commits adultery, and he who marries one who is divorced from a husband, commits adultery." The simple meaning seems devastatingly clear, but reading the silence around Luke 16:18, Yeshua's first hearers would have mentally added "for any matter" to again rescue the statement from nonsense within their Agreement. With silent words replaced and considering that the subjunctive mood of even the Greek translation of this verse merges divorce and remarriage into one continuous motion, common sense is restored: "Everyone who divorces his wife (for any matter *in order to*) marry another commits adultery, and he who marries one who is divorced from a husband (in order to marry again), commits adultery."

Just as Yeshua seemed to equate thinking angry thoughts with physical murder and thinking lustful thoughts with physical adultery in Matthew 5, he's not violating common sense there or here; it's all about the intent of our hearts—and the Law is not a fig leaf we can use to cover bad intentions. Through these sayings, Yeshua is trying to shock us into seeing God's original intent of *shalom* in relationship, to go beyond the mere following of a code all the way to the gates of Kingdom.

For us, not knowing all this, not being part of this Agreement, hurts real people, when as in this case, we run with the simple meaning that divorce always was and is only allowable in the case of "indecency," which meant many things to ancient Jews, but we interpret as adultery alone. We put the full authority of Scripture and the Church behind the misunderstanding, and divorce then becomes the new unforgivable sin as, except for adultery, divorce becomes unacceptable and remarriage becomes adultery itself. Marriage is to be endured even in the face of emotional and physical abuse and the failure to provide necessities of life—food, clothing, and love: all of which (along with infertility) were understood as grounds for divorce under the ancient Jewish Agreement. If we are going to give Scripture this sort of power over people's lives, we certainly need to understand Yeshua's message, and we need to understand it as literally as his first hearers did.

Yeshua was speaking through his Agreement, to people who understood his words in a certain way. If he didn't redefine the terms he used, then he was tacitly approving the Agreement, the agreed-upon meaning of the people listening right in front of him. Did he? Did he redefine some words that he wanted them to understand in special ways and let others stand in the Agreement?

Absolutely; yes and yes.

The whole of Yeshua's teaching is built upon his concept of the Kingdom of Heaven. It's the symbol and framework on which his entire message hangs. You could effectively argue that all of Yeshua's teaching is really the definition (or restatement) of what Kingdom is. By Yeshua's day, the concept of "kingdom" among the Jewish people had morphed from its original meaning to a popular definition: that of the reestablishment of the physical throne of David, the expulsion of the Roman occupation and the return of Israel's national identity. If Yeshua merely used the word "kingdom" without qualification, this is the image he knew would be painted in the minds of his hearers. But his concept of the Kingdom was radically different, and he never lost an opportunity to paint image after image and tell story after story to allow glimpses of his Kingdom to form in the minds and hearts of those who chose to listen. He was trying to bring the people back to the original intent and meaning of Kingdom in their Agreement.

Yeshua's definition of the Kingdom of Heaven, his Aramaic meaning, is preserved in the Gospels, but there is much more that is left unsaid. With his silence, he approved images already in the minds of his hearers of such critical concepts as "sin," "salvation," "forgiveness," "Gehenna," even "good" and "evil," and only redefined those concepts such as "law," "righteousness," and "kingdom" as needed to get the right meaning across. Reading the silence surrounding these concepts, discovering what the unwritten Agreement says about them, is the only way we'll ever know what Yeshua really intended to say.

So again, regardless of any special knowledge Yeshua may have possessed, understanding as much as possible of the first century Aramaic perspective into which he poured his message will give us great insight into the shape of our Fifth Way journey. But it's easier said than done. We as modern Westerners see the world in such a radically different way than an ancient, Eastern people such as the Jews that the very words from Yeshua's lips to our ears change in meaning as they come through the filters of our worldview. There is virtually no major concept of Yeshua's message and teaching that we can take at face value, that we can read as a "simple" meaning once translated into our own language. It's not that our translations are bad; they're amazingly accurate. We have the right words—we just don't know what they mean anymore.

> So even though the words are accurate,
> for us, they may not be "true."

I had been inches from a clean getaway.

>So close to finally being on the inside looking out, part of something that felt like home and kept the wolves at bay. Kicked back out of the nest with all the old anxiety on the rise, a decision had to be made. On the one hand was the pain in Marian's eyes. On the other was the fact that all my life I'd been running from one thing to the next, efficiently eliminating processes, but getting no nearer the truth I so desperately needed. I'm not sure I made the right decision; Marian's pretty sure to this day that I didn't, but I decided to stay in the warehouse with the big piano at least until the elders made a decision on our marriage.

Marian decided to stay with me.

>Back in search mode, I started reading everything I could lay my hands on dealing with Christian divorce and remarriage. Marian called a pastor from a nearby church right out of the phonebook and asked for help. When he said she should be speaking to her own pastor; she replied between sobs that her pastor was the problem. He agreed to see her, then me as well a few days after. His position was similar to our pastor's, but a bit softened and nuanced—it's his style and manner more than his substance that I remember.

>I found a book that in one volume held four views of biblical divorce and remarriage from four separate scholars—each interpretation of the relevant scriptural passages different from the other three. A light began to glow in the back of my mind: that spoken truth, truth reduced to words, whether by nuns in the first grade, monks in a house of formation, or pastors in a warehouse with a piano, was actually more of an opinion, an expression of an experience, a construct of a concept that wasn't necessarily absolute or even true...having billions of

people over thousands of years continue to express their truth in a particular way certainly made it compelling.

But not truer.

>There is that moment in a rollercoaster car, after tense minutes of slow ascent, you reach the crest of the first hill and look down into forever and realize you can't exhale. You may wish you never got in the car, but there's no turning back; there's only onward—through the maze of hills and turns you can't even see coming. And no matter what you think you know about rollercoasters or what anyone has told you about the ride, you'll never really understand until you arrive back where you started—screams subsiding with the jolting stop, hair standing at attention.

The Kingdom of Heaven

Think of this chapter as the fulcrum of this book.

JUST AS AN ACROBAT BALANCES ON A PLANK OVER A BARREL, shifting her weight, rolling and seesawing the plank back and forth, this chapter is the barrel over which all else is balanced. A chapter on Kingdom had better be the fulcrum of a book on the Way of Yeshua, because the Kingdom of Heaven is the fulcrum of all Yeshua's teaching—the barrel on which his entire message is balanced.

The most important things in a person's life are the things on which they spend the most time. If you read the words of Yeshua, there is one phrase that will stand out because of its sheer repetition and depth of explanation, and that phrase is the Kingdom of God—called the Kingdom of Heaven in Matthew's Gospel. The Kingdom is at once the sum and the theme of all of Yeshua's teaching; it is the framework, the central image, the lens through which Yeshua's message must be viewed if it is to be understood at all.

How can I emphasize this enough?

I can't. It can't be. But let me try...

In what way is a sailor a sailor without a ship? The ship is the framework, the little world within which everything it means to be a sailor is acted out. What is a baseball player without bat and ball and glove? Those items are at once both the very image of the game itself and the means by which it is made possible. And what is an astron-

183

omer without a telescope, without the lens through which the object of study can be apprehended at all?

Yeshua's Kingdom is all of these. It is the framework, the world in which everything it means to be a child of God is lived out; it is both the image of and process by which this life in God is made possible, and it is the lens through which that life can be viewed, understood, and apprehended. And it is at least one thing more.

As the container into which Yeshua pours all the content of his teaching, the Kingdom of Heaven is the *context*, the parameters within which all Yeshua's sayings must be understood. Just as the only thing separating a sailor from a drowning man is the deck of his ship, the only thing separating us from gross misunderstanding of Yeshua's message is a standing upon and within the true concept of Kingdom. It will be for us as the deck of our ship, the bat in our hands, the scope at our eye: *nothing Yeshua says can be understood apart from his concept of Kingdom because everything he said was said within the context of Kingdom.*

When Yeshua says at Matthew 5:20 that "unless your righteousness exceeds that of the Scribes and Pharisees, by no means will you enter the Kingdom of Heaven," he is at once giving us the topic sentence of the entire Sermon on the Mount (Matthew 5-7) and describing the context, the boundaries within which we are to explore his meaning. To infer any meaning from Yeshua's sayings beyond the scope of Kingdom as he described and understood it, is to do violence to the message itself, to wrench it out of the only soil from which it can bring life. Yeshua's message was designed for Kingdom use, and for that alone. So before we can know anything more about his Way of Kingdom, we need to know exactly what he meant by *malkutha dashmaya*, Aramaic for the Kingdom of Heaven.

Is this really so difficult? The phrase appears to translate itself quite clearly. If you ask the average Christian what the Kingdom of Heaven is, you'll get the answer "heaven," as in the place in the afterlife we go to be with God after physical death. It is, after all, called the Kingdom of *Heaven*...to our ears the meaning is implied in the name itself. But here is another instance where the simple meaning, the meaning we think we already understand about Kingdom does great harm.

If we understand the Kingdom to be the heaven of the afterlife, then what are we to make of all Yeshua's statements about which types of behavior will take us in or keep us out of the Kingdom? Doesn't Scripture also tell us that we are saved, which we understand as admission to heaven, only by God's grace and our faith and not our works, our behavior?

It's confusing when there seem to be two Yeshuas in the Gospels. There is the Yeshua who accepted and sat at table with anyone regardless of social or moral standing, who would heal bodies and forgive sins without condition and sometimes without even being asked. Then there is the Yeshua who said unless you exceed the righteousness of the Scribes and Pharisees or convert and become like children, you won't enter the Kingdom at all. How do we square these two? How do we square the Yeshua who said in Matthew 11, "Come to me, all who are weary and heavy-laden, and I will give you rest... For my yoke is easy and my burden is light," with the Yeshua who also said that it was easier for a camel to go through the eye of a needle than for a rich man to enter the Kingdom and "If your eye causes you to stumble, throw it out; it is better for you to enter the Kingdom of God with one eye, than, having two eyes, to be cast into hell." How is God's love and acceptance unconditional and yet at the same time hyper-conditional, dependent on our behavior? How is our salvation a free gift, based only on faith and yet also dependent on our works?

Further, if we understand the Kingdom of Heaven to be the heaven of the afterlife, then where is our focus? Necessarily, it's on the future, the place of eventual comfort and ultimate reward—and on the past, on the often bloody trail of our behavior that we constantly monitor in hope that we may somehow measure up to the impossible standards Yeshua sets for us as in Matthew 5:48, "...be perfect, as your Father in heaven is perfect." How do we even begin to cope with a standard like that? And what is the quality of life like, living somewhere between the promise of the future and the condemnation of the past?

There is a wonderful scene in Shakespeare's Hamlet that is quite instructive, as Shakespeare often is. Hamlet, wanting revenge on his uncle for killing his father and marrying his mother, comes upon him in the castle at his prayers. With his uncle's back to him as he kneels unaware, Hamlet has the perfect chance for ambush, draws his sword and begins quietly advancing. But all the while, his inner thoughts are arguing that if he kills him now at prayer when he has made his peace with God, Hamlet would be sending him straight to heaven. What kind of revenge is that? No, Hamlet reasons as he puts up his sword, it is better to wait for a better moment:

> *When he is drunk asleep; or in his rage;*
> *or in the incestuous pleasure of his bed;*
> *at gaming, swearing; or about some act*
> *that has no relish of salvation in it;*
> *then trip him, that his heels may kick at heaven;*
> *and that his soul may be as damned and black*
> *as hell, whereto it goes.*

For Hamlet, getting into heaven is a what-have-you-done-for-me-lately proposition: in or out, up or down, day by day, and moment by moment. Though it may sound humorous put in just this way, as it should, this is just what life is like with one eye fixed on the future and the other on the past. How many Christians who after years of following the faith, still question the reality of their salvation, their ultimate acceptance by God? And what does that do to their smile-point, the point in life that Lou found where love becomes play and not just hard work?

If we understand Kingdom to be the heaven of the afterlife, there is a mixed message in Yeshua's words that is being reflected in the quality of our own lives day by day—from a vague uneasiness, like a low-grade depression, to a bi-polar, Jekyll and Hyde alternation between faith and works, acceptance and condemnation. How can our entrance to heaven ever be secured in the face of Yeshua's detailed descriptions of what behavior gets us in or keeps us out of the Kingdom? How do we ever know for sure? And because of this mixed message, many if not most Christians remain fully focused on the future and obsessed with the acquisition of heaven, while fearing the record of the past and *completely missing the present.*

There must be another Way, and there is.

>I learned something rereading several entries going way back. That I spend far too much time apologizing for lack of writing. From now on I will try to remember and try to actually believe that I will write when I write and when I don't, that particular page will simply be spared until it's not. And however many pages are covered by the time I'm done will be just exactly the correct number.

>It has been a beautiful night. Full moon lighting up high clouds to a pearly luminescence. But with stars burning uncharacteristically brightly in between. Now, as it is twelve-thirty, it is an overcast morning. A light rain has begun to fall. Every once in a while a big, five-pointed leaf falls past my window caroming off almost bare branches on its way down. There was a total lunar eclipse last night. I knew about it in progress. Could have gone out to look. Probably should have, but decided not to. Just like many things these last few weeks.

>This is a simple entry. I like it this way tonight. Simple, quiet, unaffected. Peaceful and unchallenging, too. What a relief. The early morning is still. Rain has stopped. The office around me is littered with incomplete work that, for the moment, doesn't call me in the least. My mind is only engaged just enough to keep the pen moving. Thought up, word out, period, next thought.

>To make it complete would be if you were asleep in some impossible position on the futon in the next room. And I could go out and brush your hair out of your face and kiss your equally impossibly smooth cheek and look at you for a moment and wonder who you'll grow up to be and pray for you before I turn out the light. Another night.

Unity and Herenowness

When the tsunamis barreled over the land encircling the Indian Ocean on the day after Christmas 2004 killing hundreds of thousands of people, it had all begun with an earthquake under the Andaman Sea, the body of water between the coast of Burma and Thailand and the string of islands extending north of Sumatra. But living there at ocean-zero, the island-dotted Andaman Sea, for hundreds or maybe thousands of years was a people who didn't lose a single person to the tsunamis. A people so intimately connected with the sea that they read the signs and ran for higher ground or paddled to deeper water before the waves struck. These sea nomads, who call themselves the Moken and who are called "sea gypsies" by others, spend as many as seven to eight months a year on the water and have become truly amphibious. Their children learn to swim before they can walk, and compared to us, they can see twice as clearly underwater and can actually lower their heart rates at will in order to dive deeper and stay underwater twice as long. They are among the peoples of the earth least touched by modern civilization.

As they came into media focus in the wake of the tsunamis because of their ability to read the ocean and survive the disaster, it was their culture and worldview that delivered the greatest shocks. The Moken people have no words in their language or concepts in their worldview for "want," "when," "hello," or "goodbye," among others. This is not an isolated phenomenon as the Moken are not alone in this: other Indonesian tribes also have similar missing concepts in their languages; the Apayao tribe in the Philipines who have no words for hello or goodbye either, also have no word for "thank you."

Stop for a moment and try to conceive of daily life without words or even the notion of want, when, hello, goodbye, or thank you. Each Moken has no idea how old he or she is. There are no birthdays or birthday parties. Without a concept of when, there is no concept of past or future at all, no sense of the passage of time, just the endless alternation of day and night, the unchanging sea, and an eternal present moment. There is no recalling and recounting of days past or planning and anticipating future events. When someone leaves, there is no sadness, no tender hugs goodbye; that person is simply not present anymore. And when a person returns, even after a long absence, there is no joy at the reunion, no celebration or words of greeting; he or she is simply present again, moving seamlessly in and out of the shared moment. There are no tears at departure or shouts and smiles at return because there is no sense of disconnection or separation at all, as if physical presence is an unimportant detail, one that has no bearing at all on true connection and unity.

Not having words for want or thank you also means there is no conception of personal ownership. There are no words for "giving" or "taking," "my" or "mine." Everything is shared and owned by all, so there's never a need to express gratitude for things freely exchanged as needed, never an impulse to gather or amass anything, no sense of lack, no feelings of envy, greed, or miserliness. These are a people who are so connected, so symbiotic, so reliant on each other and nature for their very existence and survival as to be more like one organism with many moving parts than individual people with separate and competing agendas trying to live and work together. How does a single organism sense separation from itself? How does it feel gratitude toward itself or desire to withhold anything from itself? Such concepts don't exist, and so the need to have words in their Agreement to express them doesn't either.

We can express admiration for these people, saying that they exhibit qualities that we should emulate, that they occupy a higher moral ground than the rest of us "civilized" types, but that is not only untrue, it misses the point entirely.

When I was discussing the Moken with a study group one night, a woman sat there just shaking her head. When I asked her what she was thinking, she said she couldn't imagine not celebrating her daughter's birthday, feeling sadness at her departure, and wanting to run and hold her on her return. Other heads started nodding in agreement, because to her and to us, love itself is experienced and expressed *through* remembrance of the past and anticipation of the future, through the sense of loss during separation. To us, the lack of these emotions and notions among the Moken can make them seem somehow less human, less able to express the full range of human interaction, more animal-like, or at least immature, child-like, in their dealings with each other and ability to love fully.

That's how it is with a clash of worldviews. We attach moral valences, "good" and "bad," to activities and attitudes within our own worldviews and cultures, but how can those labels possibly apply to other cultures and worldviews? There are certainly both good and bad Moken people, but their goodness or badness or ability to express full humanity is not measured by our standards of generosity or greed or expression of joy at a person's return; they have their own measures that would also possibly be just as other-worldly to our sensibilities.

On the other hand, the culture of a people like the Moken is tied to a time in our past when the pressing needs of survival, of living a subsistence life in a difficult environment required the kind of communal and collective cooperation that would ensure the continuation of the group, when the needs of the individual were only important to the degree that they served the needs of all others in the group. The technologies and abundance of our civilization mask the underlying need for such cooperation and communal connection between us as individuals, but that doesn't mean the need has ceased to exist.

In fact, in all cultures, very young children exhibit an aboriginal inability to sense the passage of time (call it herenowness) or perceive separation between themselves and others (unity). Considering the link Yeshua repeatedly drew between children and Kingdom—unless you become like children, you will not enter the Kingdom—there is definitely something about unity and herenowness that Yeshua is trying to teach us about his Kingdom.

But entrance to Kingdom is not based on an inability to grasp such time and space concepts as with the Moken or a child; it's the willing submission to new realities, as with the servant, that is the key. The Aborigine people of Australia, possibly the oldest continuously maintained culture on earth, do have a concept of linear time—past, present, and future moving forward as if along a line segment—but that concept is mixed with what they call Dreamtime, or all-at-once time that one anthropologist calls *everywhen*. Dreamtime is the past, present, and future all co-existing together in the present moment, and to the Aborigines, this Dreamtime constitutes the absolute, objective reality of the universe, while linear time is only the subjective way we experience that reality—just the opposite of our Western conception where linear time is considered objective reality and Dreamtime is subjective experience.

We are inching closer to Kingdom.

Yeshua was no Moken or Aborigine, but as an ancient Jew, his people shared some of the same cultural markers. The ancient Jews, like Eastern cultures at large, were a communal, collective society where the individual existed to serve family, tribe, and nation. There really was no survival apart from the survival of the group, and the destruction of the group was tantamount to the death of the individual. The Jewish identity, the way the people saw themselves was not in their own reflection in a still pool, but as part of the many faces around them. Their language reflected this, as there is no word in Hebrew for "family" to denote just the nuclear family of husband, wife, and child as we think of family today.

The Hebrew word *mishpachah* always includes the extended family—parents and children, uncles, aunts, cousins, grandparents, grandchildren, and anyone else related by blood or marriage. And these extended families all lived together as clans: sons bringing their wives home to live in their fathers' houses, daughters going to live with their husbands in theirs. All the imagery Yeshua used of brides awaiting the arrival of their bridegrooms to take them to the Father's house where a mansion was waiting flow directly out of these customs and social arrangements.

Just as Abraham saw the vision of his seed being counted as numerous as the stars or grains of sand on the shore, "family" was really the entire tribe and nation. Further, Torah commands that the people love their neighbors as themselves in Leviticus 19:18, and when asked, "Who is my neighbor?" Yeshua responds with the story of the Good Samaritan, extending the notion of family further than even most Jews were willing to accept.

Jewish prayer to this day is formulated in the plural, not the singular, so as to be inclusive of everyone in *mishpachah*. Even prayers of petition are prayed inclusively, in the name of all, or need to be completely reconsidered as in a Rabbinic saying: "Any prayer that cannot be prayed for all Israel is no prayer at all." When Yeshua gives his followers a model prayer, it begins with "*Our* Father in heaven," being true to the form of all Jewish prayer, a form mandated in the Talmud, which states explicitly: "Let him not pray...in the singular but in the plural number so that his prayer will be heard." There is no thought given to the needs of the individual as apart from or opposed to the needs of family and nation as a whole.

This concept of plural, inclusive prayer is completely foreign territory for us as radical, Western individualists: the week after I had discussed these aspects of Jewish prayer in a college class, a student came up to me to say that he had tried and found it extremely difficult to phrase all his prayers in the first person plural. As gently as possible, I reminded him that it wasn't about changing the pronouns of his prayers that mattered; it was the changing of his entire attitude toward the purpose of prayer itself and his relationship to everyone around him that would automatically change his use of pronouns. In our world, we are completely unprepared for the uncompromising submission to family and neighbor that Yeshua's concept of unity requires.

Submersion and submission of the individual into the unity of the group was "good," was "God" even, as *Alaha* also means unity at its root. And the opposite of unity, separation, while certainly understood as a concept, was considered sin, *hataha*, and an unclean, impure state from which a person had to be cleansed in order to return to unity with the group.

>I am not a boy anymore. It seems a little late to have suddenly realized this so strongly today, but there it is. The circumstances of my environment and life and psyche preserved the boy at the expense of the man for an incredibly long time. Doing adult things with my man's body for years couldn't flush out the stubborn boy looking out with naive, willfully uncomprehending eyes–refusing to fully accept, wrap himself around, the responsibility of his actions and years.

>Boys half my age have become men because they had to, rose to the challenges they faced while I retreated. Looking at my hands yesterday at lunch while my Pastor talked, I saw age in them. Not a boy's hands at all. It is time to be a man now, but I'm not sure what that means.

>It has something to do with purpose, self-awareness, self-sacrifice, focus, perseverance... I think this because these things are coming to me, being given to me, and they seem to be bringing my manhood with them in a way that even a wife and daughter and old hands have not.

>I feel the weight of my experience as an ally, a buoy, an advantage produced out of the sum of my life that the young can't buy at any price. I do not envy the young their youth anymore; I look forward to giving the young my age.

>I see the long, convoluted path I have taken, with all its detours and cul-de-sacs resolving out of randomness into a pattern, a cohesive whole with the thrust of an arrowhead pointing toward my purpose, my Lord. I sense the first stirrings of the peace I will have when as Merton says my vocation and my life are one.

>I'm beginning to know who I am. And I am beginning to know what to do with it. I can write. I can communicate. But

much more to the point, I can see relationships in the chaos. And if I look deeply enough and struggle long enough, I can help present enough shape and form to make the things I see visible to someone else. This is the gift a writer really gives--the words are mere convenience, conveyance.

>I can't take much pride in this, it's just the way I am. I can't help the way I think, what I see. And my thoughts won't leave me alone until I work them out. So I write. And the good words, I share.

>And now, out of all this, with the guidance of the Spirit, I am sensing the common denominator of a central theme that I could not exhaust in a lifetime, that I'm beginning to realize will occupy the rest of mine. And it's nothing new. It's just what I and everyone around me needs to consider, what many already have.

>Essence. Simplicity. Silence. Solitude.

>We have let the pendulum swing so far into noisy complexity that even our best efforts and intentions have lost their meaning. We don't know who we are or what we are about. We have to force the pendulum back, possibly too far in the other direction to make the point. To strip everything away, to mercilessly cut down to the indivisible place. And we need to do it in every facet of our lives--business, church, worship, family--to make a living statement that will present the truth without having to say a word.

>Then the silence will speak.

>I feel this is where I am coming to. I sense a growing excitement coming with the clarity. It's time to move with the broad strides of a man into a future uncertain in its detail, but with the cloud and pillar of the Lord on its horizon.

>All this has been growing inside. Sometimes it makes my chest hurt. It always makes my head swim. But it gives me hope. And it gives me purpose. It gives me absolution. And it seems to be giving me a long overdue rite of passage.

⊙ ⊕ ⊕ ⊕ ⊕

Having spoken of the Hebrew sense of unity, what sort of concept of time did the ancient Jews hold? From their writings, we know they had a very well developed sense of linear time—of past, present, and future—but it is their focus and priority that defines them as a people.

Virtually everything we know of the Jews comes from the time of the Exodus forward, after the Hebrew sojourn in Egypt. All the books of the Hebrew bible or *Tanakh*, with the possible exception of Job, date from after the Exodus, when after as long as two hundred years in Egypt, the Hebrews set off on their own into the wilderness.

Ancient Egypt was a death-obsessed culture, one so steeped in the focus on the afterlife that physical life in the present was cheapened in the process. The holiest literary work of Egypt was called the Book of the Dead, and great portions of national wealth were diverted from the people and consumed in the building of the great pyramids, tombs, and monuments with which we are so familiar. Vast amounts of time, energy, science, and technology were used in creating and perfecting the occult practices of communing with the spirits of the next life and assuring a place there for their kings and wealthiest citizens through elaborate ritual and mummification. Priceless treasuries were buried with the dead in order to pave their way into the afterlife—and all this came at the expense of the people on whose backs the system rested. In short, the Egyptians were completely focused on therethen at the expense of herenow.

Maybe it was for this reason that Yahweh God focused his people in a completely different direction: on herenow at the expense of therethen. Coming out of the land of the dead, the Hebrew Torah, comprising the first five books of the Bible and the bedrock of Judaism, focuses on life herenow to the extent that it contains no clear reference to the afterlife at all...

Surprising? Shocking? Think again about the beliefs of the Sadducees of Yehsua's day, who rejected the authority of any Scripture except the five books of Torah, and who interpreted those five books rigorously, literally, and narrowly. Since Torah doesn't define an afterlife, the hardest-line Sadducees didn't believe in the immortality of the soul, in a resurrection of the dead, in angels or spirits, or in some cases even in the soul itself. But though Torah doesn't deal with the afterlife directly, it does speak of the great patriarchs such as Abraham, Isaac, Jacob, Moses, Aaron, and others being "gathered to their people" as a separate event from their deaths or burials. In the same sense, it also speaks of others being "cut off from their people."

Even with the Sadducees on the fringes of Jewish thought, traditional Judaism firmly believes that death is not the end of human existence—Jews just didn't talk about it much then and don't now. They have never taught about it much either. There is a concerted obsession with this life as opposed to the next that pervades all of Jewish culture and theology. From the most ancient times, in their literature, history, and even their language, Jews are revealed as a robust, earthy, even abrasive people fully engaged in physical life.

There is an understanding that Yahweh God, who is *ein sof* (without end), created the earth as *hanhaga*, the meeting place between God and man, between infinite and finite, whose boundaries are defined by the instruction of Torah and whose purpose is the means by which the relationship between God and his people is acted out. This relationship is immediate, happening right herenow. Over and over again in Torah, we see cause and effect, obedience and blessing, disobedience and cursing, being acted out immediately and physically in this life, not waiting for some resolution in the next.

A classic formulation of this herenow cause and effect from Deuteronomy 28 is "...if you diligently obey the Lord your God, being careful to do all his commandments which I command you today, the Lord your God will set you high above all the nations of the earth... The Lord shall cause your enemies who rise up against you to be defeated before you...The Lord will make you abound in prosperity, in the offspring of your body and in the offspring of your beast and in the produce of your ground, in the land which the Lord swore to your fathers to give you. The Lord will open for you his good storehouse, the heavens, to give rain to your land in its season and to bless all the work of your hand; and you shall lend to many nations, but you shall not borrow. The Lord will make you the head and not the tail, and you only will be above, and you will not be underneath..."

These blessings in return for following God's commandments are immediate and physical, not deferred to a spiritual reward in the next life. And of course "if you do not obey the Lord your God" all the above blessings become negated into curses that are just as immediate and physical as the blessings.

The afterlife has no discernable effect on this earthy relationship between God and his people herenow, and spending any time thinking or dealing with the spirit world is discouraged or prohibited. The Hebrews are instructed by Torah not to speak with the spirits of the dead, so necromancy and occult rituals are prohibited. Touching or even being in the presence of a corpse is prohibited for the priests and makes a person who must do so unclean: practices such as mummification or embalming were also prohibited, seen as desecrations of the body.

Perhaps because of this attitude, early passages in the Hebrew Scriptures reflect an unknowing about the nature of the next life such as in Job 14:14, "If a man dies, can he live again?" Psalms 6:4-5, "Return, O Lord, rescue my soul; save me because of your loving-kindness. For there is no mention of you in death; in Sheol who will give you thanks?" Psalms 115:17, "The dead do not praise the LORD, nor do any who go down into silence." Ecclesiastes 9:4-5, "For whoever is joined with all the living, there is hope; surely a live dog is better than a dead lion. For the living know they will die; but the dead do not know anything, nor have they any longer a reward, for their memory is forgotten."

As in the Psalms, Torah also speaks of *Sheol*, but this word, literally meaning "landfill," was more a description of the nature of the grave or death generally, than a developed, theological understanding of the afterlife. *Sheol*, synonymous with death itself, was a shadowy place where all the dead went, whether righteous or unrighteous, and was a far cry from heaven or hell as we conceive them. But from these beginnings, there seems to have been an evolution in Jewish thought regarding the afterlife both in canonical and non-canonical writings.

By the time we get to Daniel, one of the latest books of the Hebrew Bible, there is a very well-developed concept of resurrection and life after death possibly reflecting similar Babylonian themes, as the book was written while in Babylonian captivity. At 12:2, "Many of those who sleep in the dust of the ground will awake, these to everlasting life, but the others to disgrace and everlasting contempt."

In the New Testament, Yeshua speaks of *Gehenna* and "outer darkness," often translated as "hell" in English Bibles, as is the Greek word *Hades*, which also appears in the New Testament. But the Hebrew concepts of *Gehenna* and outer darkness and the Greek concept of *Hades* are not the same as our concept of hell, and the word "hell" does not appear in the New Testament at all. *Gehenna*, like *Sheol*, refers to a landfill, specifically the Valley of Hinnom, south of Jerusalem that in ancient times was the dumping place of all the city's refuse. Fires burned constantly creating a putrid mix of acrid smoke and decomposing animal remains and garbage; it was the ultimate image of corruption and uncleanness in the Jewish mind. "Outer darkness," equated with *Gehenna* in Rabbinic literature, referred to the place of nothingness outside of all life and community beyond the ends of a flat earth where the outermost mountains held up the *raqia* of Genesis 1—the hard dome of the sky. *Hades*, the Greek equivalent of *Sheol*, referred to the abode of the dead, to which both the wicked and the righteous alike would go to lead a shadowy and powerless existence.

In these concepts, we see *Gehenna* as the image of corruption and punishment; outer darkness as ultimate separation; and *Sheol* and *Hades* as undifferentiated abodes of the dead. But *Gehenna* and outer darkness could be applied to spiritual corruption, punishment, and separation herenow as well as in the afterlife, and even when applied to the afterlife, none of these images carry a conception of "hell" in the sense of a place of eternal punishment and damnation. For even though the fires of *Gehenna* burned forever, a person who went there after death was understood to stay only for a maximum of twelve months, after which they were purified and able to move on. Of course, twelve months was symbolic of a complete cycle of purification, and in this sense *Gehenna* was closer to the concept of Purgatory than it was to hell. Interestingly, to this day the Jewish *kaddish*, or prayer of mourning is ritually prayed for a maximum of eleven months in the case of deceased parent. To pray any longer would be to imply that the parent was wicked enough to need the full twelve months of purification.

Even so, these concepts were never embraced by all Jews, and to this day there is very little teaching on the afterlife in Judaism and no set doctrine that is considered authoritative. The next life, called *olam ha-ba*—the world to come—is understood to exist less as a doctrine or leap of faith than a logical extension of God's justice herenow on earth. That is, any wrongs not apparently righted in this life here on earth, *olam ha-zeh*, will of necessity need to be righted in *olam ha-ba*...so there must be one.

But *olam ha-ba* is God's business and God's domain—not man's. It really has no bearing on life herenow: for Jews both ancient and modern, all that can be known is herenow, all that needs to be known is herenow, and all that God requires of us is herenow. Jews have always been free to believe whatever they want about the next life, and they do—from reincarnation to oblivion for the wicked to resurrection to eternal life, the gamut is run. But such beliefs are held lightly as Jews are content to let the next life lie in God's hands while their focus remains on the life lived in community with each other and God right here and now.

How does all this reflect on Yeshua's concept of the Kingdom of Heaven?

Try to place yourself in the sandals of a first century Galilean peasant listening to the words of an itinerant rabbi of whom you've heard so much recently. In all your experience as a Jew, in all your father's and his father's experience, in the great stories of your nation's experience, God's presence and interaction has always been an earthly thing—something acted out in the lifetime of living witnesses. God acts in and through history, and history is the story of God's rule and reign over his people. As this rabbi speaks of Kingdom, images flare in your mind of God's justice being acted out right before your eyes: the coming of *mashiach*, of messiah, of David's throne gloriously reestablished, of the cruelty of the Romans that you experience almost daily being put down, of the infectious resolve of the Zealots to set Israel in its proper place among the nations...and your heart races and chest heaves as you wonder if he is the One.

But certain words and phrases begin to break through your reverie and pluck you out of your daydream as incongruous images of children and widows and people of no earthly importance or power begin inheriting this Kingdom. You hear him saying you won't even see this Kingdom coming because it is already inside of you, that it is already here among the Roman soldiers, that the last at table will become the first, and that prostitutes and tax collectors will enter before Pharisees and Scribes. As you begin to shift your feet amid the murmurs around you and dart glances at the reactions of others, your confusion mounts as you try to process these new bits and pieces, trying to make sense, trying to make them somehow fit what you already think you know about Kingdom.

As a good Jew, though, whatever you might be thinking about this rabbi's strange words, and however much you may strain to understand, one place you would never take your thoughts would be out of *olam ha-zeh*, this physical life. To conclude that the Kingdom this rabbi speaks of must be *olam ha-ba*, the heaven of afterlife would be as alien to you as Dreamtime to a Wall Street executive or a birthday party to a Moken. Whatever this rabbi is saying—and he doesn't seem to be making much sense at the moment—never would such a concept enter your mind.

Whether understood physically or spiritually,
to a Jew, the Kingdom is always *herenow*.

>A new year. Another arbitrary segment of time. Step over this invisible line and change this number. Mark it down. Each year seems to mean less and less and yet brings more and more. I have heard it is the greater rate of change that feeds the perceived greater rate of speed with which it passes.

>Einstein said time is subjectively relative--dependent upon whether you were sitting on a hot stove or with a pretty girl in your lap. Physicists since him have said less sexistly that time is actually the measurement of entropy in a system. The time it takes to go to maximum disorder defines it. H.G. Wells thought of time as a fourth dimension. That anything with length, breadth, and depth still didn't exist if it was instantaneous--it had to have <u>duration</u> to exist--time defined it. Benjamin Franklin said to be in love with life is to be in love with time. Time is the stuff life is made of. James Taylor said the secret of life is enjoying the passage of time. Merton said to experience the present moment is to touch the eternity of God.

>I say they are all right. Time is all we have. Time is what we are. Time defines us. Separates us now from the Almighty...and will be taken from us when we return to him. But for now, we are creatures of it. Slaves to it. It has been freely given to us, and perhaps for that reason, though it is our most precious--no, our only--commodity, we treat it with contempt. Take it for granted. Waste it. Then later in life, horde it, guard it, try to prolong it.

>I don't know how much I have. But I have been shown that what ever I have, it is all I have. Nothing I have in this life exists instantaneously. It must have time to exist. If I love my life, if I value it, then I love my time, though I rarely see it that way. My most precious possession is my life. My life here is my time here. Time is my most precious possession. And so it is

also my most precious gift. To give my time to another. The gift of time is the gift of life, and freely given makes a statement of love that cannot be mistaken or ignored.

>Time, life, love. They are all you, Lord. They are all the same. And after all, they are all that can be truly communicated or retained.

Beyond Obedience

If Yeshua doesn't specifically redefine Kingdom for his first hearers, they will understand it as the reestablishment of the throne of David in a reconstituted, independent, political nation-state. If he doesn't specifically redefine Kingdom for us, we'll understand it as the heaven of the afterlife. Such are the biases of our two cultures and worldviews. But Yeshua does emphatically and repeatedly define his Kingdom; it's just that few of his first or latest listeners have ears to hear: such are the depth and influence of our cultures and worldviews.

Beyond unity and herenowness, what did Yeshua mean when he spoke of the Kingdom of Heaven?

First of all, why would Matthew call it the Kingdom of Heaven (*malkutha dashmaya*), when Mark, Luke and John call it the Kingdom of God (*malkutha d'alaha*)? Is there a difference between the two? Actually, they mean exactly the same thing, but since Matthew was written primarily to Jews and the other three Gospels primarily to Gentiles, God's name had to be treated differently. Jews, by tradition, do not speak the name of God, for fear of profaning it (third commandment) or showing dominion over God. They used euphemisms like *Adonai* (lord), *Jehovah* (I am), *Ha Shem* (the name), and *Shemaya*. *Shemaya* comes from the same root as *shem* (light, sound, essence, character, name), but the *-aya* ending extends it without limit into the essence and connectedness of all creation. *Shemaya* was understood as the sky, the place of the winds, but just as *ruha* (wind) also means both breath and spirit, *shemaya* was understood as the place of God's spirit—heaven. So just as we substitute "gosh" and "golly" for God to avoid profaning his name, Jews would often swear "by *shemaya*," using heaven as a polite way of avoiding the use of God's name. In other words, the Kingdom of Heaven and the

Kingdom of God are the same thing tuned for different audiences. Kingdom of Heaven really means Kingdom of God...but what does that mean?

The word standing behind the English word "kingdom" is the Greek word *basileia*, and behind *basileia* stands the Aramaic word, *malkutha*. Strong's lexicon for *basileia* tells us it's "the royal power, kingship, dominion, or rule of the king, not to be confused with the actual kingdom but rather the right or authority to rule over a kingdom." In an instance where the Greek and Aramaic agree, the primary understanding of *malkutha* is also the reign or rule of the king—some recent translations render it "imperial rule."

When it comes to the *malkutha* of God though, there is more implied in the meaning than just the authority to rule. If you look at the instances in the Old Testament where Hebrew words have been translated into English as "kingdom," you find that *malkutha* or *malkuth*, the Hebrew version of the same word, is not used nearly as much as another Hebrew word that also means kingdom—*mamlacha*. *Mamlacha* is overwhelmingly used to denote the rule of Gentile kings over their tribes and nations, and of the rule of Israelite kings like Saul who stand outside of God's divine reign. *Malkuth*, by contrast, is used to denote those reigns established by God directly or exalted reigns that operate in concert with God's reign, such as the kingdom, the reign/*malkuth* of David. When David is explaining to his son Solomon in 1 Chronicles 22 why Solomon must build the temple after David's reign is over, he quotes God's pronouncement that "He (Solomon) shall build a house for my name, and he shall be my son and I will be his father; and I will establish the throne of his kingdom (*malkuth*) over Israel forever."

In Hebrew thinking, *mamlacha* denotes more of a dictatorial rule in which the will of the king is imposed on the people, and the people are forced to obey. It's a one-way flow of power in which the command of the king goes out; it is imposed on the people, but is not reflected in them or their lives beyond mere obedience.

Malkuth then, being tied closely to God, denotes a two-way reign in which the will of God is reflected in the will of the king, and the will of the king is reflected in the will of the people. But what is that will, the principle by which God reigns? As the name of God in

Aramaic is *Alaha*, in Hebrew *Eloah*—two sister-words created from the same roots—God's name means a mighty one, a oneness, a unity. It's often noted that *Eloah* is rarely used in its singular form, rather in its plural form of *Elohim*: in Hebrew, plural forms can mean either multiple things or the greatest or largest of one thing, a sort of superlative plural. So, *Elohim* and *Alaha* both can denote a great unity of not just one thing, but multiple things *functioning* as one.

The ancient Jews always emphasized function over form to the extent that Hebrew nouns are derived from verb forms, so that a person, place, or thing was understood as something that performed a certain function or action. The Hebrew names of God describe his function: *Alaha*, *Elohim*, functions as one, in unity, so the authority or principle by which God reigns is unity, oneness—everyone in the Kingdom functioning as one.

With *malkutha*, there is the sense that it is not the king who is establishing the reign at all—it is the people themselves, having been inspired by the person and purpose of the king, who are acting on his behalf, initiating and carrying out the king's will and reign. This goes far beyond mere obedience. *Malkutha* is true partnership, where the will of king and people become one and the same...and obedience becomes *obsolete*.

In what sense are a people obeying when their deepest desire is the same as the rule they are obligated to obey? It may be obedience when I tell my son to do his homework and he does, but if he learns to love homework so much that I have to practically drag him away just to eat dinner, is he still obeying my "rule?" God's *malkutha*, his reign, is such as this: we all have the freedom to obey or not obey, but when God's person and purpose begin to resonate in us, when we begin to vibrate as God vibrates, to look and sound and act as he does, we have graduated from *mamlacha* to *malkutha*, from obedience to partnership. In this sense, God's reign and will are not carried out on earth directly by God, but by those of us vibrating with him in his kingdom—his reign and will—his *malkutha*.

This is exactly the image Yeshua is painting in his model prayer at Matthew 6: "Our Father in heaven, may your name be kept holy. Let your kingdom come, let your will be done, as in heaven, so on earth." Praying for the coming of kingdom/*malkutha*, is exactly the same as praying for God's will to be done—the two phrases are synonymous in Hebrew thought—God's reign and rule are the same as his will. And the word translated as "will," *sebyana* in Aramaic, doesn't mean will as we think of an authoritative mandate, but actually means desire, pleasure, delight, or deepest purpose. Even the Greek word used here, *thelema*, has the same meanings as the Aramaic, and together they put an entirely different spin on what it means to be in God's "will." Yeshua is instructing us to pray, to live out, to bring God's deepest desire and pleasure and purpose to fullness and completion, to make it as real herenow on earth as it already is in heaven—to bring heaven to earth and earth to heaven. It is *we* who do this. We, vibrating in resonance with the deepest purpose and pleasure of God, make *malkutha* real, right herenow.

So, the Kingdom of Heaven, *malkutha dashamaya*, is literally translated, the "reign of heaven," but as *shemaya* is a Hebrew euphemism for God, it becomes the "reign of God." But God, *Alaha*, means unity, so we finally end up most literally with the "reign of unity." The Kingdom of Heaven is the "Reign of Unity." God's reign, his will, his deepest desire and purpose, is for each one of us to be enveloped in complete unity and connection with him and each other. His pleasure, his delight, is to have us resonating and vibrating at his frequency right herenow, living and loving in such a way as to be indistinguishable from Kingdom, the reign of the king himself.

>Women and their men. I see them all the time. Airport terminals are a good place to watch. The roles, the emotions, the language is universal.

>I see a young couple from the moving sidewalk coming toward me hand in hand. One of them has just arrived. I can't tell which; the small case he carries is non-descript. They talk. She is smiling. Looks up at his eyes, back forward again. Up. Back. So much is said with her eyes. I can only imagine. I watch him. He is talking, but looks forward; she alternately at him and back ahead. What I see in her eyes he hasn't seen as long as I watch.

>They pass, and I watch their backs. I see her profile tilted up to his face, but only the back of his head--minding the tiller. I've seen this before. Why is it so much easier for women to know where to look? Where to keep their eyes? Moving through their lives with their eyes fastened to the sides, on the eyes of those who travel with them--their men more intent on destination, the negotiation of the journey. And how do women keep that look in their eyes as they search up into the profiles of their men?

>Last Wednesday night we got a video of scientists trying to teach human language to apes and dolphins. You thought it would be great to watch the dolphins you saw in the pictures on the box but were bored, as I knew you'd be when I tried to talk you out of it. Even so, a segment stays in my mind. One man, a very famous scientist, spent three years raising an infant chimp and trying to teach him sign language. He named the chimp Nim. Nim did very well. Learned several hundred signs. But funding ran out, the project was disbanded, and Nim went to a zoo or something like it. After reviewing hundreds of video tapes of his sessions with Nim, the

scientist concluded that Nim was only imitating his teachers and hadn't really learned anything. Put a big dent in the chimp-teaching business for awhile.

>Several years later the scientist went to see Nim. Hadn't seen him since funding ran out on the project. In clinical voice over, he wondered if Nim would remember him. The video camera caught Nim walking with a trainer just as he caught sight of the scientist. Immediately chimp screeches filled the TV speaker at the rate of about three per second as Nim threw up his arms and sprinted, as well as chimps can in their loping way, for the scientist who got down on his haunches and braced for impact.

>Nim leapt into the scientist's lap and threw his arms around his neck. Chimp arms being what they are, they almost went around twice. All this time and for as long as the camera held on Nim and the scientist, chimp screeches never stopped or even slowed down, chimp teeth big and bright as the scene cut.

>And I kept hearing those screeches, and I laughed and smiled and my eyes stung a little all at the same time because the scientist thought that Nim learned nothing, and Nim thought that the scientist was his father, or brother at least. Because the scientist was looking ahead at where he was going. Nim was looking at him.

>I'd rather be a chimp than a scientist.

>I'd rather be a young woman watching her man's profile than a young man watching the road.

Seeing Kingdom

As this clearer picture of Kingdom is emerging, let's put our fingers right on it...

The Kingdom of Heaven is the how of unity.

Without stretching too far, we could translate Kingdom as the *will* of the king: his pleasure, delight, deepest purpose—his reign. To be in Kingdom is to literally be in the will of the king—the will of God. We all ache to know what God's will may be for our lives, and yet here it is hiding in plain sight. As we move closer to Kingdom, we begin to realize that God's will, his herenow reign, is not what we expect: not a plan, job, ministry, profession, or spouse. In fact, it's not a "what" at all...it's a "how," the very principle by which God lives and breathes. And that principle, of course, is unity—a oneness experienced herenow within us and at the same time among us and in our midst.

We spend lifetimes obsessed over what we should do to be in the center of God's will. Ironically, I'm no longer convinced God cares *what* we do, but I know he cares deeply *how* we do what we do. With the right how, any what will do. With the right how, we get to choose what.

Kingdom is the how of living in complete unity.

The Kingdom of Heaven is the quality of here.

At Luke 17, Yeshua said the Kingdom was within, among, and in our midst—the word he used meaning all three at the same time, grounded right here on earth. Ancient Hebrews didn't draw bright lines between individual and community or between inner lives and outer lives as we do. A person of faith was someone whose interior and exterior lives mirrored each other, functioned as one. As a communal society, the individual was primarily a part of the group and existed to serve the group. So a person's interior life, voice, and spirituality only had relevance and meaning in terms of service to the productive life of the group: spiritual life only existed *within* as an action expressed outward in the *midst of* or *among* the community. This is how all these prepositions work together in Semitic thought. James expresses the same idea in his New Testament letter when he says that faith without works is dead—for him, faith also exists within only at the moment it is outwardly expressed among others.

It is the same with Kingdom. The quality of life lived by someone deeply immersed in the will/desire/pleasure of God only exists within him or her as long as it is moving dynamically outward to be experienced in the midst or among the others nearby—the literal meaning of a neighbor. A neighbor is not someone we feel any affection for; a neighbor is merely *qariba*, whoever happens to be nearby...whether we like them or not, whether they like us or not. Loving our neighbor, even when the neighbor is our enemy, changes the quality of here, carves Kingdom into our lives in community.

If you ever want to measure the quality of your relationship with God, just look at the quality of the relationships closest to you. The quality of your life within will never exceed the quality of your life out *here*—among and in the midst of those around you.

The Kingdom of Heaven is the immediacy of now.

What did Yeshua tell us? In Mark 1:15, his debut at the beginning of that gospel, Yeshua says, "The time is fulfilled; the Kingdom is near," as most English versions translate it. But the Greek word *egizzo*, usually translated "near or at hand," can also mean, "has already arrived," and the Aramaic word behind it, *metah*, does mean to arrive or reach, so a better translation would be, "The waiting is over; the Kingdom is now," not at some point in the future after we die...now.

To Jews from the most ancient times, a person is not divided up into body and spirit as we dualistically think in the West. Where we imagine our souls or spirits trapped in a physical body, Jews understood that God created man and woman as *nephesh hayyah*, "living beings." God breathes life into us, but that life is never separate from our physical bodies, from who or what we are. The *ruach* or *ruha* of God, his wind, breath, and spirit in motion is equivalent to the movement of *nephesh* and is what constantly sustains all living things.

As Marvin Wilson writes in *Our Father Abraham*, "In Hebraic thought, 'soul' or 'spirit' refers to the whole person or individual as a living being. It stands for the person himself. The Old Testament view of man is that he is an animated body rather than an incarnated soul. In short, human beings live as souls, they do not 'have' souls... For the Hebrews, spirituality did not mean turning inward; true piety was not simply the private nourishing of the virtues of one's soul. Rather, it meant to be fully human, every fiber of one's being alive, empowered in passionate and inspired service to God and humanity." For the Jews of Yeshua's time or any time, anticipating the day when their souls would be freed at death to return to an eternal heaven was not the expression and goal of their spirituality. Fully immersed in physical life and service to God and each other was ultimate spiritual expression: to be fully here and immediately *now*.

And one more thing...

The Kingdom of Heaven is the force of action.

Kingdom, like faith and God's breath, must always be in motion—and for the same reason. Life is motion: God's *ruha*, his breath, wind, spirit, is constantly blowing through us, animating us, giving us life. *Ruha* animates our faith and makes Kingdom possible. There is no Kingdom apart from faith/trust, and there is no faith/trust that is not moving outward and being acted upon, "worked out," in the lives of those nearby—our neighbors. Kingdom, as the quality of life we experience in faith/trust, is always moving actively outward as well.

We have to slow down a moment and really take this in.

There is a passivity that has crept into our Western religious worldview. Narrowing our definition of salvation to mere acceptance into heaven and avoidance of hell, we see God as doing all the heavy lifting of redemption; the only action required of us never really rises above mere obedience both mentally and physically, that is, theologically and legally/morally. As we drive carefully between the lines of our lane, we can imagine release and freedom in the afterlife therethen, but our experience of Kingdom herenow never exceeds *mamlacha*.

Firmly focused on the quality of life in motion, the herehow release and freedom of *malkutha*, Yeshua is repeatedly emphatic in the active images he paints for us. And one of his most striking images of Kingdom at Matthew 11:12 is also one of the most difficult passages in the Gospels:

"From the days of John the Baptist until now the kingdom of heaven suffers violence, and violent men take it by force."

This translation, the most common in English, goes all the way back to King James in 1611, but what in the world is meant by it? How do images of violence and violent men square with everything we know of Kingdom and Yeshua himself? The key Greek words here are *biazo*, "suffers violence," *biastai*, "violent men," and *harpazo*, which though translated "taking by force," also means to pursue, seek, grasp, capture." We need to understand what *biazo* and *biastai* mean in a Hebrew context, but in an instance where the Aramaic Peshitta translation carries essentially the same meaning, we need to find those same Greek words being used in other texts in ways that will help define them.

☽ ☽ ⊕ ⊕ ⊕

Yeshua's violent Kingdom images in Matthew and Luke are both presented in the context of a description of the role of his cousin, John the Baptist. Just two verses earlier, in Matthew 11:10, Yeshua quotes from the Hebrew books of Isaiah and Malachi to present John as the messenger of God who comes to prepare the way of the Lord. Yeshua's use of this familiar Jewish image of the one who prepares the way parallels another key passage where the same image appears in the book of Micah.

In Micah 2:12-13 we find, "...I will surely gather the remnant of Israel. I will put them together like sheep in the fold; like a flock in the midst of its pasture they will be noisy with men. The breaker goes up before them; they break out, pass through the gate and go out by it. So their king goes on before them, and the Lord at their head." Here we are introduced to the image of the breaker, *parats* in Hebrew, the one who prepares the way of the king/Lord as if breaking through the gate of a sheepfold.

Ancient Jewish shepherds would typically construct a sheepfold, a pen or enclosure for the night, by piling up rocks into a crude wall with an opening at one end. After driving the sheep into the enclosure, the shepherd would either fashion a gate or simply lie down and sleep in the opening, literally becoming the "gate" of the sheepfold. By morning, the sheep were so anxious to get out to pasture that when the shepherd opened the gate, they would all rush out at once, jostling and jumping over each other, breaking forth and usually breaking the opening wider by knocking down rocks in the process. This is the image to which Yeshua is referring as he speaks of John the Baptist as the one who breaks forth with all the people as he prepares the way of the Lord.

But how do we connect any dots from Micah's breakers back to Matthew's violent men? In the 2nd to 3rd centuries BCE Egyptian Jews translated the Hebrew scriptures into Greek, creating a version called the Septuagint. Reading Micah in this version, the Greek word used to translate the Hebrew *parats*, breakers, jumps off the page as that same Greek word, *biastai*—our forceful or violent men. The dots connect and the Septuagint becomes our Rosetta Stone in deciphering what was originally meant by *biastai* in the Aramaic/Hebrew original of Yeshua's sayings.

When this saying of Yeshua was translated from his Aramaic/Hebrew into Greek for the Gospels, the word *biastai* was again used to translate Yeshua's *parats* or perhaps *qetirana* in Aramaic. The *biastai* are not "violent men," in the malicious sense we would understand that phrase, but "breakers" who break forth with the pent-up desire and manic drive of sheep trying to get to pasture after a claustrophobic night in the pen. By extension, the "violence" (*biazo*) suffered by the Kingdom is really a "breaking forth" of Kingdom principles, and those who are breaking forth with Kingdom, are "*harpazo*," pursuing, seeking, and capturing it. In fact, there really is little distinction between the Kingdom breaking forth and those breaking forth with it, as if they are one and the same.

Now we can best translate: "From the days of John the Baptist until now, the Kingdom of Heaven is breaking forth, and those breaking forth are pursuing and capturing it."

The Kingdom within is a state of being in unity with God that is explosive, that can't be contained, and is breaking forth from each transformed heart and life to dynamically transform the neighbors, those nearby, and eventually the face of the community and even the whole world. It is *legau men*, a process beginning deep inside and moving energetically outward, and in that breaking forth, the breakers "capture" or experience Kingdom—always active, never passive. And we, as breakers, are always actively participating in Kingdom, or we're not "seeing" it at all.

When Yeshua tells Nicodemus in John 3 unless he is born again he cannot see the Kingdom of God, he is drawing a straight line between being born again, or literally born "from above" and seeing the Kingdom. But to Hebrews, seeing Kingdom has nothing to do with our eyes. "Taste and see that the Lord is good," David sings at Psalm 34, and in the way of Hebrew poetry, taste and see are repeated concepts: *ta'am*—taste, perceive—*ra'ah*—see, perceive, enjoy, experience. To merely see with the eyes is passive: to view from a distance, possibly remaining unmoved and unaltered—but to taste means active proximity: in your very mouth, intimately aware, impossible to ignore. Seeing Kingdom is to taste it, enjoy it, and through the experience be born again.

If we have ears to hear, Yeshua is telling us plainly that to be born again is to taste Kingdom, and to taste Kingdom is to be born again. Kingdom is always active and moving from inside to outside creating the same effect within and among; we can only "see" it, enjoy and experience it if we are moving with it, breaking out forcefully in the same direction.

David Bivin writes in *Understanding the Difficult Words of Jesus*, "...in Hebrew, "kingdom" is active; it is action. It is God ruling in the lives of men. Those who are ruled by God are the Kingdom of God...We see God's Kingdom when we see Him in action." And we see God's action in our lives when we are born again—transformed in such a way that we can see life again through our Father's eyes...as we once did when we were children.

214

Micah's imagery of the sheep and the gate of the sheepfold now brings us full circle, leading squarely back to the Gospel of John and one of the most enduring images in Christianity. In chapter 10, Yeshua is calling himself the good shepherd and the door or gate of the sheepfold: "...he who does not enter by the door into the fold of the sheep, but climbs up some other way, he is a thief and a robber. But he who enters by the door is a shepherd of the sheep...I am the door of the sheep...if anyone enters through me, he will be saved, and will go in and out and find pasture...I am the good shepherd; the good shepherd lays down his life for the sheep...and I know my own and my own know me, and I give eternal life to them, and they will never perish; and no one will snatch them out of my hand."

Yeshua, like the ancient shepherd who lies down in the opening of the sheepfold, is literally the door, the gate, the Way by which we, the breakers, move out into Kingdom, capturing Kingdom life in the process. There are no shortcuts, no ways around, under, or over. It is this Way or no way. And just as the sheep know the shepherd's voice, the breakers know the Way. From Yeshua and Kingdom in Matthew to John the Baptist as preparer of the way in Isaiah and Malachi to the breakers and the sheep in Micah and back to Yeshua as the good shepherd and gate of the sheepfold in John 10, the circle is complete. These and other images and allusions from both the Hebrew Scriptures and the New Testament lock into a tightly woven fabric that presents Yeshua's Kingdom for those who have ears to hear...

"The kingdom of heaven is like a mustard seed, which a man took and sowed in his field; and this is smaller than all other seeds, but when it is full grown, it is larger than the garden plants and becomes a tree, so that the birds of the air come and nest in its branches."
Matthew 13:31-32

"The kingdom of heaven is like leaven, which a woman took and hid in three pecks of flour until it was all leavened." Matthew 13:33

"The kingdom of heaven is like a treasure hidden in the field, which a man found and hid again; and from joy over it he goes and sells all that he has and buys that field." Matthew 13:44

"Again, the kingdom of heaven is like a merchant seeking fine pearls, and upon finding one pearl of great value, he went and sold all that he had and bought it." Matthew 13:45-46

Always active, never passive, from inside out, from within to among, Kingdom is portrayed as quickly filling up any container into which it's placed and then explosively breaking forth into ever larger spaces as Yeshua paints his pictures for us in the brilliant colors of the abandon with which it is lived.

>As I have sat here looking down at the tops of the clouds and, alternately, at snow covered earth reading Merton, I am reminded for the thousandth uncomfortable time that God is too big to be contained by anything I can imagine or comprehend or see or be. He is too big even to be contained in his own printed Word. God can't be contained in a book. He can't be contained in a body. He can't be contained in history. He can't be contained. Our view is too narrow, our vision too short.

>It all comes down to how uncomfortable I am willing to be with my God. He is too big for me. My mind can never contain Him. So I can either find a God that fits my mind, or I can embark on a lifetime of contortion as I continually stretch my mind to accommodate more and more of the God I find. There is no end; death only accelerates the process.

>And remembering that Jesus commanded us to make followers and not converts, this is really our task as fellow followers. To show others how to contort. How to stretch. How to live in the paradox and discomfort and indescribable joy of coming to know the Father.

>He is too big to be comfortable. He is too big to be familiar. He is too big to be seen or understood. The people shied away from the Presence on the mountain and begged that only Moses should approach. God saw that that was good and appropriate.

>He is too big for us. But at the same time, Jesus shows us that there might be identification on some level. And we want identification. We want to be comfortable. So we take Jesus and turn him into a teddy bear. A comfortable, comforting,

approximation of the man. There are certainly these aspects present in him, but there is much more, and we are selective.

>Jesus is identified with the Father--with that bigness. Jesus can't be contained in a teddy bear.

>We take the Word. We study it. Memorize it. Become familiar with it. Comfortable with its rhythm and structure and thought. But the Word was with God, and the Word is God and can't be contained in a book.

>We want to know him. That is good. But when we think we do, that is illusion. And when we institutionalize the illusion, that is deception.

☽ ☽ ⊕ ⊕ ⊕

Have you ever felt the joyful abandon of Kingdom? Of course you have. When you were in love for the first time and you looked into your beloved's eyes; when you held your first child and melted into that tiny face; when you sat watching a sunset and were transported into the scene; when you threw your head back and laughed until you cried at the punch line of a really funny joke; when children, running and playing, stopped you in your tracks for a moment, and the smile crept across your face without your permission or awareness; at prayer; at worship; listening to music that closes your eyes and stops your breath... What were you thinking at any of these moments?

Nothing!

These are moments when life makes sense. Moments so big and powerful that our sense of self breaks down, and we are left completely borderless as individuals—fully connected to everyone and everything. For once, the voice with which we talk to ourselves in our minds is hushed, and we cease to be one, separate and alone, but one of many, functioning as one together. There is no sensation of the passage of time; time ceases to exist, evaporates, as we touch the face of God, the face of eternity.

This is seeing the Kingdom of God, a Kingdom moment. This moment, right now, can be such a moment...or this one. It's our choice every moment to see the Kingdom or not. And when we string enough Kingdom moments together, we can say with Yeshua, that we are characterized by Kingdom, characterized by contentment. That more often than not, we are experiencing all that Kingdom is, and our name, our *shem*, our essence, is one with God's.

Right here. Right now.

☽ ☽ ⊕ ⊕ ⊕

Children in our societies, at earlier and earlier ages, learn two crucial lessons that forever change their view of the world, life, and themselves. First, they learn to see themselves as separate from those around them, or more to the point, they learn to see their needs as separate from and in fundamental competition and conflict with the needs of those around them. Secondly, they learn to separate their conception of past and future from the present moment. In short, they learn to *separate*.

How was it with Adam and Eve? When they ate from the tree of the knowledge of good and evil, what was it they were suddenly able to do? They were able to separate one from the other, good from evil, themselves from each other—to see their nakedness and the need to cover it. They were able to separate, to *hataha*, to sin. Before the eating from the tree, they existed in a childlike state of non-separation, of not knowing disconnection from each other or God and of not knowing any moment but the present one. Their "sin" was to know these things, because these things cause "death," the awareness of separation, fear, loneliness, despair. It seems the Genesis record preserves the memory of a time when two humans, or humans as a race and a people graduated from a more animal-like and childlike state of non-awareness to a self-aware state in which the separation of sin was possible and inevitable.

The miracle of the Moken and other aboriginal tribes who've been the least touched by the civilizations of the last six thousand years or so is that they, like children, haven't learned the twin lessons of separation as we have: to separate the needs of others from personal needs or past and future from present. They continue to lead a connected and timeless existence that we lost when we "graduated" to the separation of these concepts in our own minds.

The technologies of our civilization are creating more and more separation in our lives at an exponential rate: in our climate-controlled houses and cars, at our personal computers inside our headphones, we believe the illusion that we can thrive in isolation, that we can prosper living in the therethen at the expense of here-now, that by constantly planning and working for future accomplishment and avoiding past hurts, we can somehow create a present happiness. But somehow never arrives, and illusions are, in the end, just illusions, and our pathologies and addictions betray us as the lonely, fearful people we have become. As Yahweh told us in the Garden, on the day we eat of the tree of the knowledge of good and evil, we will surely die, and we die every day in the separation we have inherited and continue to create for ourselves.

Yeshua is calling us back to the Garden—back to a unity and timelessness we lost so long ago that we have forgotten they ever existed for us. When, unlike the Moken, we graduated to a place where our personal needs and agendas so outweighed those of our neighbors that our communities began to break down, a dictatorial rule or law, *mamlacha*, had to be introduced and enacted just to stave off anarchy and maintain some level of survival for the group. But mere obedience to this law and one-way rule is only a bandage over a tumor—creating the illusion of wholeness, but doing nothing to cure the disease. Yeshua is calling us to graduate again, from *mamlacha* to *malkutha*, from obedience to partnership, to enter into the Kingdom where our desire for ourselves and God's desire for us become one again as it was in the beginning.

It is in this macro sense that Yeshua sometimes presents Kingdom in a future setting, as yet unrealized. As each breaker actively participates in Kingdom, he or she directly affects those nearby. As those neighbors experience Kingdom in the breakers around them, they may find their Way to break forth themselves and affect others as well. Like a benign virus, slowly at first, then exponentially faster, this moving outward will eventually hit a critical mass through which Kingdom within becomes indistinguishable from Kingdom among and in the midst. The principles of the King that reign in the hearts of the breakers will become the principles by which society also governs—from *mamlacha* to *malkutha*—inside out, downside up, and backside front. But it all begins within, with a Kingdom that is already here.

Kingdom is the surrender of those things that we've come to believe are vital to our existence and happiness, but which in reality are the very things that separate us from the only true sources of life: God, each other, and the present moment. Kingdom is the re-experience of unity and connection in a timeless immersion herenow. As we begin to see the world and life again from the inside out, downside up, and backside front, the bits and pieces of non-Kingdom begin to fall off, like the stone block encasing Michelangelo's horse, until we find ourselves spending more and more moments in the moment Yeshua calls Kingdom.

Our behavior has everything to do with these moments and nothing to do with a heaven we await. How we live has everything to do with our ability to see Kingdom herenow, but tells us nothing of therethen. How could it?

> Life is always herenow and never therethen—
> and therethen never exists at all—
> until the moment it becomes herenow.

As the reflection and resonance of God's desire being acted out in our lives, our behavior is the living definition of Kingdom. But loving behavior doesn't "save" us in the next life any more than unloving behavior damns us. God's ultimate acceptance of us is not based on such things as we can produce: obedience is not Kingdom, but it is a crucial first step, because before we can learn to love like God, we need to learn to live like him. So Yeshua describes the sort of behavior that is Kingdom-like, that will give us the exhilarating glimpses of moments vastly outside the scope of our wells...moments with the power to propel us in new and unexpected directions. Mere obedience is not Kingdom; it is only *mamlacha*, which is why we must exceed *mamlacha*, the righteousness of legalistic Scribes and Pharisees of every generation, in order to go any further.

This is the essence of the Way, the Fifth Way of Kingdom.

Few of us go by it, because few of us ever get to the point where we can trust enough in the radical conclusion and nature of God's furious love to realize that it is only in letting go of everything we trust that we find the only thing really trustworthy...or the essential truth that this Trustworthiness was herenow all along, right within our own backyards.

>I remembered seeing a cross from Pacific Coast Highway.

>Stark and white against the back of Malibu Canyon, the sign at the highway's edge identified it as a retreat center run by the Franciscans. When everything has become uncertain, sometimes you just have to go back to the last thing you were certain of. I fled to the Catholic cross on the hill, got a room for several days, and asked to see one of the priests. I was expecting the brown hooded robe of the Franciscans with the knotted white rope as belt, but instead there were the bland blacks of a Diocesan priest. In a small office across a worn coffee table, I told my story, and I can still see his fist coming down on the faded wood for emphasis as he said that the bible was never meant to be a proof text for living. It was the first of many things I would hear for the first time, coming back to Malibu as often as I could, meeting with both black and brown habits speaking their truth in ways so alien I had to keep reminding myself they were Catholic—if only because the habits were.

>Then I read about the American Catholic church, in schism with Rome and the Pope's authority: they allowed their priests to marry and divorced people to remarry and take Communion if they did. More absolutes hitting the floor. So I found an American Catholic church a few towns away and myself in another small office, telling my story and asking my questions until the priest asks me how much time I have and if I'd like to take a ride. Walking through the small Catholic bookstore, he points to this title and that, and nearly a hundred dollars later, I'm walking out of the store with my arms full of names like Merton and Nouwen and Manning that lead me to other names like Aquinas, à Kempis, John of the Cross, Anthony and the Desert Fathers and Mothers, and expressions of truth that could only be experienced to be believed.

>So I brought them out of their pages and let them loose around me. Imitating the life of the monk I never was, the monk Merton so vividly described, I kept silence and solitude as best I could in my new apartment—still spare, but furnished and unpacked with second story windows looking out over a wooded courtyard. Working primarily by phone and computer, I spent much of my day there and made it my hermitage. Up at 5AM, I was out running before dawn, with cool-down meditation at the side of the pool immediately after. Back in the apartment to journal and pray before shower and ready to work at eight—no television or radio—only the sound of my own voice and the thin ones coming through the earpiece to break the silence I was learning to love.

Understanding the Misunderstanding

The only thing we have to fear is fear itself.

THIS IS AS TRUE TODAY AS WHEN FRANKLIN ROOSEVELT recognized it in his first inaugural address three years into the Great Depression, calling it "nameless, unreasoning, unjustified terror, which paralyzes needed efforts to convert retreat into advance." Because this is true, because fear itself is the imagined separation between us and all things Kingdom, we must enter deeper into the Aramaic Agreement to begin to realize that our fears are really only misunderstandings.

Yeshua's entire mission and message was to show us the Father, the Good News of a love so utter that it can't ever be lost because it can't be gained—it simply exists. Our fears keep us from embracing such a love, which is why Yeshua worked so hard to clear up any misunderstanding. He had to use words big enough to describe the bigness of this love and the nature of our relationship with it—words not big in size but in scope. With only one or two syllables for the most part, these words carry immense power for their size. Big words like freedom and forgiveness, good and evil, sin and salvation survive in our theologies; our theologies turn on them as on hinges or hubs, but like all the other words coming out of Yeshua's Agreement, if we don't know what was meant by them, our misunderstandings foster that persistent sense of separation—fear itself.

Kingdom is a big word; so is Law. The concept of Kingdom as the synchronization of the desires of a king and his people, of God and mankind, was an ancient Hebrew concept that reflected God's intended relationship with us from the very beginning—unity and oneness. Yeshua prayed for this in his last words to his friends at John 17, "...that they may all be one; even as you, Father, are in me and I in you, that they also may be in us..." That the people had bastardized the original concepts of both Kingdom and Law into dictatorial rule and legalistic obedience, was exactly why Yeshua worked so hard on misunderstandings. There was a previous understanding that was lost over time and needed to be recovered and fulfilled if people were to be restored to their God and each other.

Why did the people lose their Way, their original understanding of God's relationship with them, their first love? Why was their slide into one-way rule and mere obedience so predictable and inevitable? And why is this same slide into legalism (the belief that obedience to the rule of law brings salvation) repeated person after person, generation after generation, and culture after culture, right into our own?

It's always the loss of trust that is the culprit—misunderstanding the all-embracing love of God that feels like separation, like fear itself. When the hurts of life, either small and cumulative or single and catastrophic, put the first dent in our ability to trust the Good News of an incomprehensibly perfect love, we have begun the inevitable.

How can we trust when we no longer see evidence of trustworthiness, when we're no longer sure the universe is a friendly place? How do we rebuild trust when distrust has become self-fulfilling prophecy in our lives? Without ultimate Trustworthiness at our backs, we are left completely on our own, abandoned like children separated from parents in an unfamiliar and threatening place. As our hands ache to be held again in a big, firm grasp, we seize on any of Four Ways to feel secure, to have a foundation under our feet and strong walls all around. But...

Security always comes at the price of freedom.

One or the other can be indulged, but not both at the same time. True freedom is priceless precisely because it is *unsecured*, because it contains the exhilaration, surprise, and risks of the unknown. Security, while providing at least an illusion of certainty, slowly starves off something in us that longs to fly over the very barriers that have been erected to keep us safe, whether a wall, a law, even a job. Somewhere down deep, we know all this, but as our fears grow, our willingness to trade freedom for security grows with them, and so we submit. Not to the God we no longer trust, but to the forms and rules we agree to imagine God has given us for our salvation, but which we have really only given ourselves—like a warm blanket we hope will shield us from our freezing fears.

Yeshua said that if we followed him along his Fifth Way, the truth would make us free. He said he came to bring abundant life. He said not to worry, that his burden was light and that he loved as the Father loved and neither would ever leave us. Fear itself is the opposite of all this: creating in us a slavish, obsessive adherence to the big words in our theologies, the codes of our rules and the folds of our blankets. And a rule, like a blanket, is really just another layer of separation between us and all that Yeshua envisions for us.

As far as we may have come in these pages toward seeing Kingdom as Yeshua saw it, misunderstandings remain. And each misunderstanding is another dent in our ability to see the totality of God's love for us, a hole in our ability to trust enough in that love to begin laying down our fears.

Continuing to explore the ground around Kingdom, six pairs of big words viewed from inside the Aramaic Agreement may help us clear up lingering misunderstanding, pull the layered masks off fear itself, and begin to trust Kingdom as both the destination and the Way of our Father's perfect love.

>Been in the air over four and a half hours. With just over a half hour left, I'm not exactly sure where we are. Appears to be the Arizona/California desert. There's a thick river empty-ing into a lake. Must be the Colorado/Lake Mead. That would mean we're over California now. Looks a lot like Arizona. There is a mountain range up ahead across the desert basin. I'm sure Los Angeles is on the other side.

>The land beneath me is incredible. The topography endlessly fascinating as it slides slowly by. I can only guess at the forces that created the patterns and formations I see--although at this distance it looks just like the rutted, washed earth in a vacant lot from standing height. I suppose many of the same forces come into play relatively speaking. We've banked toward what I believe is north, decelerating slightly.

>It was a good trip. Mostly what I expected. The time during travel to write and read has been a godsend. The physical distance between me and all I call my life has given perspective and meaning. The snowy cold of Maryland will contrast nicely with the warmth and sunshine of my reclaimed desert.

>I miss Marian. I miss you and Meg. I miss the comfort of those who know me best and love me anyway. Seeing my old friends created approximately the mix of emotions I expected. Even if certain circumstances and condition could be recreated out of my past like a natural habitat in a zoo, the interaction between people is always unique.

>There was communication and understanding on some levels, but not on others. Some of it flowed easily, some seemed forced. Some even feigned. But I learned more about my old friends and they heard more about me. The children were wonderful. We talked about them and work and frustra-

229

tions and church and God and divorce and marriage and five year plans.

>There is a blue lake in the mountains. It must be Big Bear. I return to people and places over and over the longer I live like a criminal returning to the scene of a crime. But every time I am different. I look at changed landscapes and older faces out of new eyes.

>It was a good trip, but I am not returning exactly as I left. I will step off the plane, find my keys, start my car from where I left it and resume following all the filaments of my life. Yet I am not the same person. The weekend has changed me. The distance, the snow, the conversation with my friends, my dreams, these words have all conspired to change me.

>I wonder if anyone will notice.

Mercy and Justice

"Anyone who is not a liberal by the age of twenty has no heart, and anyone who is not a conservative by the age of forty has no mind."

Everyone from Winston Churchill to Benjamin Disraeli, Woodrow Wilson to Wendell Willkie, George Bernard Shaw, Aristide Briand, even Otto von Bismarck have been credited with some form of this quote. Though giving the correct credit for authorship is really not the point here, the fact that this idea has been so widely expressed by so many people over such a long period of time is at least part of the point.

Obviously, the context of the quote is political, but as Kingdom is not, a deeper meaning rises as we allow it to speak directly to our attitude toward what should be the two decisive motivators of an ethical life. The Hebrew Scriptures call these two principles *mercy* and *justice*. We'd probably be closer to the concept by calling them *compassion* and justice, but in the end, they both boil down to love and fairness. The Hebrew word *hesed*, usually translated lovingkindness probably gets us closest to the tender fondness, affection, graciousness, protectiveness, and willingness to show favor that mercy and compassion imply. Justice on the other hand is a reasoned balancing of the scales, a calculated fairness, righting of wrongs, making things equal again when they have become unequal. The two principles move even farther apart when you consider that...

Compassion is not just, and justice is not compassionate.

Nor should they be. If you think of justice as getting what you deserve either positively or negatively, then mercy is *not* getting what you negatively deserve and compassion could be considered *giving* what is not positively deserved or at least earned. Mercy and compassion do not right any wrongs; they deliberately unbalance the scales of justice—they are unashamedly unfair in order to favor the object of affection. Justice, in order to be completely fair, must willfully ignore and suppress any feelings of affection or desire for mercy that may arise, like a judge who must follow the letter of the law even if it keeps her tossing and turning all night. But though mercy and justice seem diametrically opposed and separate in this way, at root, they are both manifestations of the same reign of unity, of God's love, and both are critical aspects of ethical decision-making. Knowing the difference between the two and when and where each must take precedence for the greatest good/*shalom,* are critical to making choices that create and preserve Kingdom.

To see that justice and fairness are the best any group can do for its members requires enough life experience to see a greater good beyond anecdotes of personal suffering or the excesses of specific individuals. It requires the ability to see that compassion, once institutionalized, requires machinery of government that can't be restrained—machinery that costs far too much in freedom for the security it provides because it places far too much power in the hands of the few who must control it, corrupting them. The need for authoritarian rule to maintain every socialistic and communistic government in history, along with the record of tyranny and atrocity each of these states has produced, should be proof enough, though hope eternally springs that next time will be different.

It's often pointed out that the early church was, in fact, communistic, and this is true. As in the book of Acts, members of the earliest congregations who met in their homes would place their food and revenue on the common table so that all could share equally. It was a beautiful expression of the desire-made-reality of the unity and connectedness they felt with each other. So what was the difference between the communism of the first century church and that of a state such as Russia in the twentieth century?

The obvious answer is that unlike anything produced by state control, the communism of the early church was *voluntary.* It flowed from the downside up, from the compassion and mercy of each individual who desired to place his or her income on the common table. No one was being forced from the top down to share. Even in the story of Ananias and Sapphira from Acts 5, who dropped dead after secretly withholding some of their revenue from the community, the point is not that the couple was being punished for withholding; Peter tells them they were free to keep whatever they wished. Their sin was in trying to increase their standing in the eyes of the community by pretending they had given their all, in moving back from Kingdom to *mamlacha*, to the legalistic and hypocritical pretensions of the Pharisees and Scribes. Without compassion within the heart of each individual, there could be no compassion among or in the midst of the group. This spiritual separation was what Peter could not endure, but even so, God didn't kill Ananias and Sapphira because of their sin; they were in sin, in separation because they were already spiritually dead—as good as dead to the community.

No group, not even the early church, has the capacity to be compassionate. Only the people within the group can be compassionate as they voluntarily act compassionately and lovingly, transforming life among themselves. The instant compassion becomes law, we have moved back to *mamlacha*, and have lost our Way. Compassion can't be legislated, and the very attempt to enforce the imagined results of compassion and mercy on people creates the injustice that ultimately kills the freedom and cohesion of the community.

Then what are we to do in the name of compassion? Was Robin Hood "right" in robbing the rich in order to give to the poor? Looking at his actions in isolation, arguments can be made either way, but when a system has gotten so corrupt and unjust that the people within it are suffering, a Robin Hood is often a necessary figure who brings the injustices of the group into crystal clarity and begins the process of reform. Wielded by individuals, compassion and mercy can move us in many directions, including that of civil disobedience, but to institutionalize and enforce Robin Hood's compassion from the top down only creates more injustice, not more compassion.

On the other hand, just as legislating compassion nullifies justice, imposing "zero tolerance" justice on each and every individual not only nullifies compassion, it nullifies common sense as well. This is why zero tolerance policies of any kind never work and always lead to such absurdities as the suspension of a child from school for bringing a water pistol or a plastic knife with which to spread peanut butter. Justice applied indiscriminately removes the possibility of common sense and compassion by removing the interaction of a human mind and heart, which are their only source. Compassion and common sense do not flow from law; only law flows from law. If we are to be empowered to really love our neighbors to the greatest extent possible, whether one at a time or in groups, these are bedrock concepts.

◯ ◐ ⊕ ⊕ ⊕

Moving beyond the political aspects of a discussion of mercy and justice to the spiritual issues beneath, a person who doesn't care about the inequities witnessed every day in the lives of others, especially as a young adult when idealism runs hottest, surely has no heart, no compassion. But that same person, if having lived twice as long, remains blind to the differing needs of the individual and the group, he or she has not thought things through to develop a true sense of social justice.

"You will always have the poor with you..." Matthew 26:11

"Give to Caesar that which is Caesar's..." Matthew 22:21

"Sell all you have and give to the poor..." Mark 10:21

"If anyone wants to sue you and take your shirt, let him have your coat also." Matthew 5:40

"...everyone who is angry with his brother shall be guilty before the court..." Matthew 5:22

"But I say to you, do not resist an evil person; but whoever slaps you on your right cheek, turn the other to him also." Matthew 5:39

How was it compassionate for Yeshua to off-handedly tell us that poverty will always be with us in response to his followers' lecture on the needs of the poor? How is it merciful that we should continue to pay taxes to a cruel and oppressive government? At the same time, how was it fair to tell someone to sell all he had earned just to give to the poor (who will always be with us anyway)? If you are being sued, where is the justice in being told to surrender more than is required, willingly and without complaint, to the point you have nothing left and are standing naked in public? And what kind of moral code demands judicial condemnation for simply being angry with a brother, yet turns around and says not to resist an evil person: when struck once, simply wait to be struck again?

Taken at face value, the "simple meaning" of these sayings seems to make no moral sense, defying the precepts of both justice and mercy. Again, we need new ears to hear. One of the reasons these sayings have been so difficult for us to reconcile and understand throughout all of church history, is that we seem to have forgotten something that Yeshua understood very well: that we live our lives on two levels simultaneously—the *micro* and the *macro*. The micro, dealing with the smallest or smallest number of things, and the macro, the largest or largest quantities of things, describe our lives as individuals relating to other individuals in the micro and at the same time to all the others in our community and society at once in the macro.

Is there a difference between the way we relate to a solitary person who is right in front of us and the way we relate to the entire population of any group—our family, our church, our company, our city, state, nation, world? Not to see that the answer is yes, to treat individuals in the same way we treat a group or vice versa, does great harm to both.

In the macro, compassion is not enough: justice must prevail, must be prized and sought beyond compassion and mercy in order for the group to survive. But in the micro, justice is not enough: face to face and person to person, compassion and mercy must prevail and be sought above justice in order for Kingdom to exist at all.

Since people don't and won't always act in loving ways, to maintain order, the basic mode of operation in the macro for the common good is justice—righting wrongs and making things equal. There must be a power in the macro strong enough to arbitrate disputes, judge offenders, and force all parties into submission.

But the message of Yeshua and all Scripture is that in the micro, balancing scales and giving only what is deserved or earned could never describe the love that God desires us to have for one another. As Yeshua said at Matthew 5, "For if you love those who love you, what reward do you have? Do not even the tax collectors do the same? If you greet only your brothers, what more are you doing than others?" Bright lines need to be drawn here: a group cannot be compassionate without being unjust, and an individual cannot merely be just to another individual without being unmerciful and uncompassionate.

>I am a divorced man. I am categorized by that. There is sin-
gle, married, and divorced. It shows up on tax forms and
credit applications. It is always a part of the earliest stages of
conversation and creates a certain look on people's faces and
a picture in their minds. It is a tattoo, a label of status that is
indelible, a category to live in that I can't escape. I can't check
the single box ever again. That is not accurate. I can check the
married box again at some point, but it seems that there is
only one real marriage followed by re-marriage. And that is a
category too.

>I hate divorce. As perfectly as I can do anything, I hate di-
vorce. Only God hates divorce more than I do. He is perfect;
I am not.

>What happens to my leg if it has to be amputated? It means
a lot to me as long as it's attached. I've spent years caring for
it, feeding it, exercising it, sunning it, washing it, walking on
it... But once it's lying in a stainless steel tub, what good is it to
me or anyone else? When they take it out of the room, where
does it go? Into one of those "Hazardous Medical Waste"
containers to be shipped--where? To be burned, buried,
ground up for mulch, freeze-dried for burial with the rest of
me someday?

>I've often heard that amputees can't believe their limb is really
gone at first. They can still feel it, have to see the stump. Then
spend large parts of their lives missing it, wondering where that
piece of them, that was so integral, has gone. Going to great
lengths to function as whole, but knowing they will never be
whole again. Fighting through the shock, the bitterness, the
physical therapy, fittings for prosthetics--to finally get to the
other side, of acceptance of new limitation, and of course of

new possible opportunity. But no matter how nobly or shamefully the experience is handled--the stump remains.

>Amputation cannot properly be considered a solution--or a cure. It is simply the transference from one situation or set of circumstances that is not survivable, to one that is. But survival comes at a price. Sometimes so high, some of us would not be willing to pay.

>So as I sit here with this tightness in my chest because I've had you here with me for five days and I can still see your face and feel your cheek as I said goodbye and I love you and how you came running back out of the classroom to shout goodbye Daddy across the playground at me as I was walking back to the car--I am seeing my stump.

>Divorce is no more a solution or cure than amputation. It may be necessary. It may even be justified; it may be the only survivable course, but everyone walks away with a loose sleeve or pant leg flapping. And that piece that was cut away is always just out there somewhere. The pain may go away. Acceptance can mercifully cover. Adjustments emerge.

But the absence of that piece is felt every time you try to take the next step.

☉ ☽ ⊕ ⊕ ⊕

All of Yeshua's teachings are based in the micro because Kingdom always begins in the micro, in the heart of one person at a time: inside out, downside up, backside front. Only later does Kingdom go macro when enough hearts are breaking forth. Put another way, the behavior that defines Kingdom never deals with macro issues, only micro, so to understand Yeshua's Kingdom is to understand the micro context from which it springs. And when we do, the apparent conflicts in Yeshua's teachings disappear.

When Yeshua says the poor will always be with us, he is at first making a macro statement. In the macro, within any group, there will always be those who are poor—less well off than others. No matter where or when in human history, this has been and will be true, and Yeshua is stating the obvious. But let's finish his statement at Matthew 26, "You will always have the poor with you, but you will not always have me." Yeshua shifts from the macro immediately back to the micro.

In this pericope, or little snippet of a story, Yeshua's disciples are incensed that a woman "wasted" a vial of expensive perfume by pouring it over Yeshua's head in her impulsive desire to anoint him. Their complaint was that it could have been sold and the proceeds given to the poor, but Yeshua is slapping them on the wrist, telling them they can't hide from compassion and mercy by retreating into the macro. The fact that poverty as an issue persists in the macro doesn't absolve us from acting compassionately in the micro. It's not an either/or choice that we make. Abstract macro issues like poverty will always be with us, but that's not where we live. We live our lives in the micro where the poor person in our midst *can* be fed and clothed, and a vial of perfume can complete an act of love in its wasteful extravagance. Yeshua is also telling us that no matter how hard we try, a macro issue like poverty will never be overcome *in the macro*, from the top down—but only in the micro, from the bottom up, when enough people desire to take care of each other, person to person and one on one.

The same is true when we consider Yeshua's entire statement at Matthew 22: "Give to Caesar that which is Caesar's and to God that which is God's." There is the same shift from macro immediately back to micro. In our righteous anger against the cruelty and injustice of the macro, we can't afford to lose sight of the only thing over which we really have control: our compassionate actions in the micro. If the Caesar of any age is to be brought to justice, it will only be when we are all moved to continue to give to God the things that are God's, that is, the reflection of his unity.

Conversely, the command to "Sell all you have and give to the poor" in Mark 10 is already an intensely micro injunction. Yeshua is telling one specific person who is rich and still relying on those riches for his security that he has one thing left to release before he can fully experience the freedom of Kingdom. To take that micro command and try to generalize it, to "macroize" it, is to do violence to the concept. It's not hard for a rich man to enter the Kingdom because riches themselves are evil, but because the reliance on physical wealth—whether money, beauty, talent, intellect, or power—blocks the ability to be *talya*: child and slave. Yeshua isn't saying we all need to strive to be poor, to give away all we have and lead ascetic lives as the church has often taught through the ages; it means we need to remain unattached to whatever wealth we do have, great or small, and not to let it interfere with our attitude of *talya*.

Yeshua continues to contrast the micro and macro in Matthew 5 when he says, "You have heard that the ancients were told, 'you shall not commit murder' and 'whoever commits murder shall be liable to the court.' But I say to you that everyone who is angry with his brother shall be guilty before the court; and whoever says to his brother, '*Raca*,' (worthless one) shall be guilty before the supreme court; and whoever says, 'You fool,' shall be guilty enough to go into the fiery Gehenna." This formula is used six times in the "Great Antitheses" Yeshua lays out in Matthew 5: "You have heard that the ancients were told," and he describes the macro tradition or Torah command. "But I say to you," and he describes the micro Kingdom behavior that "exceeds the righteousness of the Scribes and Phari-sees"—that which is necessary to *talya*, to Kingdom.

As long as a person hasn't physically attacked or murdered an-other, that person is safe in the macro, "innocent" in the eyes of the Law. But in the micro, in the heart of each of us, relationship has already broken down and separation has opened up the moment we become angry with another. And each escalation of that anger, from speaking it to uttering those words (like *raca*) guaranteed to incite physical violence, is a further action that destroys Kingdom...long before the Law is ever broken or invoked.

The same is true when Yeshua says, "You have heard that it was said, 'you shall not commit adultery'; but I say to you that everyone who looks at a woman with lust for her has already committed adultery with her in his heart." Physical adultery and lustful thoughts are not equivalent violations under the Law in Yeshua's thinking; he is making the same code switch between macro and micro and the same statement that once such lustful thoughts have been allowed to take root, Kingdom has already been destroyed in the marital relationship long before any physical act of unfaithfulness is committed. Stopping these separating conditions of the heart, while they are still in the heart, will restore Kingdom lost and ensure that unlawful physical acts are never committed in the first place.

And finally, "You have heard that it was said, 'An eye for an eye, and a tooth for a tooth.' But I say to you, do not resist an evil person; but whoever slaps you on your right cheek, turn the other to him also. If anyone wants to sue you and take your shirt, let him have your coat also. Whoever forces you to go one mile, go with him two." In contrast to the macro Law that demands only reciprocity, the exact paying back of whatever was taken, micro relationships demand much more in compassion and love. But once again, turning the other cheek and giving your coat as well, are micro imperatives, not meant to be generalized into the macro or self-sustaining families and groups could not exist.

Never to resist an evil person in the micro or an evil group in the macro is to become evil ourselves as we turn our backs on both justice and compassion, leaving defenseless those who are vulnerable—all for an ideal that never existed in the first place. Those who see this passage as a command to pacifism have made this very mistake. Yeshua is not calling us to absolute pacifism, the commitment never to engage in physical violence even in the defense of self or others. To be just, merciful, and compassionate, means that evil must be resisted both in the macro and the micro, at times even to the point of using lethal force.

But Yeshua's statements here move in a completely different direction, dealing with personal relationships in which we are being told not to return evil for evil in a tit-for-tat escalation of violence and hatred. The language here alludes to the Proverbs 25 image of "heaping burning coals" on the head of an enemy, a Hebraic way of saying "killing him with kindness," or destroying an enemy by turning him into a friend. Again, before the exchanges escalate, the destructive cycle can be stopped the moment one person enters Kingdom and "goes the extra mile," willingly gives more than is demanded, or turns the other cheek.

This is not the non-resistance of evil; it is the resistance of evil by disarming it with love—a resistance that is only possible in the micro relationships of our everyday lives.

⊙ ⊘ ⊕ ⊕ ⊛

As it was with the concept of Kingdom itself, it is almost impossible to over-emphasize the importance of understanding the interaction between mercy and justice, micro and macro. Not understanding that justice and mercy are both manifestations of love operating in different spheres—the tools love uses to create maximum *shalom* either within groups or between individuals—permits no end of ethical dilemmas and destroys the ability to make sound Kingdom choices in life.

The ancient Hebrews understood this intimately. Their survival as nomadic tribes depended on the macro cohesion of the tribe, the group. The individual was only as important as his or her contribution to the group's survival, so all cultural and spiritual focus was keyed to community. As modern Westerners, it's often painful to read the Hebrew bible, the Old Testament, recoiling from the wrath of an angry God or harsh, even seemingly amoral cultural practices and laws. But the Old Testament is primarily a macro account of the relationship between God and the nation of Israel; it, too, is keyed to the group where justice is essential to Israel's survival. God isn't angry, he's being viewed through the merciless lens of justice in a macro context, and every "amoral" practice of the ancient Hebrews from slavery to polygamy, wartime atrocities to sanctions against homosexuality and even infertility was aimed at procreation and group survival in a world we no longer understand.

Yeshua's genius and revolution was to begin the process of balancing spiritual relationship between macro and micro, to know God as both macro king and micro *Abba*, "daddy," into whose lap we can crawl...to begin to live our daily lives shifting seamlessly between these two great contexts in order to bring maximum *shalom* to all our relationships. The great social issues of our time or any time always straddle the micro and the macro; it's not a dualistic, either/or choice, but a unified, both/and lying at the heart of a desire for the highest good. Justice and mercy must remain on their respective thrones as long as we live between heaven and earth, and Kingdom demands that we see as much.

What Yeshua is trying to show us is that micro and macro are intertwined in such a way that they can both be successfully negotiated as a unified whole. He's trying to show us that the apparent conflict between mercy and justice and the harsh ways that individuals in groups must sometimes be treated in order to maintain the greatest *shalom* for all exist only in the *absence of Kingdom*. Once Kingdom is entered, micro and macro, mercy and justice become one—just as God is one.

In the balanced view of Yeshua, which was not new, but a "fulfillment" of the original intent of the ancient Law, the good of the individual and good of the group are not in conflict. Seeking first the Kingdom by living out mercy and compassion in the micro simultaneously fulfills the intent of the macro Law. When viewed from the inside out, downside up, and backside front, how each individual treats every other individual in the micro has everything to do with the quality of life in the macro.

When we graduate from *mamlacha* to *malkuth*, we are awarded the freedom to act without fear, to fearlessly live out our compassion and love for our neighbors without the need for a law to obey. We are also awarded the first breath of a chance to bring *shalom* to our personal relationships, which may then bring the next breath of hope that our *shalom* will break forth into our communities at large in the macro.

The hope and promise that the Kingdom within will become the Kingdom among and in our midst lay hiding in plain sight—in the space between the micro and the macro, between heaven and earth.

>Just now in the small hours it is dark. Just now in the small hours the wind is blowing. It sways in the black trees overhead; it swirls around my feet as I push stridefuls of earth behind me. Stride after stride. Street after street. Running through your darkened, concrete-covered creation.

>Only the sky is pure, untouched, untamed. Even the wind hasn't disturbed the light gauze shrouding the quartered moon and hiding the stars.

>Who is there?

>No, I run alone. Out of the depths of my aloneness. Out of the darkness and warmth of the womb. The tiny, liquid universe of which I am center. Of which I span with my arms. Of which I understand and approve and master. Through which all is supplied.

>From which I move, stride after stride. Ragged breath after ragged breath. Following the concrete rivers.

>Who is there?

>No, I run alone. Making trails into unknown places, but returning to them, making familiar places. Returning again and again, making rutted places. Tiny places of which I understand. Of which I am center.

>In which I am alone. Warm, comfortable, safe, supplied. Alone. Dark. The womb is alone. The womb is safe. Alone is the price of the womb. The price of safety.

>Who is there?

>No, I run alone. As long as I span the walls of my safety, there is no room for another. I run alone. In the tiny place.

245

The place I understand. The place I define with the length of my arms and defines me and fixes me in manageable space.

>How frightening not to touch the walls of my place. To reach out and find no boundaries. To run into void of unknown proportions. To sense bigness. To draw my own ragged breath in uncertainty. To search for center and not find it. To run. And run. And run. To run down.

>Who is there?

>Together is risk. Together is vulnerable. Together is uncertain. Together is big. Together is unmanageable. Together is unknown. Together is unfamiliar. Together is off-center. Together is not alone.

>Alone is womb. Alone is safe.
Together is better
Who is there?
May I run with you?

Law and Effect

By this point, it may seem fair to assume that Kingdom exists in the micro to foster compassion and mercy, while the Law is an instrument of the macro to ensure justice. In reality, the relationship between Kingdom and Law is not so dualistic or bi-polar...it's much more connected and beautiful.

Far from being separate forces working in different spheres, or a succession of forces, one superseding the other, Kingdom and Torah/Law are really exactly the same thing as viewed from opposite sides of the micro/macro divide. Law begins its work in the macro and filters into the micro, into the lives of the individuals under the Law, and Kingdom begins in the micro, in the heart of each individual and then breaks forth into the macro. Or alternately, Law and Kingdom can be viewed simply as a cause and its effect. Looked at this way, Kingdom does not supersede Torah/Law—Law is the cause and Kingdom is its effect...but then in the same way, the effect of Kingdom is to fulfill the Law, to make our lives look like Law, but without the need for obedience.

It's a complete circle. God's deepest purpose and desire, his pleasure and delight, is distilled down into the behavioral code of the Law, as *mamlacha*, a dictatorial macro rule for the people to obey. But Law only becomes fulfilled as it becomes Kingdom, *malkuth*, in those individuals who find their Way to write the Law on their hearts—to desire exactly what God desires. Then as Kingdom/malkuth breaks forth from those transformed hearts in the micro, it expands outward, ultimately fulfilling Law in the macro community, making obedience obsolete by turning *mamlacha* back into *malkuth*, the pleasure and purpose of God from whom it came.

Now we can understand why Yeshua said in Matthew 5 that his mission was not to abolish the Law, but to fulfill it. He was trying to bring the people back into an understanding of this relationship between Kingdom and Law, which is why he says in the next verse that until heaven and earth disappear, not even the smallest part of the Law will disappear without being fulfilled. So the Law stands firm to this day. But what is it that is actually standing?

From a macro viewpoint, Law looks like an absolute code of conduct to be obeyed on pain of punishment, but looking through Kingdom, Law's effect and result, it is a gentle hand on our shoulder, guiding and protecting along the Way. The Hebrew word *Torah*, which was translated into the Greek as *nomos* (custom, law, convention) and then into English as *law*, really means instruction, guidance, or teaching. It is really the teaching or guidance of Moses, and not "law" as an absolute instrument. In its original conception, Torah was a picture of what the relationship between God and human and between human and human was supposed to look like.

The Law is an image of the finished product—what our Kingdom lives should look like—and a Way to the finished product at the same time.

Think of Torah/Law as a mold into which you pour liquid jello. If you leave the jello in the mold long enough, you can eventually pull the mold away and the jello stands on its own, looking just like the mold into which it was poured—but in reverse. The mold is necessarily the negative or inversion of the final image we want to create, and so also is the Law. Though the Law may look and feel like a negative force in our lives, it's really just the mirror image or inverse of Kingdom. Where the Law uncomfortably or painfully intrudes and restricts, poking and pushing into our lives, surrounding areas later become corresponding extensions of ourselves, flowing outward to touch others in Kingdom. To the ancient Jews, Torah was the mold into which we pour ourselves and our lives. If we stay in the mold long enough, if we are faithful to its precepts, it can eventually be pulled away, and our lives will retain its shape. We will look just like Torah, the positive image of Torah fulfilled—Torah will remain written on our hearts.

In the Ray Bradbury novel Fahrenheit 451, books and critical thinking have been outlawed by an Orwellian government, but a group of people who love the great books humankind has produced refuses to be daunted. As the government's "firemen" relentlessly burn any books they can find, these people retreat to the wilderness, each one *becoming* a book of their choice, forgetting their former selves and even their own names as they take the name of their book, memorizing it by constantly reciting it over and over, teaching it to a child who will become that book in the next generation.

Becoming the book, becoming the Law—this is what the Scripture means at Deuteronomy 6: "Hear, O Israel! The Lord is our God, the Lord is one! You shall love the Lord your God with all your heart and with all your soul and with all your might. These words, which I am commanding you today, shall be on your heart. You shall teach them diligently to your sons and shall talk of them when you sit in your house and when you walk by the way and when you lie down and when you rise up. You shall bind them as a sign on your hand and they shall be as frontals on your forehead. You shall write them on the doorposts of your house and on your gates."

In molding the people, Torah regulated every aspect of Hebrew life. From the moment the people arose in the morning to the moment they lay down at night, almost every moment in between contained a command: what they wore, what they ate, how they prepared what they ate, how they fashioned the objects of worship, when and how they worshipped, how they related to each other, when they prayed, and how they prayed—the very tassels on their prayer shawls were knotted to match the numerical equivalents of the letters of the name of God. A contemporary Jew says that even today there is a morning prayer of thanksgiving to God for returning their souls to them for another day; there are prayers before enjoying material pleasures such as eating or wearing new clothes; prayers before performing ritual functions such as lighting candles or washing hands; prayers to recite upon seeing anything unusual like a king, a rainbow, or a great tragedy; prayers to say whenever something good or bad happens and before bed at night—all in addition to regularly scheduled prayers three times a day and those said at synagogue.

In short, without too much exaggeration, an observant Jew in the first century couldn't walk ten steps without being reminded of his or her standing under Torah. This sounds burdensome and oppressive to our ears, but really it is just the same as the New Testament injunction to "pray without ceasing." To be constantly reminded of God's presence in every moment of every day in every possible setting and activity is the very definition of unceasing prayer. The intent of Torah, of the Law, was not to "save" as we think of that term, but to make the presence of God as real as any other aspect of life. The Hebrews called it *"shekinah,"* dwelling, inhabiting, settling: the actual, felt, even visible presence of God.

It's beginning to look a lot like Kingdom...but...

As with all things that must be tasted to be seen, the original intent and understanding of Law was not transferred from generation to generation. Even in very ancient times, Hebrews interpreting Deuteronomy 6, "You shall bind them (God's commandments) as a sign on your hand and they shall be as frontals on your forehead. You shall write them on the doorposts of your house and on your gates," drifted into literalism and began actually writing passages from the Law on doorposts and gates and physically wearing phylacteries, leather boxes containing verses of Torah strapped to their foreheads and forearms. While this may have begun as a physical reminder of a spiritual truth, in time it became merely a new law to obey, a superstition even, all while God was just looking for his people to simply have every thought and action joyfully governed by the shape of Torah in their hearts.

The original intent of Law was simple. But Torah, as do all foundational documents that initially spell out the ways in which a people intend to live together, grew longer and more complicated over time. The Constitution of the United States is a perfect example of this phenomenon. The Constitution itself spells out the shape, extent, and restrictions of the federal government in just a few paragraphs, but almost immediately upon its ratification, ten amendments, the Bill of Rights, were added to further restrict federal powers. Over two hundred years later, there are now twenty seven amendments to the Constitution, but more importantly and tellingly, since the Constitution was only a framework and dealt with the law of the land in general terms, every specific instance where the law was applied had to first be interpreted by the judicial branch of the government. This process of interpretation and application of the original law has resulted in tens of thousands of new laws and millions of lines of legal code, where the original Constitution totaled only a little more than four thousand words.

Rabbinic literature describes an identical process as the Pharisees took upon themselves the legal role of interpretation and application of Torah. They were so fastidious, cautious, and determined not to break any of the commands of Torah that they created new sets of laws called "fences" or "hedges" of protection around each Law. As Ron Moseley writes in his book *Yeshua*, "The Pharisees counted six hundred and thirteen Laws in the Torah, consisting of two hundred and forty-eight commands to action and three hundred and sixty-five prohibitions. To make sure they did not break even one of these by accident or ignorance, they created a 'hedge' around the Laws. Theses hedges are called 'traditions' in the New Testament. The idea was to establish enough traditions around the Law that an individual would have to break a tradition before he could go all the way to breaking an explicit provision of the Law."

But over time, these fences, usually referred to as the Oral Tradition, became as important to the Pharisees as Torah itself, and in some cases actually *superceded* the written Law. As the influence and power of the Pharisees increased, their traditions became binding on the people as they pronounced a person's righteousness before God as the measure of his or her compliance with both Torah and their Oral Tradition, the fences. The people became incredibly burdened with hundreds upon hundreds of additional regulations that they were expected to follow to prove their righteousness in the macro eyes of the community. Yeshua's most pitched battles were those he waged against the legalism of the Pharisees and Scribes as he worked hard to redefine Torah back to its original form and intent. Though there were many points of Law on which he and the Pharisees sparred, the Sabbath, the seventh day of rest and dedication to God became a perfect focus for Yeshua to make his point.

The fourth of the Ten Commandments in Exodus 20 states: "Remember the sabbath day, to keep it holy. Six days you shall labor and do all your work, but the seventh day is a sabbath of the Lord your God; in it you shall not do any work, you or your son or your daughter, your male or your female servant or your cattle or your sojourner who stays with you. For in six days the Lord made the heavens and the earth, the sea and all that is in them, and rested on the seventh day; therefore the Lord blessed the sabbath day and made it holy."

This commandment is echoed at other places in Torah with some further detail such as at Exodus 35:2-3, "For six days work may be done, but on the seventh day you shall have a holy day, a sabbath of complete rest to the Lord; whoever does any work on it shall be put to death. You shall not kindle a fire in any of your dwellings on the sabbath day." So now we also know that kindling a fire is included under "servile work" that must not be done on the Sabbath, and we know that death was the official punishment for violation, though it was rarely carried out even in ancient times.

When it comes right down to it, what constitutes "work?" Can I take a walk without breaking a Sabbath? Can my children play, can we prepare a meal (without a fire) or, what if the fire is still burning from the day before, can I use it? Can I read, carry a book from shelf to chair, can I write? Can I deal with an emergency such as a broken bone or a hole in the roof? Can I care for my sick child? Once the letter of the Law has been separated from the spirit or intent of the Law, there is no end to the legal questions and permutations and interpretations that arise. The intent of the Sabbath Law was simple: to provide a time of rest and refreshment, of rededication to God and his purpose. The application of the letter of the Law became a nightmare as Rabbis of the Pharisaic tradition labored to define just what "servile work" entailed. The Rabbis eventually delineated thirty-nine hedges around the Sabbath Law, thirty-nine categories of activities that would be prohibited on *Shabbat*, the Sabbath.

These thirty-nine categories prohibited work that was either creative or exercised dominion over the environment and were loosely divided into four groups: activities required to make bread such as sowing, plowing, reaping, threshing, winnowing, grinding, sifting, kneading, baking; activies required to make a garment such as shearing, washing, beating, dyeing, spinning, weaving (two or more loops or threads), tying, untying, stitching, tearing; activities required to make leather—trapping, slaughtering, flaying, tanning, scraping, cutting, marking (writing or erasing two or more letters); and activities required to build a house—building, demolishing, kindling or extinguishing fire, finishing, transporting objects more than four cubits (a few feet).

But as restrictive as these thirty-nine may be, they were only *categories* of activities, each containing many more activities within them. So within each category of work, or *melachah*, there were direct derivative activites called *toledoth* that carried nearly the same legal severity as the original *melachah*. Then there were also indirect derivative activities called *shevuth* that carried much less severe punishments if violated. In this way "baking" as *melachah*, carried within it the prohibitions against cooking, poaching, and roasting— all *toledoth* under baking. Even if you weren't making bread, there wasn't much else you could do in the kitchen either on Sabbath, so meals needed to be prepared the day before. And since "winnowing" as *melachah* referred to separating chaff from grain, or making something edible which was previously inedible, it was also unlawful to filter undrinkable water to make it drinkable or to pick small bones from fish. From one commandment to thirty-nine *melachah* to dozens of *toledoth* and dozens more *shevuth*, restrictions exponentially grew. And keeping in mind that the Sabbath commandment was only one of six hundred and thirteen Laws the Rabbis recognized, starts to bring the incredibly vast scope of the Oral Tradition into view.

By the time of Yeshua, the people were heavily burdened with all this, with a system they couldn't possibly keep straight in their minds let alone live with any refreshment—a system that kept them running back to the authority of the Pharisees and Scribes for ongoing legal clarification, permission, and *validation* of their own righteousness before God, which was the source of the Pharisees' power in the first place. The Pharisees had created a new legal system on top of Torah the way one would create a new card game using the original deck of playing cards. Though the cards themselves were familiar to the people, the rules and intent of the game were solely arbitrated by these Rabbis who literally held all the cards and so also controlled the people's access to God—their acceptability to God and each other in the eyes of the community.

How much more sense does Yeshua's attitude and words now make in Matthew 23 as he rails against the Pharisees? "They tie up heavy burdens and lay them on men's shoulders, but they themselves are unwilling to move them with so much as a finger. But they do all their deeds to be noticed by men; for they broaden their phylacteries and lengthen the tassels of their garments. They love the place of honor at banquets and the chief seats in the synagogues, and respectful greetings in the market places, and being called Rabbi by men...But woe to you, scribes and Pharisees, hypocrites, because you shut off the Kingdom of Heaven from people; for you do not enter in yourselves, nor do you allow those who are entering to go in."

Is it any wonder that Yeshua was incensed as he watched his Father's love and presence become inaccessible to the people, dammed behind an incomprehensible wall of rules? What had begun with the Pharisees as a sincere effort to more perfectly follow the Way to Kingdom, had become its single greatest impediment. The righteousness of the Scribes and Pharisees, the Oral Tradition they created, formed a barrier to Kingdom as impregnable as the firmness of a person's belief that it was the Way itself. The Oral Tradition, as an expression of the Pharisees' second way of manipulation, could never lead to Kingdom; that wall had to come down, and Yeshua drew his lines sharply.

>Storm has been coming for two days.
Right on schedule, storm is here.

>Not much of a storm right now, just a gentle rain in the gray
outside my half-opened window. The rain is hard enough to
make continuous sound, but still light enough to hear individual drops. As I listen I can hear where they are falling: on concrete or the wide leaves of shrubbery, on the steel drums of
the barbecue pits. I can hear where they are in space: some
close, others falling into the middle distance of the courtyard,
others much softer, blending into delicate white noise several
hundred feet away. Little drops have made it through the
maze of barren branches to directly hit their targets; other,
larger drops have collected on branches or rain gutters and
hit with a heavier splat.

>It all makes a beautifully spacious music. I can't tell you how
pleasing it is to sit here in natural light and just be here sitting
in natural light. Sitting. Listening. Trying to write, but drifting
back off into the rain.

>This storm has been coming for two days. I heard about it
Saturday morning. After the rain Friday the air was clean and
the patches of sky between the high, shifting cumulus
formations were very blue. The way it only is here after rain.
Immediately after. And I thought about this storm still
hundreds of miles out to sea, squalling uselessly over the face
of the water, unheeded except by satellites passing overhead
and occasional ships underneath. After all, the fish couldn't
get any wetter.

>It has been coming all this time. While I had lunch and read.
While I came home and worked at the computer until 11:30.
While I was running yesterday morning before church. While
my pastor thundered his sermon. While I bought a friend a

birthday present and then worked again at the computer until it was time to go to the birthday dinner.

>And sometime while I slept, it arrived. The leading edges of the cloud system looked blindly down as the monotonous face of the water gave way to white diagonal lines of breakers dissipating against the sand and then to the strip of coastal highway beyond the sand and the six, short miles of rooftops and parking lots until it looked down and did not see the little, wooded courtyard outside my window.

>Sometime while I slept the wind picked up a bit. Sometime while I slept the first drops began to fall.

>All this without my knowledge or permission or volition. While I lived my last two days. While I slept. I simply wake up to the gift of this beautiful sound. To an hour of precious solitude with my window and my Lord and these words--that you had no idea were being written for you, while you lived your life and slept, and that have been on their way to you ever since; until the pages were placed in your hands to sit on your shelf; until you first cracked the cover and waded through page after page until you came to this very word.

>And then moved on.

>I am told the storm will last until tomorrow. Then we will have another clean, blue day. Eventually we will have another storm. I don't know when. I am glad not to know such things. To wake up and find that storms need nothing from me, but graciously include me in all they have to give.

>Eventually we will have another storm. I will try to spend some time with it also.

① ⑪ ⊕ ⊕ ⊛

From all the evidence we have, Yeshua followed Torah as precisely as any Pharisee. The fact that the Pharisees conversed with him at all, came to question him about his teachings, tells us all we need to know about Yeshua's firm observance of Torah Law. Pharisees would have had nothing to do with him otherwise; their policy was one of strict separation from anyone or anything they considered unclean. Some scholars even believe that Yeshua was actually a Pharisee himself, as there is much evidence in his teachings and life that he was very close to Rabbinical thought and practice. But even if Yeshua wasn't a Pharisee himself, he was widely called "Rabbi" by both Pharisees and other religious authorities and by the people—a title that would never have been bestowed to *am ha'eretz*, a person "of the land" who didn't follow Torah.

But Yeshua wasn't in the business of merely following Law, his mission was to fulfill it. And that meant entering Kingdom, which meant moving from the Four Ways to the Fifth Way, from *mamlacha* to *malkuth*. Though Yeshua didn't break the Law, he routinely went out of his way to break the Oral Tradition, and Sabbath was a case in point. The highest purpose of Law is to preserve life—all Jews, especially those as schooled as were the Pharisees, knew this. The Sabbath command to refrain from work flowed out of this highest purpose: to rest, refresh, restore, renew, and rededicate as essential to the preservation of life. Yeshua recognized that fulfilling the intent of Law was not so much based on what we don't do, the negative restrictions of Law, but on what positive actions we do take in the name of Kingdom. So deliberately, Yeshua never missed an opportunity to act, whether on Sabbath or any other day of the week, to restore and renew any life with which he came in contact.

One Sabbath in Matthew 22, Yeshua and his friends are walking through a grainfield. The men are hungry and as they walk are plucking heads of grain, rubbing off the chaff, and eating. This was allowed under Law even in another's field in Deuteronomy 23 as long as no sickle was used for harvesting greater quantities than could be consumed on the spot. But the Pharisees immediately object asking Yeshua why he allows this unlawful activity to take place among his followers. It's interesting to note how the Pharisees manage to be present in such unlikely places as grainfields to challenge Yeshua. One commentator has written that they always seem to be "popping up" around Yeshua in the Gospels like characters in a Broadway musical about to burst into song. The obvious answer, though, is that they also were following Yeshua, at least for a time, to better understand his teaching and ways—another reminder of Yeshua's orthodoxy under Law. In this case, Yeshua's followers had not broken Torah, but by rubbing the chaff off the head of the grain, by making something edible that was previously inedible, they had broken the Tradition, the *melachah*, of winnowing.

Yeshua reminds the Pharisees of the Scriptures that record how David and his men broke the Law and ate sacred bread that only the priests were to eat in order to preserve their lives when they were starving. He reminds them of how Torah allows the Temple priests to bake such bread on the Sabbath in order to serve the needs of the Temple, and that something greater than the Temple was present to be served—the preservation of all life. He quotes the voice of God from 1 Samuel and other prophets in the Scriptures: "I desire compassion and not sacrifice," and in the parallel passage in Mark 2, he says, "The Sabbath was made for man and not man for the Sabbath." The people were not to be broken over the very Law that was intended to refresh them and preserve their lives. Yeshua couldn't be clearer in showing that *in order to fulfill the intent of the Law, sometimes the letter of the Law must be broken.*

From the grainfields, Yeshua goes into the local synagogue and there meets a man with a withered hand. The Pharisees, still prodding, ask him pointedly whether it is permissible to heal on the Sabbath. Yeshua points out that the Law allowed pulling an animal out of a pit on Sabbath to save its life, and how much more valuable is a person than an animal? It is always lawful to do good on the Sabbath he proclaims, and with a word, heals the man's hand, earning himself the unbridled enmity of the Pharisees. The interesting part of this pericope is that Yeshua still did not break the Law. Healing with only a word did not constitute work under Torah, and healing to preserve life was not only allowed, but a duty at any time. But under the Oral Tradition, caring for the seriously ill was permitted only within certain limitations, and treating minor ailments was prohibited as it usually required certain activities that constituted work, such as grinding medications. In the Rabbis' own words as written in the *Mishna*, the first recording of the Oral Tradition, "They may not set a fracture (on Sabbath). If someone's hand or foot is dislocated, he may not pour cold water over it; but may wash it in the usual way, and if it heals, it heals." In other words, healing of non-life-threatening conditions was only permitted as a byproduct of other permissible activity. Healed directly by Yeshua's word, technically no "work" was performed, but as the shriveled hand was not life-threatening, to the Pharisees the healing was unlawful.

But Yeshua wasn't finished yet. On another Sabbath, he heals an infirm man who was lying by the pool of Bethesda in John 5 with just the words, "Get up, pick up your pallet, and walk." Here again, the healing wasn't necessarily of a life-threatening condition as the passage tells us the man had been ill for thirty-eight years and presumably could have lasted one more day. But possibly to make the point unmistakable, Yeshua not only tells the man to get up, but to pick up his pallet and walk. As the Pharisees are quick to point out, this breaks the *melachah* of transporting anything more than four cubits through a public place.

And if that wasn't specific enough, Yeshua does a fascinating thing in John 9 as he heals a blind man on Sabbath. Instead of merely healing with a word, he spits on the ground, mixes up a mud paste, and applies it to the man's eyes, telling him to go wash in the pool of Siloam. There have been many explanations in Scriptural commentaries as to why Yeshua would heal in this unusual way, but the obvious answer once again is that by making the mud paste, Yeshua was directly breaking the *melachah* against both building and kneading on Sabbath, going out of his way to make his point. Regardless of what Traditions may stand in the way, what could possibly be more refreshing, renewing, and restorative than for someone who was blind from birth to receive the gift of sight: to suddenly have light and color and full engagement in the rhythms of community life where there previously were none? There could be no more perfect fulfilling of the Sabbath commandment than this, and Yeshua knows it and literally rubs it into the face of the blind man and through him into the consciousness of anyone with ears to hear.

$$\odot \; \oslash \; \oplus \; \oplus \; \oplus$$

The Law without a human heart desiring the presence and purpose of God's love is as useless as a musical instrument without a skilled player's fingers. It could serve as a paperweight or a doorstop, but nothing even closely resembling the beauty of its original purpose.

The Law was never intended to "save" in our current theological sense of that word. Far from being the bar we must pass or standard we must attain before gaining God's acceptance, it is actually God's steadying hand on our backs, his training wheels on our bikes as we make our first trembling pushes out along the Way. From the top down and the outside in, there is no force in heaven or on earth that can help us or force us along the Fifth Way. All a legal code and its subsequent fear of punishment can do is force us to *conform*—it can never *transform*. Conformance comes from the top down and the outside in, but transformation only comes from the inside out and the downside up.

There's a wonderful story my pastor used to tell of his youngest daughter who, at a young age, was always standing up at the dinner table. After several escalating rounds of correction one night with the whole family around the table, she finally sat down, but announced darkly, "I may be sitting down on the outside, but on the inside I'm standing up."

And so it is with all of us. No matter how much we sit in conformance with outside pressures, the heart remains standing in interior defiance. Only a process beginning in the heart itself creates a "sitting down" that is true. Yeshua said at Mark 7 that it's not what goes into a man that defiles him, but what come out of his heart—therefore all foods are clean...an incredibly shocking point to make to Jews, but one that Yeshua made over and over.

Yeshua reinterpreted the Law throughout his ministry in five major ways: 1) that the Oral Tradition did not have the force of Torah; 2) that keeping the Law involved fulfilling the purpose of the Law and not just keeping the rules; 3) that obedience and disobedience are inward and not outward functions; 4) that outward forms and rituals mean nothing if the heart is not right; and 5) that Law is the expression of God's desire and purpose, and not just a code of conduct. From Matthew 5, "...if you are presenting your offering at the altar, and there remember that your brother has something against you, leave your offering there before the altar and go; first be reconciled to your brother, and then come and present your offering." The purpose of Law is to preserve life and transform it by creating more perfect relationships through which we can see the face of God. If the desire to do everything it takes to have those intimate relationships is not in our hearts in the first place, no amount of form, ritual, or conformance will put it there.

If there's any lurking illusion that the absurdly complex system of hedges and fences around the Law died with the ancient world, think again. The Pharisees are alive and well among us, and we are them. The Pharisees' first mistake was to legalize the Law, to begin to believe that the mere following of laws brought righteousness, and the more perfect the following the more perfect the righteousness. Their second mistake was to write more laws.

There's an old joke: "Why don't Baptists allow premarital sex? Because it leads to dancing."

Where is it written thou shalt not dance, drink, or smoke? Well, there certainly are injunctions in the New Testament against fornication and drunkenness, so as a hedge around those laws, it's just best not to do any activity or go to any establishment that may lead to that type of behavior. Makes perfect sense, but what happens when the hedge becomes as or more important than the law it was meant to protect? How are smokers treated in our churches today? Typically as something akin to a leper. How is social drinking tolerated in our churches? We don't even use wine with the bread at communion in Protestant circles, but substitute grape juice in order to avoid alcohol. Recently the decision to have a Valentine's Day dance at a local church caused enough controversy for some members to leave the church permanently.

Shortly after the Protestant Reformation began in the 16th century, people were actually tortured and killed by both Catholics and Protestants over the traditional issue of whether infants should be baptized and whether adults, baptized as infants, needed to be rebaptized in order to be saved. Ironically, King Ferdinand of Austria declared that execution by drowning, the "third baptism," was the best antidote to the "rebaptizers."

After Vatican II in the mid-1960s, many Catholics were disoriented and incensed that their traditions had been suddenly swept aside: the mass in Latin, the altar facing away from the people, no more fish on Fridays...when someone has eaten fish on Fridays an entire lifetime because of a law that said he or she could not eat meat, make sure you stand back before you tell them to never mind, it's alright now...

As she angrily left a Sunday service, one elderly woman guaranteed me over her shoulder that there will be no electric guitars in heaven—and churches have fractured or actually split over the type of musical instruments used in the worship service, or the style of music played, or dress, or hairstyles, or any number of cultural traditions.

Left to our own devices, we will always regress back to legalism: from the Fifth Way back to the first four, from *malkuth* back to *mamlachah*, from Kingdom back to mere obedience. It's basic human nature to see the world in two dimensions, from a flat, four-ways perspective only...to long for the false security of the thick walls of a code that "saves" vicariously and without risk. Yeshua is calling us to engage fully and look at the world and our lives from another dimension, to say as he did, that we are not here to either abolish the Law or merely keep it, but to fulfill its deepest purpose—a purpose that can be summarized by simply loving God with our whole heart, mind, and strength, and our neighbor as ourselves. Such a purpose has no kinship with a mindless following of rules motivated either by an imagined quid pro quo arrangement with God for eventual personal gain or by a continual fear of punishment. Such a purpose is perfectly liberated and free, which means it is uncharted, untamed, undiscovered, and therefore feels unsecured and risky. But it is also centered in God's love, so all risk is ultimately removed.

Torah/Law is the beautiful picture of who we really are—as God sees us, as we will become as we begin to choose relationship and enter Kingdom, as we begin to become characterized by Kingdom through the daily practice of the presence of God in our lives.

It's all here right now in Yeshua's message and vision for our abundant lives. Understanding what Yeshua meant by Kingdom and Law will clear much of the narrow path of the Way for us. And along the Way, we'll get a better view of the Father's perfect love that will keep chipping away at what's left of our fears and allow us to really begin to enjoy the ride.

>I have begun working with a client, a psychologist, who is very Eastern in her thought and spirituality. She comes at a time in my life as I grow more dissatisfied with the practice of Christianity--with the way it is practiced here in Orange County, in California. With the close-mindedness, legalism, contradictions, hypocrisies, absurdities.

>She comes at a time when Merton and Augustine have been breaking open great airy places in my heart. Places where I've come to realize that although the words are clear, who you are, Lord, is not. Who are you really? The I Am. What does that mean? The eternal, self-existence. What is that? There are no words for you. There aren't even any thoughts for you that can be entertained directly in our minds.

>We can't look you in the face. We approach obliquely. We know you only through the glass darkly. I know why most Christians, most people, stop at such a superficial level. How do you deal with that which is beneath language? Beneath rational thought? Outside of physics? The Word is clear--stick to that, order your life around it. Cling to the salvation promise by clinging to the letter of the Word thereby circumventing any deeper questions.

>And none of this is wrong, unless it leads to self-righteousness, but it is incomplete. How complete can our relationship with you be in this life, Lord? I don't know, but certainly more than I generally see around me. Again I see that you are nothing I have imagined, nothing I can imagine. But I have to keep trying to understand.

>This woman comes to me at this time of questioning, when I am pulling on myself in the midst of turmoil, and says that Christianity won't be able to contain me very long, that I will advance beyond it. And I ask rhetorically how Christianity is

being defined. Because I've already outgrown--or better, moved past--the superficiality that abounds in media and literature as the fullest expression of my personal faith. Catholicism, stripped of its government and catechism, beckons with its deep and ancient mystical roots; Zen beckons as a pure attempt to approach truth by eliminating all that is untrue.

>And flailing away at all this, I've been steadily giving ground until I am backed flat against the wall of my absolutes. But with these words, questions, I feel that wall giving way also, opening me up to 360° of confrontation, or freedom. What do I believe? Who do I believe, right now, that you are, Lord?

>In the absence of full understanding, I have to take a stand. I must have a point from which to strike out into deeper relationship.

>I believe you are love, Father. I believe you when you said you'd never leave or forsake. I drive a stake in the ground at the point of your love. Your love that can't be altered or attenuated by you or anything I or anyone else can do or fail to do. And revolving around that stake like an orbit of ever widening circles, I'll interpret everything I encounter in the light of your love and not the other way around. Whether considering your Word, the Scriptures that comprise our Bible, a personal tragedy, the world's cruelty, or a friend's requests, I'll negotiate as best I can with one hand grasping that stake. To let go of your love as the center of all gravity is to hopelessly lose my Way.

>This is a stand I can take, and from it flows a direction, a walk. I still don't know who you are, Lord. You are a moving target. Full of surprises. Your revelations come from the most unexpected places. Your truth permeates all corners of the universe, all walks of life, all philosophies, religions, codes.

>But it is here I find you most fully, with my back against the solidity of your promise. In my weakness, I pray for your indulgence and guidance. And I pray you will never allow me to become so lazy, comfortable, smug, or complacent as to

fail to recognize your truth wherever I find it. Or to tear away at the structures I have built in my mind and life when it becomes obvious they can no longer contain the God you have revealed yourself to be.

Good and Evil

It's not hard to imagine Yeshua as a small boy spending uncounted hours in his father's carpentry shop watching and helping and eventually working there himself, possibly taking over his father's business before he set off on business of his own. See his little form perched safely out of harm's way as he watches the raw lumber come in and the slow, painstaking, even organic transformation taking place before his eyes with only the roughest of hand tools being applied. See his smiles as he begins to understand his father's patient intent—parts of living trees becoming fine and finished additions to the homes of his friends and neighbors. The process is not quick, and each piece is a custom original, lovingly and skillfully coaxed out of the heart of the wood.

Yeshua was no son of a fast-paced, urban merchant, but of a rural craftsman embedded in the rhythms of agrarian life in the Galilee. These rhythms, this submission to and participation in the natural cycles of life all around became part of Yeshua's vocabulary, a storehouse of images and stories on which he called to communicate word of his Kingdom.

These are the images that abound for us in the Gospels: ordinary stories of ordinary people doing ordinary things. Yeshua speaks of widows and farmers and vineyards and wedding celebrations, of fisherman and servants, tax gatherers and sometimes kings, but always within the course of daily life that everyone recognized and experienced.

The people of the first century Galilee, just like people today living in agrarian and subsistence cultures, were intimately connected with the rhythms of nature, of the turning of the globe, night and day, the circuit of the moon through its phases, the slow progression of the seasons, the movement of wind and weather and wildlife. They lived close to the earth; they could hear its heartbeat and depended on its pulse for their very lives. To be in harmony with the land's rhythm was certainly "good;" it was critical to maintaining their lives: when to sow, when to reap, when to go out on the water, when to come in. A good crop was a ripe crop, white and ready for harvest, one that had been planted and carefully tended completely in harmony with the seasons and the land. To be outside such harmony was not only "bad," it could be disastrous when the success of a single crop could mean the difference between life and death.

Yeshua tells the story of a farmer sowing seeds that fall on good soil and bad, on rocks and the beaten path. Though the deeper spiritual meaning of his parable had to be explained, everyone immediately and intimately understood the implications of seed being planted in the wrong place, at the wrong time, and of plants dying off before becoming mature and ripe and ready.

We as modern, industrial people don't understand this anymore. We can spend years of our lives completely isolated from the rhythms of nature, in hermetically sealed, air-conditioned cars and houses, never seeing a sunrise or sunset, our bare feet never really touching the earth—even electrically isolated from the ground by rubber-soled shoes. We no longer see the quality of our lives being intimately tied to and dependent upon moving in step with the beat of the earth's heart, so our understanding of "good" and "evil" are no longer based in concepts of harmony and timeliness. These words mean something else entirely, something as completely isolated from the rhythms of nature as we ourselves have become.

For us, good and evil are moral terms dealing with the quality of interactions and behavior in human affairs or qualities that meet or fail to meet certain moral or legal standards. They are terms that describe the intrinsic nature of a person as viewed against those standards by which that person is judged acceptable, appropriate, desirable—or not.

Languages reflect the cultures that create them, and so for us in the West as the children of Greek philosophy and Roman law, good and evil are, at root, legal terms. We judge everything around us and each other according to the standards of law—and consequently we feel judged ourselves according to those same standards. When Yeshua said in Matthew 7, "Judge not, lest you be judged," he was saying exactly that—not that God would someday judge us in retaliation for judging others today, but that, "...in the way you judge, you will be judged; and by your standard of measure, it will be measured to you." If we judge another according to some standard in our minds, we have *already judged* ourselves. God has nothing to do with it.

The reality we believe is the reality we endure.

Whatever standards we apply as we judge another person's acceptability have already formed the walls of our own prison, our worldview. Those standards have become the way we see the reality of our lives, so before the first judgment of another ever enters our minds or escapes our lips, that judgment has already been applied to us. We carry the weight of that judgment ourselves long before we burden anyone else with it, and because we carry that weight, it's almost impossible for us to see God's unconditional love through the legal conditions we have already placed on ourselves.

We see good and evil through our typically dualistic eyes: as polar opposites, diametrically opposed forces with nothing in common. In the same way that we see light and dark—which we actually use as metaphors for good and evil—one is acceptable and the other is not with a great gulf in between. But remembering that in the Aramaic Agreement, light and dark, *nuhra* and *hoshech*, are not opposing forces but a continuum of necessary and complementary energies or phases of life gives us a clue to an utterly different Aramaic view of good and evil as well.

In Aramaic, the word *taba*, usually translated as "good," literally means at its roots, "ripe," the highest good a people close to the earth could imagine. Ripe fruit and crops have the power to preserve life, so if something was good, it was ripe; if it was ripe, it was good. Like the intent of Law itself, preserving life was good, so anything that preserved life was good also. When Yeshua said *taba*, good, he meant ripe, ready, mature, at the right place and the right time, in harmony with and capable of flowing seamlessly with everyone and everything. And so then, the opposite of all this, *bisha*, is unripe, not ready, immature, out of harmony and rhythm. In Hebrew also, the words for good and evil, *tov* and *ra*, respectively have analogously been translated by one scholar as "functional" and "dysfunctional," which fits very well with this Semitic mindset.

Let the significance of these words wash over you for a moment and really sink in.

When we think of being a good person, we think of someone who does "good" things, "right" things according to our standards. But a good person in the Aramaic Agreement is not someone who simply does right things, but someone who is ripe, ready, and capable of *seeing the goodness* of true relationship, the goodness of really being as one with someone else, in unity with God and each other. As a result, a good person is someone who will do everything and anything in his or her power to foster and protect that unity and those relationships. If this seems a subtle difference, look deeper; it makes all the difference in the world.

Being "good" is not about behavior, about following codes or rules; it's not even about having a standard by which to judge at all. Being good is having matured into a person who is in love with unity, who loves being one with someone else and lives accordingly. It's *mamlacha* and *malkuth* all over again, the same concept reinforcing itself. A good person is someone who is in the right place at the right time and can't help doing that which is in harmony with Kingdom and *shalom*.

Being "bad" then, being evil, is also not about doing bad things, but about being incapable, unready to see the possibility of unity anywhere, of being too unformed or too damaged to see the goodness, the necessity of true relationship in life. "Forgive them, Father, they don't know what they are doing," rings out from Yeshua with additional force, because the actions of such a person are random with respect to relationship building—harmful, hurtful, even catastrophic, because they aren't ready, ripe enough, to see what is really good. Everyone wants the best for themselves, but the ripe person understands that the best, the *taba*, is centered in unity, and the unripe person searches everywhere else, leaving a swath of destruction in his or her wake.

This is not to present an excuse for harmful behavior; it's just a statement of the facts of life, a look at the genesis of the behavior we act out and an insight into how God sees us and continues to love us in spite of unlovely behavior. Unless there is complete mental collapse, we all have choices. We can choose to learn how to move beyond the traumas and hurts of life that have damaged us and stunted our growth into ripeness and fullness, or not. The existence of the evil we create in our world should never be minimized: to do so is to trivialize the suffering and grief of those among us who have been victimized by that evil.

As we've discussed, a terrible mistake we often make today is allowing the compassion and understanding we may feel for those individuals who create evil and harm others to blunt the punishment that fits the crime. When we legislate compassion, we stop pursuing justice and therefore stop showing compassion to both victim and perpetrator. In the macro, evil and evildoers must be dealt with firmly with all the weight and force impartial justice can muster in order to stop creating more damaged, unripe people who then become evildoers themselves. But at the same time that justice is being administered in the macro, in the micro, another attitude is essential toward those same evildoers if Kingdom is to flourish at all.

A mother asks me to visit her son in central jail, desperate for something to change the trajectory of his life. As I sit at the window waiting, I look down the rows of conversations in progress: the sameness of all the orange jumpsuits on one side of the glass, every conceivable age, color, and type of person on the other. I catch sight of a young woman across an empty seat speaking to her husband/boyfriend through the telephone handset. With the look in her eyes and the smile and animation as she speaks, she is sitting across white tablecloth and candlelight—completely blind to an orange jumpsuit.

Kingdom life in a *bisha*, non-kingdom world, means that while law sees only offense and orange jumpsuits, a young woman sees only her man. What must it mean for him to see the colorblindness, the absolution in her eyes? What would it mean for us all to see that our God is orange colorblind too? Even as we serve our just sentences, the look in our Father's eyes through the glass is exactly what Yeshua is trying so hard to communicate.

Try substituting ripe and unripe for good and evil where they occur in the Gospels just as we substituted trust for faith and belief, and see what a difference it makes in our understanding of Yeshua's message. In Matthew 7, Yeshua is completing and summarizing the Sermon on the Mount: "In everything, therefore, treat people the same way you want them to treat you, for this is the Law and the Prophets." This is the summation of goodness, the "do unto others as you would have them do unto you," of the King James Version, the Golden Rule that Yeshua says includes all we need to know about the Law and the writings of the Prophets.

Then he warns, "Beware of the false prophets... You will know them by their fruits...every good tree bears good fruit, but the bad tree bears bad fruit. A good tree cannot produce bad fruit, nor can a bad tree produce good fruit. Every tree that does not bear good fruit is cut down and thrown into the fire. So then, you will know them by their fruits." But substituting the root meanings of *taba* and *bisha* gets us closer to the organic meaning: "...every ripe tree bears ripe (or beautiful) fruit, but the tree that is not ready bears unripe fruit. A ripe tree cannot produce unripe fruit, nor can a tree that is not mature produce ripe fruit. Every tree that does not bear ripe fruit is cut down and thrown into the fire."

There are no value judgments being made here, only statements of fact: either a tree is ripe or not, produces edible, ripe fruit or not, is functional and useful for preserving life or not. Something is "good," if it has the capacity to preserve life, if it is able to fulfill the intended function for which it was designed. If not, if something doesn't preserve life, or actually harms life, then it is *bisha*, evil, and its only practical use is to be cut down and burned. At least then it can function, preserve life, as fuel. A prophet is good and his or her word is good if it preserves life and relationship and increases the sum of *shalom* among the people. Look for that, and if it's not there, then, *bisha*.

In the same passage, Yeshua finally says, "Not everyone who says to me, 'Lord, Lord,' will enter the kingdom of heaven, but he who does the will of my Father who is in heaven will enter. Many will say to me on that day, 'Lord, Lord, did we not prophesy in your name, and in your name cast out demons, and in your name perform many miracles?' And then I will declare to them, 'I never knew you; depart from me, you who practice lawlessness (or wickedness, iniquity, evil).'" Yeshua is saying once again that our *behavior has nothing to do* with our acceptability to God. All the wonderful things we do in his name that we believe will certainly gain his approval are just more four-ways manipulation, more Pharisaical righteousness. None of this activity causes us to "know," to *yida* God or him to know us. We must be ready and mature enough to engage in a deeper relationship than the Four Ways can offer. It's the simple Fifth Way immersion in life and the preservation of life as *talya* that causes us to know such things and God himself.

To underscore this, the word Yeshua uses for those who practice wickedness or lawlessness or evil is not *bisha*, but *'aula*, which does mean iniquity or wickedness. But if you look up that word in an Aramaic lexicon, you find that the same base word also means "baby" or "suckling infant" when pronounced *'ula*—the word used to describe John the Baptist when still in his mother's womb or Yeshua as an infant in the manger. It also means "colt" when pronounced *'ila*—used when Yeshua is instructing his followers to bring the donkey and colt to him before his entrance into Jerusalem. What in the world do those who practice wickedness, suckling infants, and young horses have in common? They are all immature, unready, and unripe—unable yet to fulfill the purpose for which they were designed. It's fascinating to see the Aramaic Agreement expressing itself in this way, associations hardwired right into the language itself.

In the last line of Matthew 5, Yeshua says, "Be perfect, as your Father in heaven is perfect." This saying either fills us with dread because no one is perfect, could ever hope to pass such a test...or we just let it pass over and through us as one of those sweetly spiritual sayings that doesn't have a lot of meaning in the real world. But Yeshua is saying something critically meaningful and *doable* here. The word for perfect, *gamira*, doesn't mean perfectionistic or without mistakes, but complete and whole, mature, fulfilled, ready...ripe. It's the same concept. We can be as whole and complete as our Father in heaven, in the sense that we can also *see the goodness* in being at the right place at the right time for each relationship and moment in our lives. As we continue to make mistakes and fall short of whatever goals we place in front of ourselves, we can also be in love with the preservation of life and therefore "perfect," ripe, and good.

This is how God continues to love us even when we are following unlovely ways, committing unlovely acts. We may feel guilty and dirty, but God sees through the actions themselves to the seed of ripeness that lies within each of us, that he put there in the first place. He never loses sight of the possibility each one of us carries of bearing ripe fruit at any moment, no matter how immature we may be at this moment, or how much we fail to see that our unripe actions are directly defeating the purpose of finding the perfection we all crave.

Like the continuum between light and dark, there is the same necessary continuum between good and evil, between ripeness and unripeness. Like seeds and plants, we begin small and immature, incapable of bearing good fruit until we're good and ready. And as we're ripening, when we act unlovingly, Yeshua simply says, "Forgive them, Father. They don't know what they are doing." And this is literally true. For the unripe, the immature, ripeness is as beyond capability as algebra to a kindergartener.

When the student is ready, the teacher will appear, but nothing can be taught to the student who is not ready, who is not ripe. In other words, Yeshua is showing us a Father who is a patient Gardener, planting seeds and allowing his people the time they need to ripen in their season. There is no sense of urgency with Yeshua in his dealings with the unripe people around him. He always relates to them intimately, as individuals—with the compassion and love that is Kingdom. The Law will have its way with us in life, but the Father's pursuit of justice in the macro never eclipses his love for us as individual sons and daughters who are each and every one his favorites.

The Aramaic sense of good and evil is another critical concept to absorb, as it allows us to glimpse the constancy of God's love for us even when we know we are unlovely people. We *can* have it both ways, have our cake and eat it too—both macro justice and micro mercy—when intimacy and compassion are the ultimate expression of God's relationship with us. Is there any wonder it's described as Good News?

Yeshua demonstrated all this in the details of his life. Far from judging each and every action and infraction and weighing the scales of justice every moment as Hamlet supposed, God sees the finished product lying encased in whatever we've made of our lives to date, and he loves us as we are and for the people we can become. He doesn't blame us or love us less for our unripe inability to see true goodness any more than we blame a toddler for not speaking a fluent language. But neither does he create Kingdom in our lives before we are mature enough to accept it any more than we'd give an academic professorship to a five-year-old. When the student is ripe, Kingdom will appear.

⊘ ⊕ ⊕ ⊕ ⊕

As we become ready to see the constancy of God's love for us in this way, it's amazing how we also suddenly become ready to see love for others in the same light—become ready to love others right through the unripe behavior we could never get past before, to see beauty where we only saw ugliness and find companionship where we only found irritation.

In Aramaic, this kind of love is called *hab*, the word Yeshua uses when he urges us to "love (*hab*) your enemies." *Hab* conveys nothing of sentimentality or affection: related to the Hebrew word *ahabah*, it means to "kindle," and the roots point to the image of a roaring fire being kindled, coaxed, nurtured out of dry, dead bits of things; or of a plant slowly breaking through the hard, dead husk of its seed to eventually produce life-preserving fruit. Moving from inside out, this kind of love grows slowly as if from a secret enclosure—one we may not have known existed within us—but when it is ripe, transforms into *rehem*, the Aramaic word for love that Yeshua uses when he tells us to "love (*rehem*) your neighbors." *Rehem*, related to the Hebrew word for "womb," means mercy and compassion and describes a warmth and affection that pours from the depths of our spirits as if from an inner womb, like the love of a mother for her child.

As *hab* slowly becomes *rehem* deep within us, we find that enemies can be tolerated as neighbors and eventually become friends among us and in our midst. This kind of love-making—a gradual under-standing, acceptance, identification, and unity with each other—is the ripening of the very image of the Father's love in us, and that is very good, very *taba*. Though it's difficult or nearly impossible to feel affection for the unlovely, the unripe, the *bisha* among us, if we just keep showing up, it's love just the same.

And it's also amazing how feelings of affection will follow, as day follows night, the decision to love by simply living to preserve life.

Papa Pastor looked genuinely relieved.

>He was so happy to tell us that he could marry us after all, I sup-
pose you could say at that moment spirituality won out over religion—
our affection for this good man won out over our questions about his
spoken truth: questions that deepened after learning that their
decision to marry us came only after deciding that we hadn't really
been Christians at the time of our first marriages...

Did they really believe Catholics weren't Christians—that our marriages were effectively annulled over on the Evangelical side of the
room? Or was spirituality winning out over religion once again as
their personal affection for us prompted the search for a fig leaf big
enough to cover the hard line drawn between us?

>When a mountain of contradiction threatens to indefinitely post-
pone your life, sometimes you just have to choose to keep living and
climb later. And so we were married in Papa Pastor's living room on a
Tuesday morning and after a short honeymoon in San Francisco,
returned with shiny rings to our friends in the warehouse.

>I had asked one of the Malibu Franciscans why he remained in
Catholicism when he thought so little like a Catholic; he laughed and
said he'd been a priest for fifty years and would die a priest...his
laughter conveying more eloquently than the finest words that in the
end, mere mental agreement is barely noticeable against a lifetime of
relationship. To stay on with the church, to be kicked out of the nest
while still clinging to the bird seemed the necessary combination of
impetus and perseverance: to stop running and commit to a journey
that remained tethered within Christianity and our little Evangelical
warehouse without being beholden to either—a journey without an
agenda following a trail of breadcrumbs wherever they led.

Sin and Shalom

Jack is dying from cancer. Bone cancer is the most painful of all the painful cancers, and Jack has it. It started in his head and neck, but now it's in his bones. Jack is ex-navy and an ex-tugboat captain and isn't used to orders not being obeyed. But now his own body won't obey him or anything medical science can muster and that hurts almost as much as the cancer. Soon there will be so much pain that his wife and daughter will hardly recognize his face and the morphine will flow in a steady stream from the plastic bag over his head and someone will have to put nutrients in one end and clean up after the other because he will be unable to do so himself. The doctors say Jack has maybe six months, but Jack lives in Oregon, so it may be less.

Jack is fifty-nine; his daughter is only seventeen: he loves her and his wife and doesn't want to put either of them through the trauma of a six month slide into the inevitable. Oregon is the only state in the U.S. with a law that says a person has a right to die with dignity, which means Jack can let cancer take its course or he can take a glass of secobarbital, slip into a peaceful coma and be gone in two hours. It's not an easy decision, and it's not an easy process; he must have two doctors confirm he has less than six months to live and make three written requests over a fifteen day period to obtain the drugs, but he's working on it. He says he may not even use the drugs, but just knowing he has them, has some control, will help.

Jack is also at the center of a national legal battle, as the White House has instructed the Justice Department to prosecute any doctor who prescribes drugs for assisted suicide under federal law, regardless of state statutes. But that decision has been stayed pending a Supreme Court decision, so Jack presses on.

Where are all the sins here? In a situation this bad, there have to be sins...

280

Is it sinful for a U.S. President to instruct the Attorney General to prosecute and supersede state laws approved by the people? Was it sinful in the first place for the people of Oregon to have passed a law that allows us to kill ourselves legally? Is it sinful for physicians to assist in such suicides? Does Jack have the moral right to kill himself? Would his suicide be sinful even in this situation? What are the obligations of the people closest to Jack? To talk him out of it, to warn him of spiritual consequences, to let him be and make his own decision? What does Scripture have to say about suicide and its spiritual implications? Are there any circumstances in which suicide is morally acceptable and not sinful?

Did I get them all? With so many issues, probably not. Leaving macro political and legal issues aside in order to focus on the micro, what of the sinfulness of suicide itself from a moral and theological point of view? If you were raised in the Catholic church as I was, then you know the traditional teaching that suicide is tantamount to a free trip to hell. It is the ultimate expression of despair and selfishness: an unrecoverable "I don't care" to the feelings and concerns of loved ones. It is the ultimate desecration of life—murder of self—and the ultimate thumbing of the nose at God and any hope of something better. And when it *is* all these things, it's pretty bad—but what if it isn't?

After a speaking engagement not too long ago, a woman came up to me bringing another young woman by the hand, asking if I would speak to her. Haltingly, not quite ever meeting my eyes, she told me of a friend since childhood who used to be a Christian, but married a Jewish man and left the church to convert to Judaism. After a long depression, she had just committed suicide. The young woman in front of me obviously loved her friend very much and was afraid she was now in hell. The pain on her face was heartbreaking as she turned this possibility over in her mind. After all, her friend had become a Jew and then killed herself, two sins that must certainly take her out of a Christian God's reach?

At the end of her story when she finally did look at me, it was with a pleading for another alternative, another way of doing the math that didn't add up to the same answer.

○ ⊙ ⊕ ⊕ ⊕

The views we hold of good and evil, sin and forgiveness, are critical to the view we hold of God's love, and our ability to fully trust the unconditional constancy of that love is only as good as our ability to see these related concepts from Yeshua's Aramaic perspective.

By what standards do we measure sin or the severity of sin and its effect on God's love and acceptance of us? The young woman saw her friend as committing two unforgivable sins: leaving the church and killing herself—or maybe one sin eternalizing the other. In Matthew 12, Yeshua speaks of all sins and blasphemies being pardonable except "blasphemy against the Spirit." This unpardonable blasphemy means different things to different people, but in Aramaic, spirit is *ruha*, literally God's breath, and blasphemy is *gudapa*, an incision, a furrow, to cut off from. To be cut off from the breath of God is unforgivable simply and only because the sinner is no longer in position to accept the central fact of God's forgiveness. The unforgivable sin is the willful, knowing, and persistent rejection of all God has to offer. That's why there's only one, because...

God will never reject *us*. The only possible way to be rejected, is for us to reject God—and keep on rejecting him—forever.

The unforgivable sin removes the possibility of forgiveness because its *intent* is to remove the possibility of forgiveness. You can't commit it by accident or mistake. You have to actively not want forgiveness in order not to get it. Regardless of our choices and behavior, how many of us, in our heart of hearts, really don't want to be forgiven and reconciled to God? That's pretty hard to do, even if all outward appearances seem to indicate it's been accomplished in certain people. Does this kind of intent describe suicide, for instance? All suicides? Is the willful rejection of God suicide's intent?

Jack doesn't want to die—he wants to live, but there is no medical hope of that. He also wants to spare himself the excruciating pain of bone cancer and the indignities of losing all control of bodily functions. He wants to spare his loved ones the pain and trauma of watching him slowly die, the imposition of having to care for him, and the crushing financial burden of his last few months of treatment. Apart from a miracle, he's going to die within six months one way or another, and he wants his family close and connected. With no good choices left, he wants the power to choose the best of difficult alternatives for everyone concerned. But maybe if he just had a little more faith in God...maybe, but that's not unforgivable either. It comes back to intent and not just law and behavior. And that's the problem with our concept of sin—it has become just another legal term. To us, if something is unlawful, it's also sinful.

Is lying always sinful? Is stealing always sinful? They are *unlawful*, but that's not the same thing. The Law commands us not to do either, but the intent of Law is to preserve life, not to merely outlaw lying and stealing. When Germans lied to Gestapo to save Jewish lives or when a starving man steals to feed his family, we seem to understand that there are larger imperatives here. Killing another person may not be sinful either if done to preserve life in defense of self or another, and both Torah and our secular legal codes acknowledge the difference.

There are some unlawful acts so heinous that it seems impossible to separate them from sinful and malicious intent (premeditated murder, rape, and child molestation come to mind), but even so, it is not the behavior itself that is the sin; it's the intent behind the behavior and the resulting separation and devastation that make it so. Yeshua deliberately broke the Sabbath traditions in order to make that point: sometimes in order to fulfill the intent of the Law, the letter of the Law must be broken.

> Unlawful behavior is not always sinful,
> and sinful behavior is not always unlawful.

Failing to act affirmatively to preserve life, even while following the letter of the Law, can be sinful if the intent was to withhold that protection of life and *shalom* from another. On the other hand, if lying and stealing can be fulfillments of the Law when the intent is to preserve life, then what of suicide when the intent is not to die but to spare the living unnecessary pain and suffering and to preserve relationship? From a spiritual point of view, Jack's suicide may well be the most life-affirming and loving gift he can give his family and friends. Just as Paul tells us in 1 Corinthians that our good actions mean nothing spiritually if love isn't motivating them, so our "bad" actions are not sinful spiritually if they are motivated by the preservation of life: they may still be unlawful and require macro legal punishment, but they're not sinful.

Yeshua warned us about false prophets by telling us that we would know them by their fruits. If the fruit was good and ripe, the prophet's words were good and ripe also. It is the same with sin: you know it by its fruit. Sin, *hataha*, is intimately related to *shalom* by being its inverse—everything *shalom* is, sin is not. Where *shalom* is the greatest possible amount of health and wholeness and unity, *hataha*, sin, is separation and disease itself. Sin is not a behavior, it's a state of being; it doesn't lead to separation, it *is* that separation, so any action that leads to the destruction of *shalom*, is sinful, and any that increases *shalom* is not. Sinful behavior in both ancient Aramaic and Greek is seen as a "missing of the mark," whatever fails to hit the sweet spot of *shalom*, God's unity.

But once again there is a caveat here. Just as the Aramaic under-standing of good and evil as a continuum between maturity and immaturity provides no ethical excuse for our harmful actions and no legal excuse for the penalties we must pay under the law, so it is with an understanding of sin as a state of the heart, an inward intent that is separate from the choices and behavior that it creates. Com-mon sense tells us that regardless of intent, the real world conse-quences of an action or behavior can either be harmful or helpful, and just as regardless of intent, any action can have legal conse-quences. In other words, we can intend harm and do well, we can intend well and do harm, and regardless of intent, we can break the law and do time.

It's right back to the micro and macro. In the macro where justice prevails, each action we commit is judged according to the law, and punishment is sentenced. Proving non-malicious intent may soften legal penalties, but the penalties certainly remain. Ignorance of the law is not even an excuse: the harm we create is real, so the punish-ment must be real as well. We are responsible for our actions, and the scales must be balanced.

But Yeshua is again demonstrating that God doesn't relate to us in the macro with justice; he loves us intimately and individually in the micro with compassion. In John 8, when the Pharisees bring a woman to Yeshua to be judged for adultery under the Law, he is much less concerned about her unlawful behavior than he is about the intent of her accusers. "He who is without sin among you, let him be the first to throw a stone at her," he says to those holding rocks, ready to exact the death penalty required by Law. The intent of these accusers to maneuver Yeshua into breaking the Law himself and their willingness to shed blood just to discredit him, points to a sinful state of the heart far worse than mere adultery can claim. The Pharisees, though lawful, are actually living in a state of sin that is much deeper than the unlawful, adulterous woman. Yeshua deals with this deepest sin first, then he stoops back down to continue doodling in the dust of the street, ignoring the crowd as they file off one by one until he is alone with the woman.

"'Woman, where are your accusers? Did no one condemn you?' She says, 'No one, Lord.' And Yeshua replies, 'Neither do I condemn you. Go, and from now on sin no more.'" Yeshua dispenses no justice here as he trades justice for compassion; he doesn't condemn her under the Law, but at the same time, he recognizes that the unripeness that led her to adultery had first created a lonely, separated, sinful state of broken relationship and trust in her life. To go and sin no more is to go and stop missing the goodness of real unity, to live life in such a way that personal relationships are protected and revered.

No punishment on earth can make this happen; it comes only from the inside out, from the heart of a transformed life.

☉ ☽ ⊕ ⊕ ⊕

Before Yeshua heals the blind man in John 9, his followers ask him who it was that sinned to cause the man to be born blind. In logic, this is called a complex question. It's like asking when it was that you stopped beating your wife or where you hid the body. Buried beneath the question asked is a deeper question whose answer is already assumed. Did you beat your wife? Did you hide the body? Is our guilt under Law the reason for the all the ills and pain in our lives, in the lives of our children, in the world around us?

Our tragedy, our blockage to the radical nature of the Father's love is that we've already assumed a legal model for the universe. We're legalists at heart, and legalism—the belief that adherence to law makes us acceptable to God—is the default mode of our lives. It is so typical, so natural, to ask who sinned to cause the problems we encounter in life because we've already assumed a legal answer to the deeper question. And of course it is the deeper question that Yeshua answers: "It was neither that this man sinned, nor his parents; but it was so that the works of God might be displayed in him." Sin and guilt had nothing to do with the man's genetic blindness and has nothing to do with the natural tragedies we encounter in life. Our sinful behavior often creates tragedy in our lives and the lives of others, but that too, is not "punishment," as in a direct action of God in response to our choices, but a simple cause and effect—a direct result of our direct actions.

The real tragedy of our lives is the reduction of God's love to rules and regulations. To see good and evil and sin as nothing more than legal terms is to see law and our guilt under the law everywhere we look. We can't get past the fact that we will never be perfect under Law, so neither can we imagine being "perfect" under God. But being perfect—complete, whole, ripe—is being able to see beyond mere legalities: that goodness is not legal perfectionism or the righteousness of the Pharisees, but the absolute love that animates the purpose of Law—purpose that is expressed in the preservation of life and the elevation of that life to abundance.

As legalists, we are always either guilty or self-righteous; there's nothing in between, because law is like that: binary, dualistic, on or off, right or wrong, black or white. From whatever side of the legal divide we see ourselves, guilt or righteousness, we are always asking, like the Pharisees, who it was that sinned to cause every problem we see around us. Sin and guilt and law are the moving parts of the engine that drives God's punishment and reward, so we look every-where for the source of that guilt to explain the circumstances of our lives. And of course, eventually and ultimately, the evidence leads us all the way back to Adam and the serpent.

We do blame the serpent quite a bit. From demon possession to spiritual warfare to mere temptation, we've made an institution of seeing ourselves as collateral damage in a cosmic war between good and evil. But even so, the first casualty of this war was Adam, so it's only logical that Adam's first sin must be the cause of all our troubles and all our guilt. Original guilt. Original sin. We are born into it; we can't help what we are—dirty, depraved, filthy rags as compared to God's holy perfection. That's how we often see ourselves and how we live: like lepers hiding the ugliness of our disease behind shawls, shrinking back from others and warning, "Unclean."

But Yeshua simply says that no one sinned, that things happen. There is no causal connection. The ancient Hebrews had no conception of original sin; for them, it didn't exist. How could it? On the sixth day at the end of Genesis 1, God looks at his creation and sees that it is good. All is good; Adam is good, *tov*, functional, ripe. Adam's "sin," was disobedience—eating of the tree of knowledge of good and evil, but if Adam had no concept of right and wrong before he ate, how could he have been disobedient, sinful? The text tells us he was instructed not to eat, but the larger point is that his "choosing" a course of separation from perfect unity was a necessary consequence of his entrance into self-awareness and not the conscious intent to reject God. It is therefore not only forgivable, but as Yeshua says, it's also not the cause of our troubles. As God foretold, on the day Adam ate from the tree, he died to the perfect unity he knew in the Garden of his infancy as a person, but the "curse" God speaks into the lives of Adam and Eve is a simple statement of the facts of life here on earth, the way things are—that we must work for our food, that children will be born in pain—and not a punishment for growing up into sentient adulthood.

>I'm not at my desk. The apartment is empty except for the rented couch and coffee table at which I sit. My suitcase is packed by the door, clothes I won't be needing are hanging on the light fixture over what always should have been a dining area but never was. And from where I sit I can see the suit I will be married in at 10 o'clock hanging alone in the open bedroom closet. Flat and empty until I step in.

>This is the beginning of a new life. But with every birth there is a death. I take this moment to mourn the death of my old life. Of the silence and solitude of this little apartment--the place, not because of, but simply where I was when I found a measure of peace and contentment after so many thirsty years. Of the view of my courtyard in the rain. Of the warm, yellow light that highlighted the dust on my computer in the afternoon. Of your laughter at four years, then at five, six, seven, seven and a half. Of cold cereal at this coffee table in front of cartoons on those Saturday mornings after getting up slowly with you crawling in bed and talking and tickling and talking some more.

>Not so warm memories hover here too. Anguished moments. Pacing, sobbing, asking my Lord to please take me. But those are older. Softened and mostly declawed by time.

>We humans attach such significance to the things that furnish our short lives here. It's an endearing quality. A very human one. I get older. I make more transitions, live through more births and deaths. It never gets easier. Thank God. I would be less human if less affected by the comings and goings in my life. The pain is sometimes sweetened when I can remember this. And now I go to join my new wife and be father to a new daughter...

>There is such richness in the complexity of our emotions and our lives. Like the vast, never repeating weather systems that will bring us rain again this week, we flow through every conceivable combination, combinations of combinations, in infinite, God-sent variety. Full of surprises.

>Today, on the morning of my wedding day, I am a sun shower. The promise of my new family with God at the head shines brightly through the broken clouds, but cannot hold the storm of my past completely at bay.

Nowhere is the Hebrew concept of original goodness and the Christian concept of original sin more clearly contrasted than in the motivation behind prayers of blessing. Blessings, *berahkot*, have always been an immense part of Hebrew life and form the building blocks of Jewish prayer—but not at all in the way we think of them. We think of blessings as a transference of holiness or goodness from God to something or someone devoid of that holiness or goodness. In Catholic tradition, priests are called to come bless new homes or other inanimate objects such as water, books, rosaries, devotional items, or tools of trade in order to have God invest them with his holiness where it otherwise doesn't exist. People are blessed to make them holy as well: "Bless me Father for I have sinned," is the first line of the penitent's prayer in confession. In any Christian tradition, salvation itself is essentially seen as the transference of God's holiness to humans who are born without any; we bless our food before we eat it for the same reason—to transfer the holiness and goodness of God into anything that we would take into ourselves.

But as Marvin Wilson writes in *Our Father Abraham*, "The ancient Hebrews would never have thought of blessing what they ate. The idea would have been totally foreign to them; it would also have been an insult, of sorts, to God. If everything God created was 'very good' (Gen. 1:31), why should one imply that it is really unholy and profane?" Jews typically pray their blessings not before, but *after* they eat; and those blessings are not directed at any object or themselves, but are focused on blessing God himself as in this ancient Hebrew prayer: "Blessed are you, Lord our God, King of the universe, who brings forth bread from the earth." How exactly does one transfer holiness to God by blessing him? Short answer: one doesn't.

Quoting Marvin Wilson again, this time quoting Yechiel Eckstein: "The *berahkah* does not transfer holiness to the object itself, but rather entitles us to partake of the world's pleasure... We give thanks to the Lord and testify thereby that the earth is his, and we are but its caretakers." Everything in creation is already good; our petitions are not needed to coax God into making them good...again. Blessings from God are his permission for us to fully enjoy all his gifts; blessings from us are the acknowledgment of and gratitude for that permission.

This is not an attempt to settle the question of whether people are born good or bad as we think of those terms, but an acknowledgment that after we have "eaten" of the tree of the knowledge of good and evil, we are capable of either and both. To believe, as in traditional Christian theology, that we are born damned because original sin is encoded into our very DNA, is to create a passive and vicarious approach to our spirituality. We are more or less cosmic victims, and as there is nothing we can do about our innate, sinful condition, God must do it all. In complete contrast, the Hebrews, for whom all creation is *tov*, good, no such encoding exists. We must choose this day whom we will serve, as Joshua instructed, and if we choose God, we are expected to be his hands and feet on this earth. Instead of vicarious passivity, there is an air of vibrant and expectant action as the people partner with God to effect his purpose and desire—"as in heaven so on earth." The difference between seeing God as dictator over *mamlacha* and God as King over *malkuth* drives us into lives characterized either by passivity or activity, victimhood or partnership.

It is not a duality after all. There are not two things at the root of all creation, but only one. Light and dark, good and evil, shalom and sin, ripeness and unripeness, understanding and misunderstanding are not separate entities at war with each other, but different stages of the same unity. Like the caterpillar and butterfly cliché, we are on a continuous and necessary journey back to the Garden, back to Kingdom. How do we really know, *yida*, the abundance of *shalom* until we've tasted separation and disease? How do we know sweet ripeness until we've tried to pierce a hard, green surface? How will we really know we're back in the Garden until we've traveled the waterless places?

Legalism can admit none of this. Law as lawyer and judge instead of mentor and guide is by nature dualistic and therefore sinful itself in that it separates in two that which should be one. We see pain and suffering in life as evil, as punishments to be avoided at all costs, as the result of our guilty imperfection rather than the means by which we are perfected. This is all James is saying in his letter: "Consider it all joy, my brethren, when you encounter various trials, knowing that the testing of your faith produces endurance. And let endurance have its perfect result, so that you may be perfect and complete, lacking in nothing."

The blind man in John 9 was blind not because of sin, but "so that the works of God might be displayed in him." We want to automatically assume this only refers to an opportunity for Yeshua to prove himself through a miraculous healing, but on another level, blindness, like any trial, is an opportunity for each of us to overcome, experience the endurance that will have its perfect result in our lacking nothing, in our arrival back at the Garden of Kingdom.

From the perspective of legalism and dualism though, the highest good becomes the avoidance of pain and suffering (evil) rather than the moving through and beyond (good). From our self-imposed perches of either guilt or righteousness we reason: if we go back to church, do good deeds, pray harder, have more faith; if we just stop sinning, get away from all the sinful influences in life; if we go on the offensive to save our land by stamping out the sin of those who don't believe, God will take away all the problems we face. He has to after all; it's part of the contract...and so the Four Ways of yielding, manipulating, exiting, and destroying remain alive and well in our legal minds and hearts.

The hurts and traumas we suffer early in life cause us to seek comfort where we can find it, and the Four Ways can and often do provide immediate relief or at least the ability to survive. But the very success of the Four Ways in managing our circumstances installs and reinforces the dualistic notions that in turn install and reinforce legalism as the basis of all our relationships.

The Gospel according to my friend Lou exposes our lives as anxious, frightened, and guilty people. It is legalism that does this to us. Our notion of good and evil as legal terms rather than an organic progression from unripeness to ripeness creates an underlying anxiety. Our concept of Law as the arbiter of punishment and reward makes us fearful. Our view of sin as the marker of our performance under the Law, permanentizes our guilt. In the face of all this, we may still cognitively understand the concept of God's love and forgiveness, but we won't really trust it. Just how do we trust a legal God? A God who prizes justice above mercy and compassion? A God who must himself bow at the altar of his own justice, powerless to deflect for us the punishments that justice demands?

🕐 🕑 🕀 ⊕ 🕫

But at Exodus 20:5, right in the middle of the first commandment: "I, the Lord your God, am a jealous God, visiting the iniquity of the fathers on the children, on the third and the fourth generations of those who hate me, but showing lovingkindness to thousands, to those who love me and keep my commandments."

It seems pretty hard to get around this one—the ultimate expression of God as a legal God, a jealous God; a God who by the Law, by the Book, punishes those who hate him by sending generational curses, the sins of the fathers, down to the fourth generation; a God who only shows compassion to those who love him and follow his commandments. How else can we read such a verse or understand it when our worldview, the lens through which we view life, is legalism itself? We can't.

Understanding the view of God that was intended in the writing of such a verse requires a different lens. The Hebrew word, here translated "visiting," but often translated "punishing," is *paqad*. This word can be used to mean "punish," as in "visiting upon," but its primary meanings are to pay attention to, inspect, to number or reckon, to call upon (visit), and even to look after and care for. It was a word that was used to denote the taking of a census among other things. If we're still thinking we are being punished for the sins of Adam or our great-great grandparents, Yeshua is still whispering in our ears that "no one sinned." As if to confirm that, Ezekiel, at the end of chapter 18 quotes God as saying, "I will judge you...each one according to his conduct." Common sense tells us that we are responsible for our own actions, but not those of others, and as it turns out, God has common sense too.

Even so, the fact remains that the sins of the fathers *are* passed down, visited upon their children and their children's children. Children of alcoholics tend toward alcoholism or other behavioral problems and children of abuse and neglect tend to abuse and neglect...and so once again, as he did with Adam and Eve, God is simply stating the facts of life, the way things are, and not "cursing" or "punishing." Unripe people do harmful things; harmful things hurt and traumatize the children in the blast zone, causing them to take longer to ripen themselves so that they hurt and traumatize their children to the third and fourth generations, until one child finally breaks the chain of abuse. God doesn't "do" this to us, curse us with generational abuse: he pays attention to it, he recognizes it, and even looks after it and cares for it. He also forgives it, as he guides and tends and patiently waits for his children to ripen so that as soon as they are ready, Kingdom will appear, and his love and compassion will become a real presence in their lives.

God didn't give Jack bone cancer for anything he did or didn't do, but that cancer is taking Jack on a journey to ports of call even a life at sea didn't reach. It's up to Jack whether this difficult journey will ripen him further, but either way, God knows Jack's intent in wanting to be ready and empowered to take his own life. Jack's family will have to deal with the consequences of his choices, but Jack isn't choosing to hurt them any more than he's choosing to reject God or forgiveness or reconciliation; he's choosing to save himself and his family from as much pain and suffering as possible. God knows all this and his compassion for him won't waver regardless of Jack's actual choice or the consequences of that choice.

Likewise, the young woman's suicidal friend wasn't choosing to reject God when she chose to convert to Judaism. Perhaps she was choosing to follow God in a different way, or more likely she was choosing only to follow her husband and God had nothing to do with her choice. God knows this too, and if she wasn't choosing not to be forgiven, then she simply is...forgiven.

But what if her friend's suicide cut off her chance for forgiveness from God, the young woman in front of me still wanted to know? I told her that forgiveness is who God is, not what he does, and our behavior can't change that. I told her that some things are very private between God and each of us and beyond what anyone else can know in this life. I told her what Thomas Keating, a Trappist monk and author told me when I asked him a similar question while on a retreat he was leading: "I have great hopes that many things happen in the process of dying, because I don't know when they would otherwise."

There may be a whole life of time lived in just the last few nano-seconds before the lights of this world go completely out—time for realization and reconciliation; for that matter, where is it written that God has wired a hard deadline in each of our lives at the moment of physical death, beyond which there is no more for-giveness? It seems there may well be more things in heaven and earth than are dreamt of in our theologies, to (mis)quote Hamlet once again.

I'm not sure I helped soothe the young woman's grief at the moment we spoke. I could only hope and pray that as she walked away, still arm in arm with her friend, she had a few more images in her mind to help dilute the grief that she obviously still felt in her heart—a grief that was doubled by the earthly longing for her friend's presence and the spiritual fear of her damnation.

Our concepts of good and evil, law and sin, as legal terms do this to us—make us fear that our Father never really would or could forgive us, or that we've simply run out of chances. After all, God has still described himself as a jealous God—one who tolerates no unfaithfulness. How are we to reconcile that description with one of unconditional love and unlimited forgiveness? Ironically, it is from this most dissonant of descriptions, that we discover one of the most beautiful and moving illustrations of God's fierce and unwavering love for each of us...as usual, from deep within the Hebrew/Aramaic Agreement.

We have come to understand jealousy as the anger or hostility a person feels over the suspected unfaithfulness of a spouse or signifi-cant other or the threat of another's attention. Where envy is the fear of not getting something we want and another has, jealousy is the fear of losing something we already have. There are elements of possessiveness and paranoia usually associated with a jealous person, and such a person by definition is insecure with themselves and their relationships. Most significantly, the anger and hostility of a jealous person is aimed directly at the object of their jealousy. Though we would never describe our God as possessive or insecure, the rest of this definition plays right into our legalistic weakness: it's all too easy for us to imagine God being angry with us for our unfaithfulness. We deserve it; we're guilty.

But the Hebrew word translated "jealous" here and elsewhere in the Hebrew Scriptures, is *qana*. To fully appreciate the layered meanings of any Hebrew or Aramaic word is to study the two and three letter roots from which they are derived. As Jeff Benner explains in *His Name is One*, the "parent" root of *qana* is *qen* (qn), which means "nest," but which can also include the nestlings. This is the word used to describe God's protective attitude toward his people in Deuteronomy 32:11, "Like an eagle that wakes up his nest (*qen*), that hovers over his young, he spreads his wings and catches them, he carries them over his feathers."

A "child" root of *qen* is *qanah*, which means the construction of a nest, or by extension, a builder, a maker, or even a possessor. As God is described in Genesis 14:19, "...blessed is Abram to God most high, builder (*qanah*) of heaven and earth." God isn't an abstract creator to the Hebrews, but a concrete builder who roams far and wide to gather the materials needed to carefully fashion a home for his nestlings, his people: the whole of creation is understood as God's nest, a home built just for us.

Also derived from *qen*, the word *qana* itself, the one translated as "jealous," carries the meaning of "the passion with which the parent guards over the chicks in the nest." God is both *qanah*, builder, and *qana*, protector, of *qen*, the nest and the nestlings he so passionately loves, tends, and guards. In our Western minds and hearts, we see the passionate, even wrathful feelings and actions that flow out of God's jealousy as being directed toward us, when to the Hebrews those actions and feelings were directed away from us—at anyone or anything that would come between God and his beloved people.

Yeshua's heart broke over Jerusalem, over the pain and destruction and scattering he saw in their lives and mounting on the western horizon. He longed to gather and protect his people as a hen gathers her chicks under her wings, but they would not come to him. That image from Matthew 23 is the very echo of the Hebrew understanding of God's "jealousy" and his relationship with his people: the watchfulness, protectiveness, and tenderness toward us and the ferocity toward those who would raid the nest.

Somehow we must understand all this. That God is not angry with us; that he is always trying to gather us under his wings, to shelter and guard and guide. He is not even angry at our sinful behavior, though his heart may break over the pain he knows will result from our unwillingness to simply come and shelter with him.

〇 ① ⊕ ⊕ ⊛

A Catholic priest once told me a story from his time as a missionary in Laos, when local military authorities arrested him and staked him to the ground, spread-eagled and face up in a clearing outside a village in the forest. It was during the monsoon rains when drops come down as big as grapes and with the force of a slingshot. The rain felt like a thousand knives as it mercilessly pummeled him, as he vainly struggled to shelter his face, turning it side to side until he caught sight of a hen in the nearby brush. Through slits of barely opened eyes and sheets of falling water, he watched the hen just a few feet away under the leaves with her wings spread low to the ground and all her chicks huddled close under their mother's umbrella.

I can only imagine the loneliness he must have felt at that moment—the isolation and abandonment, the collapse of all his intentions and dreams. How images of being held by his own mother may have formed in his mind as he replayed events in his life that took him to that very moment of despair. I don't know these things for sure; I can only imagine. But I do know what he told me: how he longed to be one of those chicks, to slip off the ropes that held him and crawl under those wings and wait out the storm. How he finally and completely understood the meaning of God's aching desire to gather us all under the span of his protection and love.

Somehow we must understand all this.

Yeshua said, "I am the good shepherd; the good shepherd lays down his life for the sheep. He who is a hired hand, and not a shepherd, who is not the owner of the sheep, sees the wolf coming, and leaves the sheep and flees, and the wolf snatches them and scatters them. He flees because he is a hired hand and is not concerned about the sheep. I am the good shepherd, and I know my own and my own know me, even as the Father knows me and I know the Father; and I lay down my life for the sheep."

How many times, in how many ways, does God need to tell us and show us the manner in which he loves us? Maybe just once more... Or maybe we all need our moment pinned to the ground and blinded by the rain before we can begin to really see.

>I am at Serra again. Sitting on a bench at the point from which the back of the canyon looks out across the trees and creek and tennis courts and pools and stables to the ocean. It is already very light, but it is a gray day with the clouds hanging low over the tops of the hills behind me and falling like a curtain about a half mile to sea. I am not alone. A man on the next bench is reading his Bible. Another on the bench after that. Periodically, footsteps clump up the path behind me and recede again. The birds are only slightly muted by the weather--geese, dogs, coyotes, and traffic from the coast highway all make the sonic journey up to this bench.

>The solitude I had living alone is gone. Replaced by my new family. Even here, where I come to be silent for a space, I am sharing my room. How ever this sounds to you, I am not saying it is bad thing, only different. I think, though, that the change has kept me from writing, from wanting to even test whether words will come out of non-solitude that have anything to say. It is silly, superstitious even, but there it is.

>And there is so much to say. So much has happened. Mass starts in twenty minutes, so there's not much time, but I'll continue later.

>I am married again. I can feel the still unfamiliar band on my finger as I write. I ran slightly late that morning of the wedding after writing too long as usual. I was still nervous since the night before and was nervous driving to our pastor's house. Arriving before Marian, I was nervous waiting. There was only seven of us waiting for her and her maid of honor in the front room. I was nervous until the pastor's wife opened the door and my bride was standing framed in it like a beautiful painting.

>There was a moment, a breath, where we all just looked. She was stunning in her off-white, elegant, ankle-length dress. But

301

what I remember most is her eyes. In an instant, all was erased from the night before, from the night and morning of stress. Her eyes were for me and mine for her. As we stood together listening to our pastor, saying our vows, I stared into her eyes, impossibly big like a moon on the horizon. It was a scene in a movie where everything peripheral fades to black leaving one image in crystalline view.

>I got lost in those eyes. It was a moment to remember, to call up and replay when no one is getting lost in anyone's eyes. A couple of weeks ago, we got to laughing almost uncontrollably in bed before going to sleep, and when I could speak again I said let's remember this moment. Make it a touchstone, a place to come back to when we're not laughing anymore.

>And, of course we won't always be laughing. It seems hard to imagine now that we would ever let this closeness and respect all get away somehow--but then it's only been five weeks. How many other couples have said the same? That's why the touchstones. A trail of breadcrumbs laid through our lives together that can always lead back to a moment that contained a reason why.

Freedom and Forgiveness

As you sit or lie with these pages, become very still for a moment, quiet yourself, and gently become aware of your breathing... Even as these words continue to flow across your vision and through your mind, feel the rise and fall, the filling and emptying. Silent. Smooth. Effortless.

Until the moment these words called your attention to it, one of your most critical life functions went on completely unnoticed and unheeded. Unless there was some difficulty, asthma or congestion perhaps, that caused you to be aware of it, you were as conscious of your breathing as you are of your hair growing. As it should be...even in sleep your body continues to breathe, of course. You don't have to think about it, it just happens. Under normal circumstances, you don't have to plan for it, make time for it, worry about it, fight for it, and unless you're a scuba diver, you don't have to pay for it either.

God told Adam and Eve that they would have to work for their food; and almost every waking moment of the lives of most creatures on earth is consumed with obtaining consumables. We spend our lives thinking about, planning for, preparing, budgeting, and paying for our food—food is certainly not free. But breathing our air was free in the Garden, and it is still today—for the moment. In fact, that's how we know something is really free: if we don't have to think, plan, worry, budget, pay, or fight for something, it's free. It's free precisely because it's free *from* all those actions.

The things from which we are the most free, the most liberated, are those things we think about the least. Conversely, the more we think or worry about something, the more that thing imprisons us, owns us, enslaves us. When you lie awake at night worrying and planning over your finances or a big test or promotion or a relationship gone sour, that thing owns you, has you in chains. But when that thing is resolved to the point that you sleep through the night and go through your day without giving it a second thought, you are liberated, free—at least from that one thing.

Yeshua said at Matthew 6:24, "No one can serve two masters; for either he will hate the one and love the other, or he will be devoted to one and despise the other. You cannot serve God and mammon." Sometimes mammon is translated as "wealth" or "money," but mammon actually means much more than that. Mammon is the anglicized version of the Aramaic word *mamona*, which was left untranslated in the Greek manuscripts, appearing as *mamonas*. Originally, *mamona* was the name of a Mesopotamian goddess of wealth, which then became synonymous with greed and avarice, or the personification of such. But even more to the point, going back to the roots of the word, *mamona* signifies the piling up or accumulation of external things that eventually defines the person doing the accumulating. It seems that in the compulsive desire to possess, the possessor becomes possessed by the very objects of his or her desire—defined by them. That is the perfect definition of greed, avarice, *mamona*.

Mamona is the opposite of freedom and liberation, because by definition, a person in the throes of a compulsive need to acquire is always thinking and planning and manipulating everything and everyone in their blast zone to get the things they desire. This is why Yeshua says that "it is easier for a camel to go through the eye of a needle than for a rich person to enter the Kingdom." Kingdom is freedom personified, *mamona* is greed personified; greed is enslavement, imprisonment by the objects of desire. How does a slave enter freedom until and unless the chains are removed?

Yeshua tells the rich young man in Matthew 19 that if he wants to be complete, perfect, ripe, he must sell all he has and give it to the poor. But this is no moral command to be generous; it's the very practical realization that only when the rich man is no longer thinking about his wealth or looking to it for his security will he be free enough to come follow Yeshua and his Way. It's the same message Yeshua tells us all back in Matthew 6: do not store up treasures on earth where moth and rust eat at them, but in heaven where they are safe from such decay. All these are images of freedom, the freedom with which Kingdom beckons. It's not that God won't allow us to enter Kingdom because we've disobeyed his command to be generous; it's the fact of our enslavement to our *mamona* of choice that removes the possibility of experiencing the freedom Kingdom promises in our lives.

God never bars us from Kingdom; it's our own compulsions that bar us from seeing the reality of Kingdom in every moment.

① ① ⊕ ⊕ ⊛

There is a very strange parable that Yeshua tells in Luke 16 of an unrighteous manager who was embezzling from his wealthy employer until he is discovered and called to account. The manager knows he will be dismissed when the facts come out, so in order to have a soft landing after he becomes unemployed, he secretly brings in his employer's debtors one by one and systematically forgives much of their debts. By making friends in this way, he reasons, he will have new doors open to him when his present one shuts. The really puzzling part of the story is that when the employer hears what his manager has done, far from being angry, he praises him for having acted shrewdly. Then as the moral of the story, Yeshua pronounces: "...make friends for yourselves by means of the mammon of unrighteousness, so that when it fails, they will receive you into the eternal dwellings."

This story seems to make no moral sense; it goes against every ethical nerve ending in our bodies until we understand what is meant by the "mammon of unrighteousness." To the Hebrews, unrighteous mammon was not wealth that was unrighteously obtained; it was wealth that was unrighteously *retained*. This makes all the difference. There were three signs the Jews recognized as the evidence of a heart that was truly turned from sin: prayer, fasting, and charity (giving of alms). Unrighteous mammon was the profit, the wealth over and above that which a person needed that was immorally retained by the refusal to give to others charitably. The wealth that the manager embezzled was not unrighteous mammon because he embezzled it; it was unrighteous because he, his employer, or both dammed it up and did not allow it to flow outward to those who needed it.

What Yeshua is saying is that whether rich or poor or middle class, if our hearts are free enough to turn outward, to instinctively respond to the needs of those around us, our neighbors—then we are truly free. If we are holding on to our possessions obsessively, depriving others of the assistance and relief that we could give them, then while we may not be unlawful technically, we are still sinfully imprisoned. Eventually, physical riches will always fail, and if we've not developed loving relationships all around us, we will be truly alone in our time of need, still defined and now haunted by that which we no longer possess.

What we think about the most is what defines us, possesses us, and limits our freedom.

What is that? What do we think about the most? Money or lack of it? Our jobs? Our families, children, wives, husbands, a love relationship or lack of that? Our hobbies, sports, church, religion, politics, charitable activities and causes? Our next drink or fix or sexual encounter? God?... Whatever they may be, these things possess us and limit our freedom. But is a loss of freedom always a bad thing? We Westerners automatically place our personal freedom as a highest good, but some of the items on this list are also very good things by which to be beholden. Are we really supposed to be completely free—free from all law, responsibility, and obligation?

To be completely free is to be completely alone.

If I gave my wife the same amount of thought and concern I give my breathing, I wouldn't have a wife. Any relationship that is given no conscious thought, planning, tending, budgeting, or allocation of time and resources would be indistinguishable from loneliness. Just as we voluntarily trade freedom for security by submitting to laws and taxes and other restrictions in society, so we also trade freedom for relationship by submitting to the responsibilities and obligations that love requires. "Greater love has no one than this, that one lay down his life for his friends." Yeshua said this at John 15, and though we immediately connect this image to his death on the cross, laying down our lives for our friends and neighbors carries even deeper and ongoing significance.

As hard as it may be to be willing to die for another, it may even be harder to *live* for another by laying down everything that has come to define our lives, that we have worked so hard to acquire. There is no greater love than to be willing to lay down the very things we think about most for the sake of someone else—to allow thoughts about the welfare of others to completely displace any thought about our own welfare and the treasures we amass to sustain it. To trade freedom for the mutual bondedness, submission, and connection of any relationship of love is a very good trade.

In what sense then are we free in Kingdom? If Kingdom is defined by complete and perfect unity and oneness of relationship, must it not also be defined by limited freedom as well? Yeshua said at John 8:32, "If you continue in my word, then you are truly disciples of mine; and you will know the truth, and the truth will make you free." What sort of truth is it that will make us free...and from what? And how is this truth and freedom related to our sense of Kingdom? The clues are in the language itself.

Starting with the second half of the equation first, the "set free" half, there are four closely related Hebrew/Aramaic terms we need to consider, and the first is *subqana*. *Subqana* is the Aramaic word that is translated "make you free" here in John 8, and it is also the same word translated as "release" and "set free" in Luke 4:18 as Yeshua stands in the synagogue at Nazareth reading from Isaiah 61: "The spirit of the Lord is upon me, because he anointed me to preach the Gospel to the poor. He has sent me to proclaim *release* to the captives, and recovery of sight to the blind, to *set free* those who are oppressed..."

Subqana means to set free, to release, to liberate, or to *deliver*.

There is a wonderful little contemporary parable that most of us have probably heard that tells of a man on the roof of his house during a flood. The water is up to the eves of the house when a row boat comes by calling to the man to get in; they will save him. But he says, "No, God will save me." A helicopter roars overhead, throws down the rope ladder calling him to come up; they will save him. He says, "No, God will save me." Finally, a motorboat glides up with the same offer, but he declines, again saying, "God will save me." The waters rise over the roof, and the man drowns. When he gets to heaven and meets God he blurts out, "God, why didn't you save me?" God replies, "I sent you two boats and a helicopter—what more did you want?" Besides being a great illustration of unmet expectation, this story captures the Hebrew concept of deliverance and salvation perfectly.

To save in Aramaic is *heya*, which comes from the same root as the word for life: *haye*. *Heya* as salvation literally means to give life or preserve life, to deliver from that which would destroy life. Liberation and salvation to the ancient Jews were virtually the same thing; salvation to Jews, who had no clear concept of the afterlife anyway, was all about being preserved and delivered and liberated right herenow, not therethen. When Yeshua prays in his model prayer, "Deliver us from evil," he is literally defining the Jewish concept of salvation.

But there is another word from the Hebrew Scriptures that is closely related to salvation and liberation and will likely surprise many of us in the West—and that is, *judgment*. In Hebrew, to judge is primarily expressed by the word *shafat*. We as a legal-minded people immediately think of judging and judgment in legal terms, that is, a deciding, an arbitration, a legal verdict, an up or down vote. But *shafat* in Hebrew not only means to decide, but to rule, to govern, to vindicate, and to *deliver*.

If you think of the Judges who led Israel at critical points in its history before the establishment of the kings, they are not at all legal figures in the way we think of a judge. The Judges of Israel were warriors—military leaders who were called upon in times of crisis to lead the people and deliver them from the threat at hand. Figures like Deborah and Gideon and Samson were great leaders who ruled and rallied armies (and sometimes rendered legal verdicts as well) until the crisis was resolved; they then returned to their regular lives. The Judges delivered, saved, and liberated their people just as God did. Abraham calls God a "judge," *shafat*, in Genesis 18:25 when he is bargaining with him to save and deliver the people of Sodom and Gomorrah. Moses was also considered *shafat* in his role as deliverer of his people, and he also ruled and arbitrated for the people as described in Exodus 18.

It is critical for us, we legalists at heart, to understand that judgment is so closely related to salvation, deliverance, and liberation in the Scriptures. It won't be easy for us to think of judgment as a literal term of endearment for God, but amazingly, the judgment of God is also the salvation of God, the deliverance and liberation of God. The Jews knew their God in this way from the beginning, and as we continue to enter the Aramaic Agreement, the God we know as a legal God of absolute justice will continue to morph into the "jealous," protective God of compassion and mercy who guards, delivers, and preserves us under his wings, if we will only come and shelter with him.

But there is another amazing connection. When Yeshua asks his Father in that model prayer at Matthew 6 to, "Forgive us our debts as we forgive our debtors," the word he uses for "forgive" is *sebaq*, which now brings us full circle. *Sebaq* is itself a form of the word with which we started, *subqana*. Sharing the same roots, when the word used for release or liberation of the captives in Luke 4, also means "forgiveness," a connection is being made that we must not miss. At their roots, *sebaq* and *subqana* mean to loosen, let go, leave, allow—to return something to its original state. From those meanings it becomes clear how the concepts of release, liberation, and forgiveness all flow from that same word. When something or someone has become damaged, imprisoned, injured, or hurt; when any ill has befallen; forgiveness is letting it go, allowing it the freedom to return to its original state.

When Moses asks the Egyptian Pharaoh to let his people go, he is asking for forgiveness, for the freedom to allow his people to return to their original state. When a group of men lower their paralyzed friend down through the roof to Yeshua in Matthew 9, Yeshua grants their request for healing by saying, "Take courage, son, your sins are forgiven." He also physically heals him, but the point remains that forgiveness and healing are interchangeable concepts. To ask for healing is to ask for forgiveness, deliverance, and liberation, as they all have the power to return us to our original state before the brokenness and hurt and bondage took away our freedom. Liberation, salvation, judgment, and forgiveness: all equivalent terms in Hebrew thought pointing us toward the healing and deliverance contained herenow in the constancy of God's love.

To be set free, then, is to be forgiven. To be forgiven is to be set free. To be forgiven and set free is to be saved, and to be saved is to be delivered and healed from all the things that have taken our *shalom*, from all the things that would keep us from returning to the Garden, our original state of abundant life and the greatest possible health and unity—from Kingdom. All this is freedom, being set free. It is the freedom from thinking about, worrying over, planning for, stressing on, and trying to pay for our relationship with God.

How do we get this freedom? Yeshua says if we know the truth, the truth will take us there. But as Pontius Pilate asked, "What is truth?"

⊙ ⊙ ⊕ ⊕ ⊕

We'll never know whether Pilate expected an answer to his question about truth. If he got one, it's not recorded in John 18. When Yeshua tells him he was born to testify to the truth and that everyone who was "of the truth" would hear his voice, perhaps Pilate's question was just framed rhetorically, dismissively—a bared-teeth stating of his cynical experience that truth was whatever people wanted it to be; that it could always be bent to conveniently fit one of the Four Ways that all politicians understood too well; that truth was always relative, and one man's ceiling was another man's floor. We'll never know whether Pilate was sincere with his question, whether he really wanted an answer or just an opportunity to telegraph the answer he already thought he knew.

We do know that Yeshua was sincere, though. For him, truth was as real as air and sea and as personal and intimate as a warm embrace. Yeshua's truth had power—the power to heal and forgive and set free. What sort of truth has this power?

"If you continue in my word, then you are truly disciples of mine; and you will know the truth, and the truth will make you free."

Now looking at the first half of this equation, I hope I never cease to be surprised and amazed at the smallest details of life, of the impact of a single word uttered a thousand years ago, or two thousand... When Yeshua said "truth," he uttered *serara*—to be strong, vigorous, to establish, to strengthen, to believe. To the ancient

Hebrews, anything that did all that was certainly "true;" it was truth. When we look at the roots of *serara*, we are pointed toward that which liberates, opens possibilities, a right or harmonious direction.

The truth will make you free... What is truth? Yeshua says it right out loud: "If you continue in my word," if you live as I live and love as I love, "you will know the truth"—it is the ongoing experience of forgiveness/liberation that sets a right direction, opens a door that was previously shut to truth/liberation. It's a mathematical equation after all, with both sides equaling each other: it's another closed loop, and to make that loop even tighter, at the end of Luke 4:18 we read that Yeshua was sent "to set free those who are oppressed." But that is a translation from the Greek. When we translate from the Aramaic, we get, "...to *free* those who are oppressed with *forgiveness*." We've got to see the symmetry here—because the Aramaic word used for (setting) free, is none other than *serara*, the same word used for truth; and the word used for forgiveness is once again, *subqana*, the same word used for setting free. Here again in this verse, Yeshua, and Isaiah before him, are literally saying that truth will free those who are oppressed by returning them to their original state; that those who are oppressed will be freed, forgiven, saved, healed, and delivered by constantly experiencing new possibilities, establishing and strengthening trust in that which liberates—the truth.

Yeshua called that powerful truth his Gospel, the Good News. Truth is the Good News of God's nature. Following Yeshua, living as he lived, opens us to the repeated experience of God's nature, the truth that his love is free, that there is nothing we can do to lose it or diminish it, that we don't have to think, plan, or worry about it. There is nothing we can do to not be forgiven, saved, healed, or delivered unless we *choose* not to be forgiven, saved, healed, or delivered. God is always sending two boats and a helicopter. Are we willing to come aboard?

>Made the flight home with only moments to spare--about three and a half hours to go. Got a window seat this time, but wing and turbine fill all but the horizon, which is covered with clouds anyway.

>It has been so hard to write lately. I try to just put one word in front of another, but nothing gets moving. I just get one word further ahead. Maybe there's too much to say. Maybe there's not enough.

>I'm going home now. Been away five days. Haven't seen you in a week. But all the women in my life will be home tonight. My family. Not quite all together, far from all apart. When the sadness strikes, like now, that says things aren't the way they're supposed to be, I ask myself how else they could have been.

>What was the correct combination of decisions that would have yielded the correct life? Of course there is none. And most recently, when I really think about it, the only correct life I'll ever have is the one I take pleasure in. Feel the joy from all the gifts I've been given and those I can subsequently give.

>To really understand life is to feel the joy of it, or to feel the joy of it, is to understand it best.

>Maybe I'll understand better when I'm holding all of you in my arms.

Simon Peter, or Shim'on Kefa in Hebrew, comes to Yeshua wanting to know how many times he should forgive his brother when he sins against him—up to seven times? Considering that the Rabbinical Pharisees prescribed forgiveness only up to three times, seven may have seemed like a big number to Peter. But Yeshua replies at Matthew 18, "I do not say to you, up to seven times, but up to seventy times seven." Doing the math, some say this number is 77 and others, 490, but even if it's 490, at the rate we need forgiveness, that may only get us out a year and a half or so.

Peter and Yeshua's numbers are a direct analog from the Scriptures, from Genesis 4, where Cain is protected by God through a mark and the pronouncement that anyone who kills Cain will have vengeance taken on him sevenfold. Upping the ante, Lamech, Cain's fifth generation grandson boasts that if Cain was to be avenged sevenfold, then he would be avenged seventy-sevenfold. Yeshua is matching the number of times vengeance would be taken with the number of times forgiveness will be granted. Seventy-seven? Four hundred and ninety?

Remembering the symbolic meaning and use of numbers, we get a very different figure. Seven is the number of spiritual perfection and completion, and ten is a number signifying the millennium or eternity. If you factor it out, the number Yeshua is giving us is essentially perfection times perfection times eternity...it's like saying forever and a day. There is no limit, no end to the times that God will forgive—there is no moment when the absolute bedrock of our relationship with God is not based in forgiveness, restoration, reconciliation, healing, deliverance, salvation. Yeshua's attitude and conduct toward everyone with whom he came in contact certainly bears this out; Yeshua's first instinct was always to accept and beckon close, to heal and forgive.

Continuing on in Matthew 18 though, we're in for a shock. In the verse immediately following the seventy times seven figure, Yeshua begins a parable by saying, "For this reason the Kingdom of Heaven may be compared to a king who wished to settle accounts with his slaves..." For what reason? For the reason that there is no limit to forgiveness. But in the parable, a slave who owed the king a debt that ran into the millions of our dollars is forgiven his debt through the compassion and mercy of the king. So far, so good—especially considering that to the ancient Jews, a debt was the same as sin. Like sin, a debt creates a state of imbalance, anxiety, and limitation, a lack of freedom that requires restitution or forgiveness to restore the original balance. But in this story, restitution is not an option as Yeshua has the king forgive a debt so great that the slave would never have been able to repay.

The forgiven slave, though, immediately turns around and refuses to forgive the debt of another slave who owed him only a few dollars, throwing him into prison until he pays. When the king hears of this, he is enraged, reinstates the first slave's debt, and hands him over to the torturers until he should repay every last cent. Yeshua's parting comment is that, "My heavenly Father will also do the same to you, if each of you does not forgive his brother from your heart." How could Kingdom possibly be compared to this? And if this is not clear enough, at Matthew 6 Yeshua has already stated that, "...if you forgive others for their transgressions, your heavenly Father will also forgive you. But if you do not forgive others, then your Father will not forgive your transgressions."

So which is it? Is forgiveness free and unlimited or conditional and limited to our willingness to forgive others?

The answer lies again in our ability to think within the Aramaic Agreement. Just as sin is not the behavior that leads to separation, but the state of separation itself, forgiveness is not the action of forgiving, but the state of being free, delivered, and restored to wholeness.

God's pronouncement that the sins of the fathers would be handed down to the children to the forth generation, was not a punishment, but a statement of the facts of life: that harmful behavior harms those close, causing them to harm those close in turn. God doesn't "do" this to us; he doesn't "curse" us with such punishments. It's just what happens in life as effect follows cause. And what is true in the negative with sin is true in the positive with forgiveness. Forgiveness is the state of being free from all the hurt, anxiety, anger, frustration, fear, and separation that imprison us when a relationship is broken. But a relationship is never broken from God's perspective. God is perfect Unity, so God's side of every relationship is perfect Unity as well—part of his own definition. God is never in the business of withholding forgiveness; restoration is always right there waiting, as available as the air we breathe. Our willingness to enter into the state of being forgiven, though, is completely up to us, not God.

The moment we forgive another, release the hurt and anger caused by that person, is the moment we are forgiven—released and set free ourselves. Not to forgive, not to release, to continue holding on to the hurt and anger is to remain unforgiven—outside the state of being free and restored to our original condition. God doesn't "do" this to us, we do it to ourselves, but it is still true to say that until we ourselves forgive, we are not forgiven—we remain victims by choice in the state of being oppressed and undelivered.

As with everything else, we want to think of forgiveness in legal terms, of course, in passive and vicarious terms: but Yeshua is telling us that it is *our* responsibility, not God's, to forgive the broken state of our hearts—that we are the only ones who can allow them to be restored to their original state at all. Whether we are perpetrator or victim, debtor or creditor, the process is the same because forgiveness lies far beneath both action and blame.

When we are hurt, deeply or slightly, physically or emotionally, and we lie awake at night replaying angry scenes in our minds, staring at the ceiling, rehearsing what we will say and do next: thinking, worrying, planning...we are enslaved and imprisoned by that over which we obsess. Removing that obsession, "forgiving" it, has nothing to do with an apology extended or received; it has nothing to do with the other person at all. And Yeshua is telling us it has nothing to do with God either. From God's point of view, we are *always* forgiven—seventy times seven—but that's only half the equation. We are the other half.

Forgiveness is the surrender of our victimhood—taking back the full personhood that was stripped from us by another or ourselves. Either we find our Way to let go of the victimhood of unforgiveness or we don't. Either we stop thinking, planning, worrying about it and become free from it, delivered from it, or we don't. God won't do it for us, won't violate our right to choose. Until we forgive, set ourselves free with truth, we are not forgiven, set free. And the only way we know we are really forgiven is when we can sleep through the night again, when we no longer give the problem a second thought— and not a moment before. God is waiting with open wings. All we have to do is come in out of the rain.

○ ○ ○ ○ ○

There was a moment in my life when I was more completely betrayed by someone I thought I loved than I had ever been before or have been since. I remember the sleepless nights and waking obsession with each detail and event, the plotting and planning, the worry and the tears. And I remember when the final cut came, when the realization of the completeness of the betrayal hit me, something in me just let go. I'm still not sure what triggered it. Maybe at the moment I realized there was nothing left to lose, I realized there was nothing left to hold on to either. Maybe I was just tired and worn out. Or maybe since I had acted like every other man in her life, I had simply been treated like every other man in her life, and I could finally admit that love had never been part of any of it.

Whatever the reason, in that moment, it all left me. If you've ever seen a scene in a movie where an aquarium is shattered, where in just a second or two all the water gushes out like an extended sigh, leaving fish flipping and flopping amid the plants and gravel on the floor—that was it. That was what I felt, sitting there as if I'd been shattered, emptied, with all that fear and resentment and anger left gasping on the floor. At that moment, and from that moment, I was free, forgiven, delivered. I slept again, I thought of other things again, I took care of business again. And all this happened without an apology offered or accepted, without any face-to-face contact at all. It may have even happened without my consent, but it happened, and it made all the difference.

When I was ready, when I was ripe, forgiveness appeared.

I never said the words, "I forgive you." I never heard the words, "I'm sorry." It didn't matter; not one of us can ever forgive anyone else, and no one can ever forgive us. We can express what has already occurred in our hearts, but that's not the same thing. Forgiveness is not a commodity that can be traded, transported between individuals or groups. Forgiveness, like everything else along the Fifth Way, moves from inside out, and if a person's heart has not already been forgiven—delivered, restored, saved—no apology will make it so, though it may begin the process. It is simply a choice we make. We can accept the free forgiveness that is always available or not; it's not something God or anyone else does for us.

We are not forgiven because we forgive.
We forgive once we know we are always and already forgiven.

Years ago, there was a terrible shooting at a school in Kentucky—a Columbine-type shooting, before there was Columbine. Several students were killed by another student, and the grief of the parents of the victims and the entire community was thick as everyone desperately tried to make sense where there was none. In the midst of all this and in the glare of national and worldwide media coverage, a group of Christians took to the streets in front of the school with signs saying that they, as Christians, forgave the student who shot the others. The parents of the dead students were furious. In the midst of their grief, they were certainly not ready to utter the words of a forgiveness they had not yet experienced, and perhaps have still not to this day. Their babies were dead—someone else's baby took their babies away, and their lives would never be the same. A sign in the street, on a TV screen, didn't change that; it only deepened the grief.

A wounding as deep as losing a child begins a journey that has a life of its own and must be followed to its end if there is ever to be restoration, a return to the original state. There are no shortcuts, and the length of the journey is determined only by the readiness of the journeyer. When the student is ready, forgiveness will appear and not a moment sooner. We can't take the journey for another, we certainly can't forgive *for* another by proxy, and there are no words to make it all go away. The mistake of the Christians-with-signs was in thinking legally, passively, and vicariously—as if they could write a forgiveness contract on a sign and transfer or confer it on the world; a sort of vicarious forgiveness without any further action to make it so, to make restoration a reality.

More recently, another school shooting occurred at an Amish schoolhouse in Pennsylvania. A distraught and deranged man killed five little girls and wounded as many others before killing himself. The Amish community circled close around its fallen and grieving brothers and sisters as it has for centuries. There were no signs in the streets, no press conferences, and no media coverage that wasn't shot through a telephoto lens. The grieving ones uttered few recorded words of forgiveness, but they sent a group to the widow and children of the man who shot their babies, comforted them, and even set up a charitable fund for them, just as they comforted and cared for the families of the girls he shot.

This is forgiveness in action flowing from an already released heart, forgiveness as it is worked out in real time. The evidence of true forgiveness is the freedom to continue to act lovingly despite the hurts and tragedies we endure. As the return from victimhood back to personhood, forgiveness is active and personal; it creates choices and behavior that at once create and reflect the freedom, deliverance, and salvation that already exist in the heart of every forgiving/forgiven person.

It's our knowing of the truth that accomplishes all this. To know truth, *yida* truth, is the same as knowing God—not with a mental construct, but with the experience of our lives. Truth: that which is strong and vigorous and has the capacity to liberate, is the same as God. God is truth personified. God is love; God's love is free and true. God is Garden, the place of our original state of complete freedom and unity. Forgiveness is a return to Garden, to God, to Unity. God is Unity, and as such, our relationship with him is never broken or even diminished from his side of the equation. For God, as the perfection of love and Unity, every relationship with him is also perfect—how could it be otherwise? That we *experience* our relationships with him and each other as something less than perfect, less than forgiven, is not a punishment, but a choice: our choice alone, as we are the only ones with a choice to make. God has already made his. In terms of how we typically understand for-giveness as an action or a legal decision...

God doesn't "forgive" anyone—ever.

There is no need. We are always already forgiven, and there is nothing we can do to alter that fact. Forgiveness isn't something God does—it's something he *is*. All we can do is accept it or not, realize it or not. Come in out of the rain or not. But we have to be ready to accept forgiveness for it to appear. We have to be ready to accept freedom, which is the same thing. And most of us are not.

How often do we hear of inmates being released from prison only to quickly commit new crimes in order to be returned to the confines they know rather than the freedom they fear; of alcoholics, once detoxed and rehabilitated, turning back to drink; of lottery winners squandering their sudden wealth to return to their former poverty; of celebrities who've struggled long to achieve success only to have their personal and professional lives fall apart once they do; of men and women leaving abusive relationships and marriages only to begin new abusive relationships and marriages; of churchgoers being saved and baptized, but continuing to live in the fear and shadow of hell?

God, love, freedom, deliverance, salvation, and forgiveness are always and forever available and free. We need to be ready to accept that reality of life, or it will never become real in our lives.

① ① ⊕ ⊕ ⊕

There is one more wonderful and pointed story at the end of Luke 7 in which a Pharisee named Simon, Shim'on, invites Yeshua to dinner. During the meal, a woman known throughout the city as a sinner, enters Simon's house weeping uncontrollably. Standing behind Yeshua as he reclines at the table, she wets his feet with her tears, dries them with her hair, and anoints them with expensive perfume. Simon watches all this from the head of the table, thinking to himself that if Yeshua were really a prophet, he would know what sort of woman was touching him. Thinking as a Pharisee, Simon knows that to be touched by someone unclean was to become unclean as well, which a Pharisee would never do. Either Yeshua doesn't know who is touching him or doesn't care, making him neither prophet nor Pharisee.

Yeshua, perhaps while continuing to dip his food and eat, casually announces, "Simon, I have something to say to you." Simon replies, "Say it, Teacher." Yeshua: "A moneylender had two debtors: one owed five hundred denarii, and the other fifty. When they were unable to repay, he graciously forgave them both. So which of them will love him more?" Simon: "I suppose the one whom he forgave more." Yeshua: "You have judged correctly." Then turning toward the woman, he continues: "Do you see this woman? I entered your house; you gave me no water for my feet, but she has wet my feet with her tears and wiped them with her hair. You gave me no kiss; but she, since the time I came in, has not ceased to kiss my feet. You did not anoint my head with oil, but she anointed my feet with perfume. For this reason I say to you, her sins, which are many, have been forgiven, for she loved much; but he who is forgiven little, loves little."

Is this really true? Does the size of the forgiven debt really translate directly into the amount of love and gratitude experienced by the one forgiven? Looking at forgiveness as we typically do, as a legal transaction passively and vicariously coming to us from the outside in, it would seem that size does not really matter: the wicked slave forgiven of a debt he could never repay in a hundred lifetimes could still not find it in his heart to forgive even the small debt of his fellow slave. In our collective experience, it seems more likely that people will not be radically changed to realize love and gratitude in their lives when they dodge a bullet of any size—at least not for long.

But the truth—Yeshua's point here—is that forgiveness, like everything else along the Fifth Way comes from the inside out—never from the outside in. As long as we continue to think legally and contractually, our view of the value of forgiveness is directly related to our view of *ourselves*, not our view of the forgiver or the forgiven debt. It's our view of ourselves, our performance under the Law, that dictates the amount of love and gratitude that will be generated by forgiveness. Under law there is only guilt and self-righteousness with nothing in between: the woman knows she is guilty; Simon, who believes he is legally blameless, is self-righteous. Our ability to return to love and freedom after being forgiven depends directly on whether we see ourselves as guilty or righteous; whether we feel we've *earned* and are now *entitled* to forgiveness or whether it was freely given in the first place. But the truth that Law was never meant to be a legal instrument at all means we never earn anything by it anyway—forgiveness is always and forever free.

If we earn forgiveness by following the Law, forgiveness isn't free; if it isn't free, gratitude is not an appropriate response. If we think we have earned it, then by God, everyone else had better earn it as well: after all, we suffered long under the law to earn our place, just as the elder brother of the prodigal son suffered in his father's fields while his younger brother was off playing with his family's money. If we think forgiveness isn't free, there is no joy in what is given to us, only resentment over what is freely given to others.

It's not how much we are forgiven that makes us love much—we are always and forever forgiven; it's whether we realize that we are *freely* forgiven that brings wellsprings of love into our lives, whether we can drop our legalistic tendencies long enough to see and begin to know the truth: that we have earned nothing and are entitled to nothing and yet are *denied nothing*.

Returning to our story, Yeshua says to the woman: "Your sins have been forgiven." Those around the table begin to say to themselves, "Who is this man who even forgives sins?"

Even here, they misunderstand. Yeshua does not say he is forgiving anything, and he is not. He is merely stating the reality of forgiveness already accomplished—confirming what the woman has already realized—that she is free from all the worry and concern and fear with which her broken life had burdened her. Then, as if to clear up any possible misinterpretation, Yeshua completes the scene by saying to her, "Your faith has saved you; go in peace." Not "I have saved you," or even, "The Father has saved you..."

We should know by now enough of the original intent of the key words here: "faith," "saved," and "peace" to be able to interpret Yeshua's meaning from within the Aramaic Agreement. He is saying to the woman and to all of us by extension:

"Your trust and knowing of the truth of God's absolute love and acceptance has made you free from anything that would stand in the way of the greatest possible health and wholeness and Unity in life; go live it."

> The Truth will make us free.
> The Truth is Gospel.
> The Gospel is Good News.
> The Good News is: there is no bad news.
> Freedom is forgiveness and forgiveness is free.
> We're as forgiven as we want to be

>The house is finally quiet. You and Meg are asleep in your
bunks and I am alone with only the gas fire and my roaring
thoughts. Marian is in Idyllwild on retreat with sixty or seventy
women from our church. Practically had to push her out the
door. Very apprehensive. Wondering if she'd fit in, be
comfortable. Her first retreat. Gotten two phone calls from
her since last night when it started. Sounds like she needn't
have worried, as I expected. Often the things we need the
most are also the most frightening.

>It has been a long day. A good day with you two, but long.
I'm glad to be alone for a moment--well, at least quiet. I know
now I'm not cut out for full-time three-year-old chatter.
I promised we'd go fishing, so we bought little poles and reels
and went to the lake. Didn't come close to a bite and you
both got bored. Turned out to be more an exercise in casting.
Me casting for Meg, you for yourself. You caught right on,
casting far out into the middle of the little lake, making me
watch you. Meg making me watch her reel back in. Trying to
give both of you a healthy respect for what a fish hook can do
to a finger.

>As usual, you were off and running on your own looking for
the best spot to fish--Meg staying close by my side, but always
calling to you. And there was this one moment, one image I
caught of you about 50 yards away--on your haunches right at
the water's edge, looking down at your line, backlit by the sun
with that halo around the edges of stray hair and fabric,
sparkling water reflected in your face. I stared, recording
every detail in my mind, willing to trade half a year's pay for a
loaded camera and telephoto lens.

>I have been a little short tempered. Well, OK, very short.
It's not you. The business partnership has been extremely

stressful. Problems with money (not enough), problems with the work (missed deadlines), and worst, pretty serious disagreements over the nature of the partnership itself.

>I didn't think that we, as partners and friends and brothers in faith could lose our common bond and vision so quickly and completely. I don't know why I thought that, but I did. So once again I have been surprised. And as angry as I can remember being for a very long time. It's not over. Every time I think it is, it starts again. I have the weekend as respite, but it starts again on Monday. I'm not sure that at least one of our partners will survive in the group. I'm not sure I want him to, although I've been friend and co-worker to him for over seven years. I'm also not sure why this is happening, but I am learning to be tough, firm, uncompromising in certain areas where my absolutes meet the road.

>In that peculiar way I seem to have of being able to look at myself from some certain height as if I were someone else, it has all been fascinating to watch. I see transformation in myself, willingness to embrace the necessity of confrontation when confrontation is required. Of doing the very disagreeable tasks when they are clearly my responsibility. I haven't been altogether pleased with myself, though. My anger and resentment–though possibly justified to an extent–have still been ugly. And I have talked too much. My problems with anyone else should have been kept to those directly involved except where necessary.

> I hope to learn from this, to understand more of what the Desert Fathers have been trying to tell me about love and silence and the connection between the two: "I have often repented of having spoken, but never of having remained silent." Abbot Arsenius speaking to me from his ancient world to a world where everything and nothing has changed; from his deep silence to a non-silence I have come to expect.

Bread and Blood

God's relationship with each of us is *always* intensely personal, *always* played out in the micro and not the macro, *always* defined by compassion and not justice, and *always* freely forgiven as God continues to guide us into ripeness.

Mamlacha and *malkuth*, micro and macro, justice and mercy, law and guidance, good and evil, sin and shalom, freedom and forgiveness create a layering of principles that all reinforce each other and present a unified view of Kingdom. Or perhaps a better way to describe the interaction of these concepts from an Aramaic perspective is to say that they are all multiple ways of looking at the same thing. Every one of these pairs points to an inside-out process by which an individual, transformed not by the macro pressures of law and justice but by the micro attraction of compassion and mercy, breaks out into community from the downside-up to live a life that is "good" and "sinless" and "perfect," while being completely free of the law that normally would govern such things—free to live from the backside-front without fear of abandonment. All these pairs of concepts are different views, different facets of the Fifth Way to Kingdom.

But there is one more pair to consider...

Bread and Blood.

① ① ⊕ ⊕ ⊕

There's an old saying that at the Protestant Reformation, five hundred years ago, the Catholics took the Bread and the Protestants took the Book, and they have never been together since. It's sad but true that at that moment in history, the mysticism, liturgy, and tradition of the ancient Roman church seems to have been formally divorced from the integrity and common sense of the Scriptures.

Like two parents fighting over the same child without the wisdom of Solomon to guide them, Protestants and Catholics actually did split the baby in two, with both walking away poorer as a result. It's as if the Roman church, in taking the bread, the mystical sacraments and traditions, took the heart of the church; the Protestants, in taking the book, the strict reliance on and faith in the Word of God, took the mind. But heart and mind need each other, and once again in the West, what was once one became two—with both halves losing touch with Unity.

In reality, the Roman Catholic church had lost its foundation in the Scriptures long before the Protestant Reformation; it can be argued that the early church had severed its ties with all things Jewish—the context of Scripture—by as early as the second century CE. In fact, the disconnection and dissonance between Catholic dogma and practice and the message of Scripture was ultimately the flashpoint that ignited the Reformation itself. But a wounding as deep as a Reformation also creates a journey that has a life of its own, and the life of a journey as big as a Reformation is impossible to control.

To his dismay, Martin Luther couldn't control the forces he unleashed when he nailed his ninety-five complaints to the doors of Castle Church. So the pendulum that the Roman church had allowed to swing too far in one direction was pulled back by the Protestants too far in the other. It was classic escalation of the Four Ways: Luther never originally intended to break from the Catholic church, but when his first way attempts to yield, to work within the Catholic system, became unbearable, he switched to the second way and attempted to influence the church. But when his "influence" became too threatening, the Roman church went directly to the fourth way, trying to destroy Luther's voice and message, whereupon he resorted to the third way and exited.

As the fight escalated and blood was shed, the two sides hardened their lines and broadened the distinctions between them. Whether Evangelical, Calvinist, or Anabaptist, the Protestants retreated further into the literalism of their various interpretations of the Book, while the Catholics moved further into their traditions at the expense of the Book. And perhaps nowhere is the evidence of these distinctions more apparent than at the table of the bread and the blood: Communion, the Eucharist.

Beginning with the Anabaptists and in strict accordance with Scripture, contemporary Protestants see the bread and wine as "emblems," symbolic of the sacrifice of Yehsua to be used "in remembrance" of him. In stark contrast, Catholics, in their tradition, see the bread and wine as being supernaturally transformed into the body and blood of Christ at the moment of consecration, a belief called "transubstantiation." Luther himself offered the middle ground of "consubstantiation," the belief that the bread and wine were not actually transformed, but were mixed with, brought in union with, the body and blood of Christ. As different as these three interpretations are, they are also similar in that they all focus on the death and sacrifice of Jesus, and as they all originate in a Western setting, they are typically legalistic, passive, and vicarious—missing the deeper point being made by the Aramaic context.

When Yeshua says during his last meal with his friends in Luke 22, "This is my body which is given for you; do this in remembrance of me...This cup, which is poured out for you, is the new covenant in my blood," there is not much doubt that he is casting himself in a sacrificial light. The inference is clear that Israel, who killed many of her prophets including John the Baptist, would certainly strike again when feeling threatened by Yeshua's message. Yeshua knew this, of course, and is also clearly drawing lines between his impending death and the Temple sacrificial system where the blood of animals was shed to cleanse the sin of the people: Yeshua's blood would form the basis of a new covenant, one that would have the power to liberate, deliver, and forgive—not legally and temporarily, but transformatively and permanently.

But where we see these allusions legally, passively, and vicariously through the lens of Yeshua's death, the Aramaic Agreement would have us impose a very different meaning: an active and personal message based in compassion and mercy as seen through the lens of Yeshua's *life*.

The Jews celebrated life, not death, and still do today. To a people completely focused on herenow as opposed to therethen, death was a tragedy, not an escape from an inferior physical life to a better, spiritual one—and death by crucifixion was anathema. For as long as there was a Jewish presence and influence among the early followers of Yeshua and the Way, the cross as a symbol of God's redemption was abomination, and they never adopted it. Rather than an image of death, they used images of life and the preservation of life such as the fish, the anchor, and concentric circles signifying the eternal life of Father and Son. The cross did not become the symbol of Christianity until as late as the third or fourth centuries—well after Christianity had completely separated from Judaism. Participation in the action of life rather than the fact of death was the focus and unifying force of their faith.

But in terms of Yeshua's imagery at the Last Supper, it probably goes without saying that the eating of human flesh and the drinking of any creature's blood was expressly forbidden by Law, so imagine how hard it was for Jews to understand Yeshua's words not only at his last meal, but at John 6 right after he had multiplied five barley loaves and two fish to feed a huge crowd: "I am the bread of life; he who comes to me will not hunger, and he who believes in me will never thirst...Your fathers ate the manna in the wilderness, and they died. This is the bread which comes down out of heaven, so that one may eat of it and not die. I am the living bread that came down out of heaven; if anyone eats of this bread, he will live forever; and the bread also which I will give for the life of the world is my flesh."

How were Jews to understand such words? Like Nicodemus in John 3 who thought that to be born again meant he would have to re-enter his mother's womb, and like the Samaritan woman in the next chapter who wanted Yeshua's living water so she wouldn't have to carry that heavy jar out to the well every day, Yeshua's listeners this day thought they would have to literally eat human flesh in order to receive eternal life: "Then the Jews began to argue with one another, saying, "How can this man give us his flesh to eat?" But Yeshua pressed on: "Truly, truly, I say to you, unless you eat the flesh of the Son of Man and drink his blood, you have no life in yourselves. He who eats my flesh and drinks my blood has eternal life, and I will raise him up on the last day. For my flesh is true food, and my blood is true drink. He who eats my flesh and drinks my blood abides in me, and I in him. As the living Father sent me, and I live because of the Father, so he who eats me, he also will live because of me. This is the bread which came down out of heaven; not as the fathers ate and died; he who eats this bread will live forever."

Many of Yeshua's followers stopped following that day.

Yeshua is portrayed in John's Gospel as the "bread of life" in chapter 6, "living water" in chapter 7, and the "light of the world" in chapter 8—all images of the preservation of life; all substances that needed to be ingested or taken into ourselves; all substances working from the inside out to free us from hunger and thirst and darkness—to free us from worrying about tomorrow. But Yeshua's sayings here are so outrageous to a Jewish audience that they misinterpreted them and couldn't get past the imagery that was trying to point them toward truth. Interestingly, as many of Yeshua's first hearers missed the mark of his meaning by literalizing his words; we today miss the mark by legalizing them. Between the extremes of cannibalism and contract, the clues to meaning lie once again in the language itself for those who have ears to hear and can think beyond the first Four Ways.

Yeshua uses bread and blood as another in a series of images to get his point across. During that last meal, he takes bread, breaks it and passes it out saying, "Take this and eat; this is my body." Bread, *lakhma* in Aramaic, doesn't just mean physical bread, but as it shares roots with *hokhmah*, the word for wisdom, it also means the source of all sustenance—physical, emotional, spiritual—the very wisdom and provision of God, everything we need or will ever need. Yeshua is saying that that wisdom, that provision, resides in him; it is who he is; it is his body, as he and the Father are one. Everything that the Father is, Yeshua is—there is no daylight between them, no desire or action not identical. So he invites us to eat, to take into ourselves this sustenance from heaven, to become one with him just as he is one with the Father. To become "perfect," ripe and complete, as he and the Father are perfect and complete. "Take this and eat;" make it who we are as well.

And at the end of the meal, he takes the cup. The cup of his *dama*, his blood. But *dama* doesn't just mean blood, but also juice, sap, and essence. To the ancient Jews, the blood was the life force; it was that which carried life, and so was sacred. It was literally the essence of all that a creature was, which was why it was unlawful to drink it. But Yeshua tells us to drink his *dama*. Take this life force, this essential animation of who he is and make it who we are as well. The wine, also a juice, the Jewish symbol of joy and celebration mixed with the essence of Yeshua's oneness with the Father is the powerful symbol Yeshua is using to bring us to *taba*, the ability to see the goodness and rightness and truth of such things.

① ① ⊕ ⊕ ⊕

Yeshua often uses the phrase "in my name." He uses it specifically in terms of prayer many times, as in John 14: "Whatever you ask in my name, that will I do, so that the Father may be glorified in the Son. If you ask me anything in my name, I will do it." In considering such passages, it is we who now literalize and miss Yeshua's meaning by thinking if we simply pray the words "in Jesus' name," our prayers will be heard and answered. But affixing the words "in Jesus' name" to the end of every prayer can either be a beautiful reminder of a deeper truth or just extra words. The Aramaic word for "name" is *shema*, which can mean light, word, sound, reputation, character, essence: it is the essential or visible characteristic by which something is known as itself—as distinct from anything else. A name, a *shema*, in ancient Hebrew life was not just a word by which someone was called, it was always indicative of whom he or she was. Yeshua's name, probably a shortened form of the Hebrew *Yehosua*, literally means "Yahweh is salvation" and points to his mission and purpose.

To pray in Yeshua's name is not to simply invoke words that will guarantee God's favorable action; that is superstition. To pray with or in Yeshua's *shema*—character, essence, reputation, light—is to be completely identified with Yeshua, who is completely identified with the Father. It means to pray exactly as Yeshua would pray, who in turn, is praying exactly as the Father is praying. To pray for the same purpose for which the Father prays is by definition an answered prayer. Yeshua is calling us, either by prayer in his *shema* or by drinking his *dama*, to become one with him in desire, purpose, and action.

To see this drinking of *dama* as the unlawful drinking of physical blood is to literalize the meaning and exit the relationship; to see it as the symbol of a contract in blood, which guarantees God's favorable action, is to legalize the meaning and become passive in the relationship. To see the drinking of *dama* as identification with the essence of Yeshua and the Father is to vibrate at the frequency of the King, to enter Kingdom, *malkuth*, to know truth and become free.

Ancient Greek Christians called Communion *anamnesis*, "unforgetting," or as we would say, remembrance. Communion is remembering who we really are, before our fear changed us. When we eat and drink, when we enter into the oneness of Kingdom, we remember Yeshua, as he asked us to, in the fullest sense of that word's meaning. The remembrance is not what we do in worship service or liturgy—that is only symbol. We remember not just by passive thoughts in our minds, but by every action, choice, and the living out of each relationship in our lives—every moment of our lives. True remembrance is bringing the past into the present, taking our *lakhma* and *dama* into the streets and making that truth as real as our own body and blood to all those with whom we come in contact.

Lakhma and *dama*—bread and blood, wisdom and essence. These are words and symbols Yeshua used to help us become complete. But words lose their meaning with time and translation. Symbols lose their ability to point to truth as they devolve into ritual and superstition. It's up to each of us to keep the meaning written on our hearts. Not to content ourselves with the simple following of cold rules and forms, but to graduate from *mamlacha* to *malkuth*, to see the goodness of each face and life we encounter. And if we will truly eat the *lakhma* and drink the *dama* of Yeshua's life, we take our place as a *taba* people, a complete people—full of ripe fruit—ready, willing, and able; present at the right place and the right time to celebrate the unity we experience with God and each person who shares this moment with us.

There is no other Kingdom than this.
This Kingdom is all there is in Unity with the Father.

It all happens herenow. We enter Kingdom herenow. We live Kingdom herenow. If we desire transformation in our lives, that transformation is herenow. There is no therethen to await for our transformation...Yeshua is telling us that our transformation, our rebirth, our ingestion of living water, bread, and blood, is always imminent, always present and possible—it's always right on the tip of our tongues.

And make no mistake: Yeshua is also telling us: If we can't find it herenow, we won't find it therethen.

> Heaven is not where Kingdom begins—
> heaven is that into which Kingdom *extends*.

THE LIFE

ON THE WAY

>A few days ago, I decided to run some errands during the middle of the day and went to a store to see if I could find a filing cabinet for Marian. I turned down an aisle looking for furniture and out of the corner of my eye, caught sight of a woman pushing a cart toward me. Something about the figure she cut made me look. The way she carried herself, her smooth stride, striking profile as she looked across the aisle. Beautiful woman. It was a full second or two before I realized this was the woman I hold in bed every night. Unbelievably, inexplicably it was Marian...

>It was a full day or two before I realized what a gift I had been given. To see her as she is without me, without my influence. To see her as if for the first time and feel what that was like all over again. To be attracted, intrigued by her as if a stranger. To be reminded in a way that can't be planned or arranged why our paths have become one. A very great gift.

>But a gift not given in isolation. I just started a book yesterday, The Everlasting Man by G.K. Chesterton, whose premise states,

>...we see things fairly when we see them first... We must try to recover the candor and wonder of the child; the unspoiled realism and objectivity of innocence. Or if we cannot do that, we must try at least to shake off the cloud of mere custom and see the thing as new, if only by seeing it as unnatural. Things that may well be familiar so long as familiarity breeds affection had much better become unfamiliar when familiarity breeds contempt.

>And this is how it works: the soil broken up at Serra with words I heard again for the first time, seeds planted with my stranger-wife in a department store, and the onset of the storm of irrigation with Chesterton. It's uncanny. But so subtle. So easy to miss. To let be disguised, unrecognized as an unre-

lated series of events. And I suppose they are, until I make the connection. Hear the Lord's voice in the white noise. See his will in the randomness. Find his purpose in what I could so easily mistake as the meaninglessness of my life.

>And yet, in these rare moments of clarity, I know that the purpose and meaning I crave in this life are as nothing compared to maintaining the finding of a simple state of childlike openness, of potential acceptance. I am more convinced every day that God will be like nothing I would ever expect, like nothing I could ever be truly prepared for; that my whole job here is just to learn to see everything and everyone as if for the first time and love them with a first love something like an infatuation--a wild, heart-pounding, high school crush.

>Because only with that life-view in my muscle-memory as automatic response will I ever hold the possibility of accepting what I see as mine when I see it in God's face. He would never turn his back on me, but I may turn mine on him, or simply miss him completely in my inability to believe my own spiritual eyes.

>It really is so simple. It's not about saving souls or doing good or learning great mysteries. It's just about seeing with the eyes of a child the undistorted, unvarnished, thrilling truth that washes over me; living a lifetime of joyful rehearsal, that when the ultimate truth appears, I will run to embrace it.

The Question

Sometimes the hardest thing to do
is just the thing you do next.

WHAT HAS BEEN THE SENSATION OF HAVING READ THROUGH THIS
book? Sitting there reading, you've no doubt been leading with your
head, your mind. Some concepts and ideas may have been interesting, enlightening, even liberating—others you may be resisting,
remaining skeptically distant either reserving judgment or having
rendered it already. But the most important thing to realize is that
whatever your sensations or reactions, you're still *sitting there reading.*
Leading with your mind.

It's what we naturally do as Westerners.

You have been considering Yeshua's message intellectually, trying
to stream the straight rays of *nuhra*, of enlightenment, down into the
curved well of your particular worldview. And though opening the
mind, breaking the stranglehold of the mind's view of life and
reality is an essential step, it's only one step.

We are not saved by the mind.

So Yeshua's message, if it saves, is not intellectual at its core. The
wind blows where it wishes and we hear the sound of it, but we
don't know where it comes from or where it goes—our minds are
limited by what we can conceive, but we were built to live and

breathe far beyond mere conception. If you have allowed the images, stories, and wild sayings of Yeshua to reach beyond your mind, to creep into a deeper experience and begin layering up underneath like those shovels full of dirt raining down on your head, you've begun to form the foundation of a structure beyond conception, one that will hold and shelter whether mentally conceived or not.

Standing a few feet higher at the bottom of your well, what now? What next? The Way is not clearly stretching out before you; it doesn't do that. But deep inside your well, even the slightest glimpse of an endless horizon demands a next step.

If you leave all this new information neatly packed in boxes or displayed in a glass case, what is merely catalogued or debated among friends changes nothing, touches nothing that really matters. If you, like Nicodemus, have come this far alone by night or, like the rich young man, have come by day trailing servants and friends, you now stand before Yeshua—his full gaze on you alone.

This is your moment. What is it you want to ask? What is that most important question, the one on which it seems your whole life depends?

If you, as they, sense that something is missing, that even if you've lived a very ethical or religious life, there must be more than you've experienced or done; if you, as they, are hearing the call, reaching the threshold of the pain you can endure, or losing the desire to feel anything at all, then you as they have formed the same question:

What must I do to obtain eternal life?

Isn't that it? Two thousand years ago, yesterday, today—isn't that the question? Is what we see around us all there is to life or is there more? When we die, is that all there is to life or is there more? Is the universe a friendly place? Is there really a hand to hold in the dark or are we on our own, alone? *Eternal life.* The phrase heard over and over in Yeshua's stories encompasses all this, all these deeply human questions, questions of which fear is made.

But like everything else we've encountered along the Way, eternal life is also a part of the Aramaic Agreement, and so means one thing to us and another to Yeshua and his first hearers. When we imagine eternal life, we are thinking of salvation, of the forever of a heavenly existence somewhere, somewhen in the future. We should know enough by now to know that this is not what Yeshua or any good Hebrew is thinking.

The word for eternal, *alma*, also means *world* as at John 3:16—for thus God loved the world/*alma* so as to give his only begotten son that whoever would believe in him would not perish but would have life that is eternal/*alma*; it means era, age, generation; its roots point toward never ending cycles of newness and diversity, which is why it's used to convey both eternity and the face of our ever-changing world. Eternal life, *hayye d'alma*, is not only life that continues beyond death, it's life right herenow that is always new, fresh, exciting, fulfilled, complete, alive. Yeshua said he came to bring us life and life abundantly—*hayye d'alma*. Salvation and eternal life are both spiritual liberation...beginning right now and here as always.

What must we do to obtain *hayye d'alma*, to fill in the missing pieces and begin to experience our lives as always new and alive, each turned corner a surprise? Our minds alone, like the jet plane that while the greatest mode of travel across earth can't get us into lowest orbit, will not take us there. To find this kind of life we must stop thinking and start acting; if we want to go somewhere we've never been before, we need to start doing something we've never done before—the doing, the experiencing, is the *hayye d'alma* we seek.

> Obtaining life that is eternal only becomes possible the moment we become present to the life that is now.

We think of eternity as a large amount of time, but really, all time is just one moment, eternally. God is everywhere and every-when, but everywhere is just one place—here—and everywhen is just one moment—now. We'll never find God, the source of eternal life, anywhere else because we can't *be* anywhere else except where and when we are. To be fully present to this moment and all it contains is to be present to the *hayye d'alma* that is our Father. Practicing presence *is* the Fifth Way, the Way of Yeshua, the only way to the Father.

Yeshua is *yihidaya*, translated as "only begotten" at John 3:16, but which at root means single, solitary, united in all aspects of being. We would say integrated, having integrity. As son of God—*son of Unity*—Yeshua, the completely integrated man, is the personification of presence. All his thoughts, actions, deepest desires function as one and are completely connected to his moments. How much of Yeshua's Way would be traveled simply by making sure our thoughts match our present duties, that we are actually and only thinking about what we are doing at the moment?

Why do we love extreme sports, thrill rides, falling in love, making love, making music, beautiful people and places? Because they all do the same thing: they integrate us. They focus all our parts, all our aspects of being on one thing, one moment. They make us feel alive—*hayye d'alma*—by being so intense as to banish anything that is not relevant, essential to the experience. To jump out of an airplane with a bedsheet strapped to your back or hang from a cliff face by your fingertips is not to be wondering whether you left the porch light on or even whether your child's lab results are in. With no room for error there is no room for anything separated from the moment.

We feel alive and renewed when we are not separated from anything or anyone; separation is sin, so sinlessness, connection, is experienced as life eternally new and now. Prayer beads, meditation, contemplative prayer, worship music, and all religious rituals are designed to take us to the same integrated place by distancing us from the ever-present monologue in our minds. Yeshua said: seek first the Kingdom, *the Way of presence*, and God's righteousness, *unity*, and all else would be added. When we do whatever we do, whether in kitchen or cathedral, if we bring our full presence with us, we get it all.

Typically, we say that the essence of spirituality is love, but what is love without presence? Thomas Merton wrote that love, beyond feeling or behavior, is actually *identification with the beloved*. When the line between us and our beloved has become so thin we can no longer see where we end and the other begins, when we've in a sense become the beloved, anything we do is done as if to ourselves and the beloved at the same time. Identification is presence and presence is identification. "I and the Father are one," is the expression of the pure presence of Yeshua. And presence is indistinguishable from love, love that makes us feel alive, eternally.

What must we do to obtain life that is eternally alive?

The Question

⊙ ⊘ ⊕ ⊕ ⊕

> Relationship occupies the spot where the line
> between heaven and earth is the thinnest.

A lifetime ago when I was trying to learn how to sing, a vocal coach said something that seemed very odd at the time, but has stuck with me, becoming truer as the years go by. He told me he couldn't teach me to sing correctly; he could only teach me what it *felt like* to sing correctly. Knowing that this distinction would be lost on me, he went on to say that when you are learning any external instrument—piano, guitar, saxophone—you're dealing with fingers, hands, arms, lips, teeth, tongue, body parts you can see and consciously control. You can watch teachers and other players and imitate their movements and technique. It's not that such a process as training visible muscles is ever easy or quick, as in training for any sport or physical skill, but at least it's out in the open. You can see what it is you're trying to do.

The point he was making was that in singing, the instrument is within us, requiring the use of muscles that can't be seen. You can't see yourself or anyone else controlling the interplay between diaphragm and vocal folds, the position of the larynx, resonance of tone in chest or head or anywhere in between. But you can certainly hear the difference. As teacher, he would be able to hear the difference between when I was producing a tone correctly and when I was not, so his process of teaching would be to describe the sensations of correct singing and try to get me to experience those same sensations as I sang. When he heard the right result, the right sound, he would tell me; my job was to memorize that sensation, and then simply continue to reproduce the sensations that would reproduce the right sounds.

It did seem odd at the time, an unnecessarily long way home. But the longer I live, the more wisdom I see in such a process, such a view of the workings of things.

We can't see any of the muscles of the spiritual world, and unlike singing, we often don't even feel them working. Thomas Keating wrote that "the spiritual life doesn't need to be felt, but it does need to be practiced," noting that some of the most spiritually mature people he'd known had never or rarely felt emotional response to decades of spiritual practice. And from its earliest generations, the ancient church also recognized that though emotional response—understood as spiritual *consolation* and *desolation*—is an essential and beautiful part of our spirituality, it is not a gauge of spiritual progress. That though it has definite and discernable effects in the physical life, the spiritual life is largely an unfelt process.

A millennium and a half later this distinction has been lost. We think that of course we feel our spirituality—it's how we know it exists. But the ancients remind that our emotional responses to the workings of the spirit are just that: physical responses to nonphysical connection. They often occur together, but to become mature in our faith is to keep showing up to the practice of it, confident that spiritual progress is being made whether we feel it or not. To confuse emotion and spirituality is to run the risk of merely seeking emotional responses that, like an addict with a drug, will certainly create emotion, but not necessarily spiritual encounter.

And if we can't feel spiritual muscles working, we won't see them working either, even in the place we've always been told to look...

Religion and spirituality are very different things.

To run the clock back to the beginning of any religion is to see that before there is religion, there is a direct experience of God's presence deep enough to transform the life of an individual or group. Religion begins as the *expression* of that experience, and if it survives, grows to include the manner in which followers live their faith together, creating a culture of rites, doctrine, and symbol. But very few of us begin at the beginning, and those who join a religion are first confronted with an intellectual, cultural, and emotional expression, not the spiritual experience itself.

The fearful attitudes, emotions, and behavior that limit the quality of our lives will not change until we have directly experienced the Good News of God's nature. So when Yeshua is asked, his Way is not confined to religion; it begins right here and now with the daily details of human relationship: loving each other as we want to be loved. In each loving detail are Law and religion fulfilled because relationship building *itself*, presence in action, is the spiritual life, the Fifth Way. Functional religion ushers us into these loving details and direct spiritual encounters; dysfunctional religion becomes an end in itself, symbol without meaning, a form of corporate narcissism blind to deeper connection.

When Yeshua as singing coach told Nicodemus, "The wind blows where it wishes and you hear the sound of it, but do not know where it comes from and where it is going; so is everyone who is born of the Spirit," he was trying to get these distinctions across. We can't see the wind, but we see its effect on the world around us; we can't see the Spirit, but we can see its effect on how we live our lives and engage in relationship.

Learning to live spiritually begins as a learning to memorize and reproduce, not specific feelings or religious culture, but a *quality of relationship* that is the evidence of "correct" spiritual engagement. It's a way of sneaking up on unseen Spirit by placing ourselves directly in the spot where the line between heaven and earth is the thinnest—the spot occupied by good relationship.

God is the unseen unity, the simplicity that embraces all the diversity and complexity we see every day, and Yeshua is showing us how all our relationships are one and the same, flowing both toward and away from that unseen connection. In this life, the quality of heavenly relationships is defined by the quality of earthly ones. When Yeshua tells us to leave our rituals at the altar and first go fix a broken human relationship, when he says what we do to the least of these around us we do to him, he is saying that when we tend to the relationships among us and in our midst, we are at the same time tending to our relationship within.

Or as John wrote in his first letter, "If someone says, 'I love God,' and hates his brother, he is a liar; for the one who does not love his brother whom he has seen, cannot love God whom he has not seen." And if James is right—that faith without works is dead—then he and John, as bluntly as possible, are telling us that *our love for God is only as real as our love for each other*.

Again from John's first letter, "God is love, and the one who abides in love abides in God, and God abides in him... There is no fear in love; but perfect love casts out fear, because fear involves punishment, and the one who fears is not perfected in love. We love, because He first loved us."

If you find yourself wondering how you're doing with God, about the quality of your relationship with him, just take a look at the quality of your relationships with those closest to you, those whose toothbrushes hang next to yours. The amount of stress, anxiety, anger, resentment, frustration, jealousy, envy in your life directly measure your fear—they are all manifestations of it. It is always fear that breaks down relationship, forces us into Four Ways strategies that treat others as object and expose our distrust of God's presence and promise. Our relationship with God is realized in relationship with each other, and our love for each other leads inevitably back to the God who loved us first.

The moment our desire becomes greater than our fear, desire for another's *shalom* becomes greater than fear of our own loss, the journey from fear to love becomes suddenly possible with presence as vehicle. The moment we begin to take pleasure in *leaving people better than we found them*—even if all we give is a smile in a grocery aisle—it is enough; it will introduce our presence to God's presence and, with nothing more emotional or religious than this, bring us to the trailhead of the Way.

Standing at the trailhead, the Gate to the Way of Yeshua, the string of moments we've deliberately spent experiencing connection and presence have begun the work of dismantling our natural Four Ways worldview and have led us here to the edge of life that is spiritually and eternally alive. It is just a beginning...the beginning of a beginning because as far as we've come, we've only traveled the part of the path we can see stretching before us. Both Nicodemus and the rich young man had followed the rules of good relationship as well as they could within the confines of their religion and culture—yet were still aware that something was missing, that they'd fallen short of experiencing eternal life. Yeshua called both men to look beyond the walls of their wells, rise from the constricted security of the familiar to face the endless horizon of a different world. One man did and one could not, walking away saddened at the prospect of selling everything he knew and understood for a fall into the unfamiliar.

If you're on a recognizable path, a familiar path, you're most likely not on the Fifth Way, but one of the other Four. Like the rich young man, you've crept back from the edge of the familiar in fear of too much unseen space. No need for shame; we all do this. If Yeshua's Way really does bring us back to Father, then it also brings us radically beyond everything we think we know, because that's where Father lives. We won't see the path stretching out before us, planned and understood—it doesn't do that, but remains eternally new and unanticipated...unsettling, disorienting, disturbing, dangerous yet exhilarating, breathlessly materializing under our feet with each step.

The line between the familiar and unfamiliar, between the Four Ways and the Fifth, between earth and heaven, is the edge from which Yeshua is calling us to fall if we really want to experience life that is eternally new. It will cost us everything we have accrued and come to trust, everything that blinds us to the radical truth within, among, and in our midst. Yeshua's last instruction to his friends before his execution—to simply "love each other as I have loved you" is the key, but only has power to lead us to our rebirth in spirit when the radical notion begins to dawn that loving as Yeshua loved means loving everyone, equally, all the time.

Yeshua tells us that if we only love those who love us, what have we really accomplished? If we're only kind to those who are kind to us, what have we learned of his unfamiliar Way? For Yeshua, loving the *enemy*—identification and presence with another even in the absence of affirming feelings or understanding—is the central effect of radical transformation, of being spiritually reborn with the ability to see the unity of eternal life everywhere we look. But if loving the enemy is the effect of being born again spiritually, what is the cause? In his typically paradoxical fashion, Yeshua is telling us in every way he possibly can that *the effect is also the cause.* That becoming unoffendable and unjudging, to place love where it is not deserved leads both to and from the spiritual awakening of our second birth.

Two thousand years of rehearsing Yeshua's teaching to love the enemy has done the job of making the unfamiliar seem familiar and domesticated: no longer dangerous or able to shock us, move us beyond the edge of what we think we know. But for Yeshua's first followers, the law of the land was retribution, an eye for an eye and a tooth for a tooth. In an honor-shame society where tribes were bound to exact revenge for transgression, the people were taught to love their neighbor but hate their enemy; to hold the "serpent" in their hearts—the anger and resentment that fueled such retribution; that to grant forgiveness before contrition and restitution was not only foolish but immoral. Yeshua's first hearers would have been as scandalized and outraged as the elder brother of the prodigal to hear love for the enemy being identified as the essence of Yeshua's Way.

The truth is, for all our two thousand years of familiarity with Yeshua's teaching, we no more love our enemies than the Jews who listened first. Who is our enemy? Yeshua would say anyone we see as *other*, who doesn't think, act, or look as we do: from an irritating co-worker to a legal adversary to an unfaithful spouse; from someone in a different political party, ethnicity, church or theology to an illegal immigrant or the person who took our job; enemy is the one who offends us through action or mere existence, the person we absolutely believe is going to hell: thief, addict, pedophile, child rapist, suicide bomber. We fear our enemies, judge them into categories that strip them of the basic humanity we reserve for ourselves and those we understand and approve—those who understand and approve us.

Not that we don't defend boundaries and borders and those who can't defend themselves—even with lethal force when necessary. But when we do what we must in the moment to preserve life and relationship, can we leave our defense of the moment *in that moment*—careful not to carry it with us as the defining terms of yet another person or group we will forever see as *other*, unworthy of our love?

Can we do this? Hold heaven and earth in one embrace?

When Yeshua tells us not to resist an evil person, to offer our left cheek as well when struck on the right, to offer our coat as well when sued for our shirt; to walk a second mile of servitude when obligated only to go the first, he is telling us that being lawful and right is not enough. Being lawful and right is merely familiar, not Godly or God-like...does not show us the Father as Yeshua did with his fierce identification with the least of these. Being lawful and right is just a beginning, the barest beginning of a beginning.

God is love—doesn't do love as a verb, *is* love as a noun. Our behavior means nothing to such a love; it just is, exists as itself, can't be attenuated or diverted it in any way, is never withheld. When Yeshua reminds us that sun and rain, the warmth and provision of the Father's love, fall indiscriminately on both the just and the unjust, the righteous and unrighteous, if we're not offended and outraged, we haven't been paying attention, haven't moved even within the vicinity of the Father's radical conclusion. Love that is earned or reciprocated is familiar. The Father's love is neither earned nor familiar, continues whether reciprocated or not. We can stand in shade and shelter, deny its existence, but we can't stop the falling.

This is outrageous, unfair, unjust. *Exactly.*

God's love is not fair. God's love is not just.

God's love deliberately unbalances the scales of justice in favor of the beloved. Always in favor of the beloved. If we really want to follow Yeshua's Way, the only Way to the Father, we will have to pass through outrage and offense, let our outrage at the furious nature of God's love burn until there is no fuel left within. Yeshua is telling us that *nothing happens in the first mile,* the familiar mile of obligation, of law and rule. It is in the second mile, the voluntary mile of undeserved love, that we learn something of our Father in heaven and ourselves on earth. Loving our neighbor brings us to the edge of all we cling to in fear...

...loving our enemy puts us in freefall.

Love like this cannot be transferred. Too radical, too perfect, it must be experienced to be believed. When we feel the first stirrings of compassion leave our heart in the direction of someone we believed impossible to love, when that compassion allows us to lower justice and blood pressure long enough to give whatever is most needed in the moment, it's then we first glimpse the equally impossible love our Father has for us. We will never really believe we can be loved and accepted until we experience giving love and acceptance away to someone equally underserving. If we can't love the enemy, we'll never know how God can love us. If we can't forgive the enemy, we'll never know how forgiven we really are.

The only way we can freely give something away is if we already possess it in the first place. And the only way we know for sure whether we possess a thing is if we can freely give it away. No strings attached. We can only love because he first loved us.

Doing everything we've learned to do in presence and relationship brings us to the edge of all that is familiar, stands us up before Yeshua, his full gaze on us alone. This is our moment, our moment to ask the question...ask what we must do next to obtain the life we know still eludes. But in asking, we are faced with even more pressing questions: while living and breathing here on earth, are we prepared to accept an answer that comes directly out of heaven? That turns everything we think we know inside out, downside up, and backside front? Are we ready to sell all we think we possess for a fall with Yeshua into life that is eternally new?

Can we do this? Hold such seemingly disparate truths as heaven and earth in one embrace? Learn to love the oscillations of life: day and night, joy and loss, ascent and descent? Can we learn to live with unresolved mystery? Laugh at our compulsive need to explain? Lose everything, our very lives, in order to find life? See purpose in pain, acceptance in imperfection, strength in vulnerability, accomplishment in inaction, community in silence and solitude? Can we walk the agendas of the Four Ways while riding the blissful dependence of the Fifth, realizing that the objects of our deepest desire can only and ever be *received*...never taken?

Can we do this?

Yeshua says yes.

And he says it most absolutely and emphatically from the cross— the ultimate mystery of life in death, beauty in cruelty, power in abject weakness.

Yeshua says yes.

And until *we* say yes, we will not follow him along the Way.

The Four Ways give us the things we need to live.
The Fifth Way gives us life. Life that is eternally new and alive.

>How do you prepare for a journey without an agenda?

>You don't. Preparation is agenda in thin disguise. Committing to simply follow a trail of breadcrumbs left by others who simply followed has led to places I didn't know existed because I was finally free to find truth where it was and not where I expected it to be. But choosing to follow rather than run from pain pinned me to truth's brutality—the ruthless disorientation and near panic of feeling that last intellectual wall at my back fall away, spinning around to three hundred and sixty degrees of landless horizon.

>The journey back across the arc of Christian thought led emphatically to Hebrew thought and began building bridges in my mind: between modern and ancient, East and West, mystical and intellectual, religious and spiritual. They all had value—all necessary parts of the whole. In the written words of those I would never meet and the spoken words and faces of those I met as often as possible, I sensed bigness, a vantage that promised much more than I could ever hold in two hands.

>Through every book and ancient word study, I could feel myself slipping more and more snugly into the sandals of those who followed first. And there among the silent pages, I found a Jesus I'd never met before—not in church, school, monastery, warehouse, or anywhere in between. Like the first smile you coax out of a child peeking around her mother's hip, this Hebrew Jesus, so outrageous and unattractive at first, became slowly responsive, then understandable, comforting. Inevitable. Here was a Jesus who spoke in a language without contradiction. Here was a message grounded in the daylight details of common sense yet as expansive as the nighttime sky. Here was someone I could follow with abandon for the rest of my life.

>It was all coming down to identity, who and what I thought I really was—and as far as I'd come, I still didn't know what such questions even meant. I was still neurotic, still chasing things out beyond my windshield, but now my neurosis had one advantage: this Hebrew Jesus had opened a space in my mind large enough to drive an experience through, large enough to let Merton and Brother Lawrence, John of the Cross and the Desert Fathers lead me inward to a silent place where facts became faces attached to living relationship. Imitating them, I practiced the silent presence of God until I found there really are moments when life makes sense.

>Sitting alone one night on the deck behind our rented townhome, there was suddenly a thought in a certain place in my mind where there hadn't been before. Just words. Not even words spoken out loud. I'd heard them many times before of course, but at that moment they became real, alive, giving me permission to entertain the unthinkable and begin to know what couldn't have been transferred any other way.

I was loved.

>I was loved with a love that couldn't be lost because it couldn't be gained. It just was. It self-existed. I could either accept the freely roaming gift or move on, but I couldn't change the fact of it. My behavior didn't matter to such a love: at my worst or my best, it was all the same to the Father who simply waits for my return.

>I'd always been told and had come to believe that you can't have the good news without the bad news.

>But the Good News is...there is no bad news.

>I was as loved and forgiven as I wanted to be. God's choice had been always and forever made.

My turn.

Smilepoint

It's not what you think.
It never is.

AND THE MORE YOU THINK, THE LESS IT RESEMBLES ANYTHING
close to what really is.

Like an anticipated, important conversation you worry over, play
over and over in your mind, running down every possible twist and
turn, reply and rebuttal: no matter how many times you live that
conversation in your thoughts or how many versions you create, the
real thing is always different and unexpected—and you remain
unprepared.

Sometimes just the slightest gesture or look, a fragrance or a stray
lock of hair can derail, deflate, and defuse even the best-laid plan.

It never comes out the way you think.

① ① ⊕ ⊕ ⊕

Across the line between the first two chapters of Mark, Yeshua heals
a leper, forgives a paralytic, and calls Levi out of his tax booth in
back-to-back succession. These three encounters placed together tell
us that Mark sees them as connected. All three men are outcasts: the
leper is banned from coming into contact with anyone until
declared clean by temple priests; the paralytic's disability, viewed as
the direct result of sin, leaves him suspect and utterly dependent,

unable to take his place in the community; Levi as a toll-tax collector is hated as a Roman collaborator, a "beast in human form" excluded from any social interaction or religious fellowship.

Yeshua is obligated by all the religious and social codes of his Agreement to respect the boundaries placed between him and each of these men. Yet with all three, Yeshua goes out of his way to break through those boundaries in order to connect with them.

He breaks ritual boundaries: by extending his hand and touching the leper before he is healed, he makes himself ritually unclean, and by declaring the leper clean, claims authority held only by the temple priests.

He breaks theological boundaries: when the paralytic is lowered to him through a hole in the roof dug by loving friends, Yeshua calls him "son," a member of his own family, and before there is any evidence of repentance, declares that his sins are forgiven, apparently claiming authority held only by God.

He breaks social boundaries: by calling Levi to his inner-circle before he's willing to leave his tax booth, his seat of dishonor, and going to his house later that day, he shocks bystanders—reclining at a table full of other tax collectors and those who stand wildly outside the Law.

When Pharisees accuse him of legal violations, you can almost hear his sigh as Yeshua pulls out yet another striking analogy: that like a good physician, he would always be found among those who are sick, of course. Where else would he be, could he be but in a house full of outcasts? He quotes the prophet Hosea mouthing the words of Yahweh, *I desire mercy and not sacrifice; I delight in knowledge of God, not burnt offerings.* "Go and learn what this means," Yeshua tells them as a final appeal to experience the utter irrelevance of Law in the face of the allness of God's compassion and acceptance.

Where Law requires healing before restoration, Yeshua reaches out, touches and connects before any healing takes place; where Law requires evidence of repentance and restitution before forgiveness, Yeshua declares kinship and recognizes that loving relationship itself is all the evidence of forgiveness we ever need or receive; where Law requires exclusion and separation, Yeshua calls out for companionship and sits at the table of lifelong commitment.

Try to imagine the faces of these three men as the realization dawns that nothing in their encounters with Yeshua is coming out the way they thought. That nothing could have prepared them for the immensity of Yeshua's trademark smile, the one that seems to split his face into two halves and says: *you are the only person in the world at this moment.* It's not anything any one of us could ever think, but once experienced, pulls us into our own face-splitting grin.

A sociologist who spent a decade studying vulnerability, courage, empathy, shame comes at human relationship from the viewpoint of connection. Humans are all about connection, she says. Through thousands of letters and interviews, the data emerged that there are two groups of people in the world—those who connect and those who don't. More to the point, there are those who believe they are worthy of connection and those who don't...and the line between the two is only as thick as *shame*—the fear of disconnection. It's the fear of disconnection that ironically keeps us from connecting, forever driving us to find ways to be accepted. But the moment we believe we have to work to be accepted is the moment we also believe we are not worthy of connection right here and now, that we must somehow be other than we are. And if we're not now worthy, what will ever make us so? How much is ever enough to be sure?

Thousands of letters and interviews revealed that all that separates those who connect and those who are always wondering if they are good enough is simply a sense of worthiness. Those who feel connected and accepted, *believe they are worthy* of connection and acceptance in spite of all their present imperfection. Imperfect and worthy at the same time... Imagine.

Acceptance before healing, before repentance or restitution.

This is the deep, deep truth that Yeshua is telling us to go and find for ourselves, because no amount of telling will suffice. As long as we believe there is *anything* we need to do to gain God's acceptance, then it's all and only about what we do. God's love and acceptance is either absolute or it's not; it can't be just a little absolute. Only along the Fifth Way will we experience that God is nothing like Law. Either our behavior makes us acceptable, or we already are and have always been, and for anyone raised to earn salvation-as-obedience under Law, the sense of unworthiness has been driven so deep, no legal version of the Gospel will do anything but reinforce the pain. And the shame.

We have always been taught to believe that Jesus came to save us from sin. As true as that is, there are layers. When we see Yeshua leading with acceptance, accepting first and asking questions later, the realization begins to dawn that to save us from sin, he first had to save us from *shame*.

It's another long way home, but as Yeshua said, it's the only Way...through him, through the perfect love and acceptance that casts out fear. To lose our shame is to lose our fear of disconnection. To lose our fear is to lose our aloneness, our sense of separation and all the sinful behavior that separation necessitates.

☉ ⊙ ⊕ ⊕ ⊕

Up in the mountains, up the hill, as the men like to say, I was speaking about some of these things at retreat.

We retreat to the mountains to escape the routines of life. From Friday afternoon to Sunday morning we disappear from friends and family—for as long as Jesus was in the tomb we hide in the hills to see whether we can be resurrected as well, or at least resuscitated. We go to find a way to begin again; we go to find God.

But God is not in the mountains any more intimately than he's in our marriages or finances or jobs, and whatever we bring to the mountains is what we find there. Though things may appear changed and invigorating in the thin air and pine-covered context, mountaintop revelations can quickly morph back into familiar patterns upon our return, as if the mountain gave them life and takes it back again, or like fish out of water, they can only gasp a short time without their native atmosphere. We don't live on mountaintops. We live on the plains and in the valleys; it's there we need to learn how to live.

When I had finished speaking, a friend I'd known for many years wanted to talk, wanted to know how to do it, how to start, how to change. He really just couldn't take much more of the pressure, and it seemed to him there was something I'd said that triggered a glimmer somewhere that looked a bit like a Way out or through, but wouldn't lie still long enough for him to know for sure.

I tried to tell him it wasn't what he thought—it never is. I tried to tell him it wasn't something you could take by the throat or mount on your wall. It was as different an experience from anything you'd expect as night is from day, as far as east from west. Actually, I didn't say it quite like that, but I could still see the bit of light fading from his eyes. Whatever he sensed I might have had for him was not coming forth in usable form. Like vitamins you can't absorb fast enough, I could see my words passing right through him, spilling out onto the rough planks of the floor.

I suggested we get together for lunch after the retreat so we could talk, that there was much to say, and he agreed.

That was April, in the mountains; by the end of August he was dead. Sometimes when people say that they can't take the pressure anymore, they really mean it. But how could we have known there was so little time left? I did call him when we got down off the mountain, off the hill: week after week and month after month there was always a reason why not until the beginning of summer when I decided to give it a rest and wait till maybe he had more time. But there wasn't more time.

I didn't exactly fail him, but I didn't exactly help either. I think about him often—see his picture at my desk every day. The program from his memorial service, with his face in a soft oval on the cover, has been hanging on my filing cabinet since the day I brought it home. I put it right next to the program I had brought home from Lou's memorial service three years before. Lou has been watching over me as well with that big grin beaming out from his own soft oval up on the filing cabinet, reminding me daily that it's not at all what I think. It never is.

These two men, side by side on my cabinet, looking out from above the dates that mark their span with us, are even now representing choices in life. Both were good men, equally respected and loved. Both laughed and smiled and cried and died, but one found his Way out or through to reach the smilepoint, to become characterized by contentment; the other did not. One answered the call, was completed by his journey and touched the face of God, falling deeply in love with all creation, learning to play within it, while the other worked hard, chipping away day in and out to the end. Both were lovely men, good friends who decided to live their lives in love, equally desiring to please God and equally loved by him—but one knew the manner in which he was loved and the other did not, and that made all the difference.

☉ ⓘ ⊕ ⊕ ⊕

Lou lived in a mobile home park with his wife and his diabetes. You wouldn't have looked at him twice in passing, but he was a hero because he set out, released the last thing to which he was clinging, and returned to us with his hair whitened by the sight of God's countenance. He was a hero because he returned with God's deepest purpose and desire written in God's own hand, not with ink, not on stone tablets, but in the transformed smile of his life—and in his ability to state that purpose and desire with authority, straight from his heart, in only twelve words...

Love each other...just love each other.
And kid around a little.

If you ask me how to do it, how to start, how to change; if you just know there's something more or can't take the pressure much longer and you're looking for a Way out or through; it begins with twelve words. We spend entire lives trying to find God. We work so hard we forget why we were looking in the first place.

Yeshua and Lou are trying to tell us it's not what we think.

It never is.

Live your life. Love your life. Love life. All life.
Love each other, enjoy each other, kid around a little,
and forget about finding God.

Once you're on the Way, God will find you.

>Two months. Happy 60-day Anniversary. From the great perspective of two months, I can't help wondering how many anniversaries there will be. And how long before I can balance all the pieces of my new life. Life has begun again. Life is two months old. Life will never be the same. Again. And again.

>Almost ready to turn off the desk lamp. Last, brave little star fighting to be seen through the lightening blue between upper branches. Cold morning. Cold, dark apartment. Very quiet. Little girls asleep in the other room. Just like the first entry here with you asleep. Not 41 days old, but 7 years. A person. You are who you are. I know who that is. You'll reinforce it from here, modify it, but not fundamentally change.
This is a good thing.
You are a good person.

>The little star is gone now. Had to give up the fight against the big star coming up the other side of the sky, just starting to color the treetops. Light off. Cool, blue cast over the pages now. So warm, knowing you're here with me. Sleeping peacefully. Trusting me supremely, fully to keep you safe. Allowing yourself, through me, to be a child. To defer growing up for a while longer because you can.

>Quarter to seven. Time to shower. Time to shave. Time to wake you as slowly and gently as possible. Time for stretching and dressing and donuts on the drive to church. Time for the noise to begin. The day to rise up, roll over us, grow old, fade to evening to give us just enough time to gather enough strength to get up and watch the little star lose its fight once more in the coming glare.

>And just now, in my silence, looking for next words, feeling the weight of the emptiness of not knowing exactly what to say, feeling myself at the end of myself, with nothing else to of-

fer this page or anything or anyone else, I hear soft footsteps, bare footsteps in the carpet behind me and I turn to you, stumbling toward me, eyes half closed, arms out. I gather you into my lap. Warm, smooth. Hold tight. Whisper in your ear.

Groggy whispers back.

>Don't you see, this is life. I hold it in my arms. Precious, fleeting, unpredictable, untenable. It comes unbidden, stays as long as it desires. Changes form without notice.

>When we think it's over, when we think there is nothing left, soft footsteps come up from behind and flow warmly into our laps and breathe new words into empty pens.
New thoughts into empty minds.
New fire into cold hearts.

>The little star is not lost. It is still there, burning with the intensity of a thousand suns. It simply gave way for a time, a short time to let us have day, warmth, variety, life. But it is still right there, between the branches, between someone's branches as this ball turns.

>You are like this, Lord. Burning brightly beyond the light blue veil. Giving way to our daylight for a time while we live. I keep forgetting that you are here. That the veil is much closer than the sky. That I am not all there is. That when I am over, your soft footsteps will come and bring new life and words if only I will pull you into my lap and hold you as though my life depended on it.

>Oh my God. My Lord. My Life. Thank you. Thank you for the tears on my cheeks. Thank you for my little girl sleeping again in my lap. For my littler one in the next room, my bigger one away in the mountains. Thank you for this cold, clear morning, for the doves sitting in the top branches of the lightening trees. Thank you for my pen. Thank you for reminding me of my life.

>You are the unexpected, Lord.
You are the ultimate surprise that keeps us guessing, interested, and alive.

Selected Sources and Additional Reading

HEBREW/ARAMAIC LANGUAGE, CULTURE, WORLDVIEW

Benner, Jeff. *His Name is One: An Ancient Hebrew Perspective of the Name of God.* VirtualBookWorm, 2003.

Bivin, David, and Roy B. Blizzard. *Understanding the Difficult Words of Jesus.* Treasure House, 1994.

Borman, Thorleif. *Hebrew Thought Compared with Greek.* W.W. Norton & Company, 2002.

Bruce, F.F. *Hard Sayings of Jesus.* InterVarsity Press, 1983.

Douglas-Klotz, Neil. *The Hidden Gospel: Decoding the Spiritual Message of the Aramaic Jesus.* Quest Books, 2001.

Douglas-Klotz, Neil. *Prayers of the Cosmos: Meditations on the Aramaic Words of Jesus.* HarperSanFrancisco, 1993.

Friedman, David. *They Loved the Torah: What Yeshua's First Followers Really Thought About the Law.* Messianic Jewish Resources International, 2001.

Moseley, Ron. *Yeshua: A Guide to the Real Jesus and the Original Church.* Messianic Jewish Resources International, 1998.

Munk, Michael. *The Wisdom in the Hebrew Alphabet.* Artscroll, 1986.

Stern, David H. *Restoring the Jewishness of the Gospel: A Message for Christians.* Jewish New Testament Publications, Inc., 1988.

Wilson, Marvin. *Our Father Abraham: Jewish Roots of the Christian Faith.* Wm B. Eerdsmans Publishing Compay, 1989.

Young, Brad. *Jesus the Jewish Theologian.* Hendrickson Publishers, 1995.

LEXICONS AND GRAMMARS

Benner, Jeff. *The Ancient Hebrew Language and Alphabet: Understanding the Ancient Hebrew Language of the Bible Based on the Ancient Hebrew Culture and Thought.* VirtualBookWorm, 2004.

Benner, Jeff. *Ancient Hebrew Lexicon of the Bible: Hebrew Letters, Words and Roots Defined Within Their Ancient Cultural Context.* VirtualBookWorm, 2005.

Kaufman, Steven, ed. *Comprehensive Aramaic Lexicon.* Hebrew Union College, cal1.cn.huc.edu.

Jennings, William. *Lexicon to the Syriac New Testament.* Oxford at the Clarendon Press, 1926.

Smith, J. Payne. *A Compendious Syriac Dictionary.* Wipf and Stock Publishers, 1999.

Aramaic Lexicon and Concordance. The Way International, 1989. Aramaicpeshitta.com.

English Dictionary Supplement to the Concordance to the Peshitta Version of the Aramaic New Testament. American Christian Press, 1985.

The Concordance to the Peshitta Version of the Aramaic New Testament. American Christian Press, 1985.

Strong, James. *Strong's Exhaustive Concordance of the Bible.* Hendrickson Publishers, 2007.

BIBLE TRANSLATIONS AND COMMENTARIES

Barnes, Albert. *Barnes Notes on the Old and New Testaments.* Baker Books, 1983.

Clarke, Adam. *Commentary on the Entire Bible.* Baker Book House, 1971.

Daniel, Orville. *A Harmony of the Four Gospels.* Baker Books, 1996.

Gill, John. *Exposition of the Old and New Testaments.* Baptist Standard Bearer, 2006.

Jamieson, R. *Jamieson, Fausset and Brown Commentary on the Whole Bible.* Zondervan, 1999.

Lamsa, George M. *Holy Bible from the Ancient Eastern Text.* Harper Collins, 1968.

Peterson, Eugene H. *The Message.* Navpress, 1988.

Stern, David. *Complete Jewish Bible.* Jewish New Testament Publications, 1998.

Stern, David. *Jewish New Testament.* Messianic Jewish Resources International, 1989.

Stern, David. *Jewish New Testament Commentary.* Messianic Jewish Resources International, 1992.

Younan, Paul. *Aramaic/English Peshitta Interlinear New Testament.* Peshitta.org, 2000.

Eight Translation New Testament. Tyndale House Publishers, 1974.

Vincent, Marvin. *Vincent's Word Studies in the New Testament.* Hendrickson Publishers, 1985.

ORIGIN OF SCRIPTURE/CHRISTIANITY, CHURCH HISTORY

Barnstone, Willis, Ed. *The Other Bible.* Harper & Row, 1983

Cairns, Earle E. *Christianity through the Centuries.* Academie Books, 1981.

Cameron, Ron, ed. *The Other Gospels.* The Westminster Press, 1982.

Mack, Burton L. *Who Wrote the New Testament?* Harper Collins, 1995.

Mack, Burton L. *The Lost Gospel: The Book of Q and Christian Origins.* Harper Collins, 1994.

Maier, Paul, L. *Josephus, The Essential Writings: A Condensation of Jewish Antiquities and the Jewish War.* Kregel Publications, 1988.

Mead, Frank S. *Handbook of Denominations in the United States.* Abingdon Press, 1995.

Miller, Robert J., Ed. *The Complete Gospels.* Polebridge Press, 1992.

Pagels, Elaine. *The Gnostic Gospels.* Vintage Books, 1979.

Sailhamer, John H. *How We Got the Bible.* Zondervan Publishing House, 1998.

Wegner, Paul D. *The Journey from Text to Translation: The Origin and Development of the Bible.* Baker Academic, 1999

Vermes, G. *The Dead Sea Scrolls in English.* Pelican Books, 1962.

Zondervan Handbook to the Bible. Zondervan Publishing House, 1999.

CHRISTIAN SPIRITUALITY

Manning, Brennan. *The Ragamuffin Gospel: Good News for the Bedraggled, Beat-Up, and Burnt-Out.* Multnomah, 2000.

Manning, Brennan. *Ruthless Trust: The Ragamuffin's Path to God.* HarperSanFrancisco, 2002.

Manning, Brennan. *Abba's Child: The Cry of the Heart for Intimate Belonging.* Navpress Publishing Group, 2002.

Nouwen, Henri. *Life of the Beloved: Spiritual Living in a Secular World.* Crossroads General Interest, 2002.

Nouwen, Henri. *Return of the Prodigal Son: A Story of Homecoming.* Image, 1994.

Nouwen, Henri. *The Way of the Heart: Desert Spirituality and Contemporary Ministry.* HarperSanFrancisco, 1991.

Nouwen, Henri. *Out of Solitude: Three Meditations on the Christian Life.* Ave Maria Press, 2004

Yancey, Philip. *What's So Amazing About Grace?* Zondervan, 2002.

CONTEMPLATIVE PRAYER, SPIRITUAL JOURNEY

Anonymous. *The Cloud of Unknowing.* HarperSanFrancisco, 2004.

Bochen, Christine M., ed. *Thomas Merton: Essential Writings.* Orbis Books, 2000.

Brother Lawrence. *The Practice of the Presence of God.* Whitaker House, 1982.

Cunningham, Lawrence S., ed. *Thomas Merton: Spiritual Master.* Paulist Press, 1992.

Keating, Thomas. *Invitation to Love: The Way of Christian Contemplation.* Continuum International Publishing Group, 1994

Keating, Thomas. *Open Mind, Open Heart: The Contemplative Dimension of the Gospel.* Continuum International Publishing Group, 1994

Merton, Thomas. *The Seven Storey Mountain.* Harcourt, 1999.

Merton, Thomas. *The New Seeds of Contemplation.* New Directions Publishing Corp., 1972.

Merton, Thomas. *The Wisdom of the Desert: Sayings from the Desert Fathers of the Fourth Century.* Shambhala, 2004.

Merton, Thomas. *Thoughts in Solitude.* Farrar, Straus and Giroux, 1999.

THEOLOGICAL ISSUES

Enns, Paul. *The Moody Handbook of Theology*. Moody Press, 1989.

Instone-Brewer, David. *Divorce and Remarriage in the Bible: The Social and Literary Context*. Wm. B. Eerdsmans Publishing Company, 2002.

Lewis, C.S. *The Great Divorce*. Fount, 2002.

Lewis, C.S. *The Problem of Pain*. HarperSanFrancisco, 2001.

Merton, Thomas. *Opening the Bible*. Fortress Press/The Liturgical Press, 1970.

Virkler, Henry A. *Hermeneutics: Principles and Processes of Biblical Interpretation*. Baker Book House, 1981.

POSTMODERN ISSUES

Kimball, Dan. *Emerging Church: Vintage Christianity for New Generations*. Zondervan, 2003.

McLaren, Brian. *A Generous Orthodoxy*. Zondervan, 2004.

Sweet, Leonard. *Aqua Church: Essential Leadership Arts for Piloting Your Church in Today's Fluid Culture*. Group Publishing, 1999.

Sweet, Leonard. *Soul Tsunami*. Zondervan, 2001.

Sweet, Leonard. *Out of the Question, into the Mystery: Getting Lost in the GodLife Relationship*. Waterbrook Press, 2004.

MISCELLANEOUS ISSUES

Brown, Brene, *Daring Greatly: How the Courage to be Vulnerable Transforms the Way We Live, Love, Parent, and Lead*. Gotham Books, 2012.

Brown, Brene. *The Gifts of Imperfection: Let Go of Who You Think You're Supposed to Be and Embrace Who You Are*. Hazelden Publishing, 2010.

Campbell, Joseph. *The Hero With a Thousand Faces*. Princeton University Press, 1973.

Chesterton, G.K. *The Everlasting Man*. Ignatius Press, 1993.

Copi, Irving M. *Introduction to Logic*. Macmillan Publishing Company, 1982.

Davies, Paul. *The Mind of God: The Scientific Basis for a Rational World*. Simon and Schuster, 1993

Dawson, Raymond, trans. *Confucius: The Analects*. Oxford University Press, 1993

Frankel, Viktor E. *Man's Search for Meaning*. Washington Square Press, 1984

Giles, Herbert A., trans. *Chuang Tzu: Mystic, Moralist, and Social Reformer*. AMS Press, 1974.

Hawking, Stephen. *A Brief History of Time*. Bantam, 1998.

Henricks, Robert G., trans. *Lao Tzu: Te-Tao Ching*. Ballantine Books, 1989.

Merton, Thomas. *The Way of Chuang Tzu*. Shambhala, 2004.

ARTICLES

Christ Among the Partisans, Gary Wills, NY Times, 4/9/06.

Cut, Thrust, and Christ, Susannah Meadows, Newsweek, 2/6/2006.

Jack's Death, His Choice, Nicholas D. Kristoff, NY Times, 4/10/2005.

Turtles All The Way Down, Paul Campos, Rocky Mountain News, 8/9/2005.

David Brisbin, MDiv/RASI is teaching pastor at theeffect faith community and recovery ministry in San Juan Capistrano, CA. He is also executive director of Encompass Recovery, an addiction treatment center, and president of America's Children, a non-profit organization focused on the education and nutrition of children. He lives in South Orange County, CA with his wife, Marian and their children.

For more information about theeffect or to book David Brisbin for a speaking engagement, please visit:

www.theeffect.org

Made in the USA
Middletown, DE
09 August 2023

36415237R00231